The Arts and Youth at Risk

The Arts and Youth at Risk: Global and Local Challenges

Edited by

Angela O'Brien and Kate Donelan

Cambridge Scholars Publishing

The Arts and Youth at Risk: Global and Local Challenges, Edited by Angela O'Brien and Kate Donelan

This book first published 2008 by

Cambridge Scholars Publishing

12 Back Chapman Street, Newcastle upon Tyne, NE6 2XX, UK

British Library Cataloguing in Publication Data
A catalogue record for this book is available from the British Library

ISBN (10): 1-84718-632-7, ISBN (13): 9781847186324

TABLE OF CONTENTS

ACKNOWLEDGMENTS

First of all we would like to thank the authors who contributed to this edited collection. While this book is global in conception, it is the first volume of articles about arts-based interventions for "at risk" youth to focus on the Australian experience. These contributions show the depth of research being undertaken "Down Under" and the complexities and challenges associated with the range of school, community and institutional contexts discussed in this volume.

We would also like to thank Professor Shirley Brice Heath, who has been a source of inspiration and encouragement to us in this work. She has outlined the significance of this volume in her Foreword. She provides a global context for readers, identifying past, current and emerging trends in social and educational interventions with young people. Thank you also to Dr Peter O'Connor, our other international voice, whose personal and professional reflections conclude this book. When he remembers the good ladies who provided charity to his childhood family he asks himself if he is doing more harm than good in his contemporary work with troubled young people. This is the ethical challenge for all of us locally and globally; it is the question that underpins most of the articles in this book. We hope this book will challenge you to question your own motivations and practices.

These chapters are elaborated versions of papers that were first presented and discussed at the *Risky Business* Symposium held at The University of Melbourne, Australia, 20–22 October 2005. The symposium was the culminating event for *Risky Business*, a four-year research project into the impact of arts-based interventions for young people "at risk". The *Risky Business* project was funded by the Australian Research Council and a range of industry organizations, all stakeholders in this area, including the Australia Council for the Arts, Arts Victoria, the Melbourne Magistrates' Court, the Victorian State Government Departments of Justice and Human Services (Juvenile Justice), VicHealth and providers of youth services: Whitelion, Visycares and St Luke's, Bendigo. We are grateful for their financial and in-kind support. We could not have done the research without this funding.

As you read these chapters, you will be aware that none of the research projects discussed could have been completed without financial backing from government and non-government organizations. On behalf of those who research this area in Australia and our authors, we acknowledge that support. We hope that this book will generate interest in arts-based interventions for "at risk" youth and will increase structural and financial support across the sectors that focus on young people, including health and wellbeing, justice, education and the arts.

The *Risky Business* Symposium was funded by VicHealth, the Victorian Health Promotion Foundation that is the peak body for health promotion in Victoria, Australia. VicHealth advocates health promotion as a powerful, cost-effective and efficient way to maintain a healthier community. Rather than focusing on people at risk for specific diseases, health promotion involves the population as a whole in the context of their everyday lives. Activities are geared toward promoting health and preventing ill-health. Community arts funding is a priority for VicHealth who recognize the potential of arts participation and engagement to build wellbeing and social connectedness.

We are grateful to a number of people who assisted us with the preparation and running of this Symposium and this subsequent publication. Tim Stitz, the *Risky Business* Administrator organized the Symposium with characteristic flair. He has also been our publication manager. *Risky Business* doctoral student Kiersten Coulter worked with industry partners Judy Morton from Arts Victoria and Susan Ball from VicHealth on the Symposium steering committee. Thanks are also due to Diane Brown, the copy editor, Kimba Griffith, the formatting editor, and to Cambridge Scholars Publishing.

We were fortunate to have the opportunity to meet and work with an exceptional group of community and professional artists throughout the life of the *Risky Business* project and a number of them spoke about their work at the Symposium. We also had the opportunity to meet with many of the young people involved in these programs and to share their arts making and something of their life stories. This book salutes the dedication, energy and courage of the contributors to the *Risky Business* project.

Angela O'Brien and Kate Donelan
April 2008

FOREWORD

SHIRLEY BRICE HEATH

I am pleased to have a role in this philosophically complex and pragmatically provocative book. The editors and authors take the brave stance of interrogating the consequences, trajectories, and effects of participation in the arts by young people – especially those who carry labels such as "at risk". In this foreword, I attempt to underscore and extend some of the central tenets of this volume. I do so by calling attention to the critical need to consider contextual background as well as an international perspective on children and youth.

Contextual framing

This volume steps into a fast-moving stream of international concern about the health and welfare of children and young adults ignored or not adequately cared for by their families and the State. Experts in human development as well as policymakers within the United Nations, World Health Organization, and national and regional governments look beyond family, school and the justice system to find contexts that can effectively fill the non-family and non-school hours of young people in nations across the economic spectrum. Economically powerful nations, such as Australia, Canada, Germany, Great Britain and the United States, increasingly face the perplexing question of why so many of their young find their way into trouble – most often with alcohol and other mind-altering substances and through reckless experimentation that leads to conflict with legal authorities. Impoverished nations, whose children have suffered from ethnic warfare, famine, refugee life, and the absence of educational and medical benefits, know that their future depends on the young who desperately need dependable support that families, international agencies, and nation states cannot now provide.

In the wide range of contexts of need from economically advanced nations to impoverished and war-torn states, new channels of learning, reconciliation, and meaningful apprenticeship must take up critical roles. They have to do so within the simultaneity of despair over environmental degradation and elation over the rapid spread of technology and popular media around the world. Ironically, the coupling of these phenomena, acknowledged widely in the first decade of the twenty-first century and certain to continue throughout the century, pushes for another unlikely connection – that of the arts to acknowledge exploration in the sciences, especially the environmental sciences.

A turn to the arts as a source of help for and with the young is not new in developed nations. In nations facing famine, ethnic rivalries, political unrest, and inadequate educational and economic opportunities, the potential of the arts has been only minimally explored, for participation in the arts is likely to be judged as unaffordable, irrelevant and ineffectual. However, it is not unreasonable to expect that increasingly international groups and independent social entrepreneurs will look to the arts as platform and partner in knowledge advancement among the young in nations that lack state will and resources to enable their educational systems to meet societal needs.

In the past two decades, a similar kind of recognition led well-meaning change agents in economically advanced nations to put forward participation in the arts as remediation and redemption instruments of personal and social change for young people. Arts "programs," "projects," and "experience" were promoted for their potential to bring changes – emotional, social, and academic – to the young. Arts opportunities were praised for "giving" the young "empowerment," "voice" and "confidence" (cf. Hetland et al. 2007).

In these nations, much ink and many bombastic speeches have claimed these benefits from the arts as well as improved self-esteem, growth in understanding and positive life-changing consequences. Yet little social science research backs these claims. Until now, few critics have stepped forward to point out this fact. Even more infrequent have been critical examinations of the potential of the arts for children and the young in developing nations, and how learning in the arts might work in these contexts to deepen and spread environmental, educational, and health information and skills. This refreshingly honest volume gives us the direct, thoughtful, and insightful background that will lead us to look closely at not only the political and economic contexts for the work of the arts with and through young people, but also the extent of substance and innovative power actually available through the arts.

It should be evident that the local learning environment and circumstances of arts opportunities make all the difference on the question of whether or not the arts are appropriate, inclusive, and effective in meeting local needs. Are possibilities voluntary or mandated (often as part of juvenile justice or education rehabilitation or remediation programs)? Is the work in the arts only short-term entry-level work in which the young never have the chance to struggle through the intermediate and advanced work that builds expertise in performance and aesthetic judgment? Do the offerings receive professional instruction and critique that will bring excellence of achievement, enable the work to move beyond the local, and sustain the means by which the young can become expert enough to pass on their skills and knowledge to younger learners?

Advocacy of the arts, often through enthusiasts who have themselves found life values in their own work in the arts, has taken precedence over long-term theory-based examinations of arts learning environments – both within and beyond schools. Fundamental flaws in excessive and exaggerated claims for the arts have resulted primarily from three misguided notions:

1. Learning is monolinear in direction.
2. Positive learning experiences "naturally" transfer to other circumstances.
3. Learning in art forms enhances individual achievement that can be measured in ways similar to quantifiable achievement in other domains.
4. The arts, more than other "subjects", offer "diversionary" as well as "compensatory" opportunities for learning.

Those who wish to claim educational advancement through arts participation have been particularly susceptible to these fallacies, for these four notions occur routinely in academic curricular and assessment thinking.

Research that could offer "clean" evidence on the effects of the arts demands one or more control or comparison groups with which individuals in arts "treatment" or "intervention" can be compared. In addition, some kind of equivalency of "treatment" has to be delineated, along with identification of outcomes that can be measured or quantified. Any pre and post-tests need to be normalized on a representatively sampled population. Ideally, such research is longitudinal as well as cross-sector, with follow-up that can exclude other "interventions" in the lives of individuals that might well have overtaken any "effects" of the arts.

Such studies are expensive, require cross-disciplinary collaboration, and need to promise some kind of economic return for a constituency powerful enough to push for policy change. Artists have historically held little political power as a group, and their professional identity has never been wrapped in either stable or high financial returns. Thus research that "finds in favor of artists" is unlikely to enlist a constituency powerful enough to persuade political and financial forces to turn positive research results into accepted practice.

Underlying the arguments of this volume is recognition of the above factors and many more. This book makes clear that if the arts as agent of change for individuals and their communities are to carry long-term effects, certain conditions for participation in the arts have to be present. Regardless of type of organization (e.g., school, museum, youth association or community group), day-to-day within program contexts and conditions need certain consistent features (cf. Heath 2007, 2006; Heath and Smyth 1999). These will ensure that children and the young learn in environments that offer the following:

1. Sustained co-learning with adult professionals as expert mentors over long periods of time.
2. Meaningful reliance on referenced knowledge from written, curated, demonstrated, and performed sources and models.
3. High-risk expectations for collaborative exhibition, performance, or production.
4. Opportunities for the practice and guidance needed to move from beginning levels of skill to explore intermediate and advanced achievement.

Though different art forms require different periods of time for reaching satisfactory levels of performance or production, achievement in all art forms takes hard work, study, practice, and sustained access to good models and tough-love guidance. Moreover, high expectations have to hold, meaning that those who plan and implement opportunities for the arts with the young must know and respect the capacity of children and adolescents to undertake and often to lead in thinking through the arts (cf. Matthews 1999).

Two points regarding the arts and learning stand out historically – in Western and Eastern history as well as in studies of the role of artists in indigenous societies. First is the close tie between work in the arts and knowledge of science – whether botany, animal anatomy, architecture, astronomy, or technology. Second is the need for apprenticeship with periods of scaffolded learning that carries meaning and receives critique from within the local community. The scientific and sustained bases of the arts demand that learners have sustained opportunities to draw upon their observational, mimetic, and critical skills throughout their stages of learning (Austin 2001; Perkins 1994). Artists across history and societies have often been innovators, forecasters of change, spiritual interpreters, and cautionary voices on human greed and disregard for the environment. These facts tell us the world needs artists, and the young need the arts.

International youth perspective

The dichotomy between rich and poor nations set out in the preceding sections does not go far enough in cautioning us to ask some comparative questions about how children and young people get defined under different circumstances, and what difference these definitions might make for learning in the arts. Here it is essential that we note the place of young people in their local and broad social-relational systems and the extent to which the young are subject to the stresses of economic, political and educational forces.

In the past two decades, nations such as Australia, the United States and Canada, as well as many European nations, have drastically increased expectations for the percentage of secondary school graduates and even university enrollments. For those who do not complete secondary school or do not enroll in advanced or higher education, social consequences follow. Information-based economies demand of their labor force a facility with oral and written language, as well as numeracy and technological skills. Service skills and manual labor, though acknowledged as essential to the smooth operation of information-based and high-tech societies, fall to the bottom of the list of "desired" occupations. Some attribute this "inequality" to social causation, while others say it is a matter of self-selection. The arts, long associated with "crafts," are often left with little regard except for their leisure-time benefits or entertainment value. Thus there may be a deep-seated sense of "appropriate" in the choice of the arts in the past two decades as an educational or esteem-building means for the young who have already been labeled "at risk" of not achieving school completion and successful university education.

In economically advanced societies, it is primarily the elite who are likely to value academic achievement over manual adeptness. Such a view carries with it an implicit acceptance of a scope-and-sequence linear path of achievement as critical to school achievement. In contrast, manual dexterity and a handy way with machines, technology, the arts or "people skills" rarely come in a predictable trajectory. Early facility or bursts of achievement mark the latter, leaving highly unclear just how those talented in these areas fit into maturation trajectories. Because such individuals often select what they want to do over what others set out for them to do, their maturity and judgment are often seen as inadequate, wrong-headed, or just plain "dangerous" for these individuals and those around them.

Yet a variety of theories of human development, including ecological theory (Brofenbrenner 1979), socio-historical theories (Vygotsky 1994/1930; Bakhtin 1986), and critical race/ethnicity theories (Cross 1991), urge researchers to take into account how young people internalize the values and practices of social systems. This kind of attention is essential when young people's individual talents or cultural/community norms differ from those dominant in the society. To be sure, youth and society are interdependent, but in cases in which the maturation and judgment, as well as the chosen talents or directions of youth, do not match those of educational systems, researchers have to look beyond individual differences to political and economic factors. Much of what we do in society moves us along toward unquestioning social reproduction with little or no attention to adaptive or transformative factors. We have to consider the extent to which this kind of reproductive push places stress on young people who see no reason to value this blind drive toward more of the same from the past.

We see this point demonstrated, for example, when young people take up functions in some communities that adults either cannot or do not want to serve. The young fill gaps that adults neither see nor may wish to be filled. In various parts of the world, young people step forward to help provide economic support for their families, work for environmental and social justice, and advocate for community sustainability. In Boston, Massachusetts, the only all-green building in the city was initiated by a group of young people who had established a community arts organization for young people (Heath 2005, 2000; Heath and Street 1999). In Mumbai, India, street children persuaded a group of elite women to establish Child Line, a free help line for street children in need of assistance (Heath and Robinson 2004). Today the functions of that group have been included in regional governmental responsibilities, and the concept has spread to other nations (Elkington and Hartigan 2008).

In almost all instances, when young people initiate such programs, the arts figure centrally in their mission and communicational effectiveness. Children and the young express their own and their communities' "need to know" through the arts, and they move toward social change with the arts in full partnership. Moreover, the arts enable empathy – the willingness to see the positions of others and to get to know them when older members of a society may wish to forget, reduce their reflections, or ignore what is "different" or "other". Young people in nations where hatred and fear have held people apart for centuries often want to explore the past, talk about it, and find new ways to express and represent it (Daiute et al. 2006). The young who opt out of conventional school norms of achievement or who have been denied opportunities for schooling are often those who find their way to the arts and alternative ways of making a difference in their societies.

This book is designed for readers who care about their communities and are willing to create institutions and negotiate for meaningful roles for young people (cf. Rabkin and Redmond 2004). Explanations supported by theory and research from across the disciplines address the need to think and to think hard about where and how the arts and young people fit together and in concert with moral reason, societal inclusion and environmental justice. To do otherwise is to risk denying the benefits that can come from the ingenious insights and seemingly endless energies and imaginative powers of the young. This book calls on us to think beyond "using" the arts for instrumental redirection of young individuals seen as being out-of-step with the larger society.

We simply must expect more from both the arts and the young. Creativity, adaptability and transformation lie at the heart of the arts. So too do these same elements lie deeply within the sciences. Yet arts programs for the young rarely couple science and arts. Knowledge of the body and the way it works figure centrally in the life of dancers, martial arts specialists and actors. Information and theories about chemical components and conditions of exposure figure centrally in the work of visual artists. Musicians work with mathematics and the physics of sound through their instruments. Sculptors and illustrators know deeply the geological, botanical and anatomical elements of the objects of their portrayals. Why is it that arts programs for the young leave aside the long-standing inextricable interdependence of the sciences and arts? Could it be that this acknowledgment would mean having to take the arts and the young *too seriously?* Could it mean that doing so would bring *too much* respect to both the arts and the young? These are critical questions for arts advocates.

What happens when facts challenge value? For too long, it may be that complacent valuing of the arts has led us to ignore facts – historical, sociological and cognitive. Let the next steps in our rethinking the arts and youth not begin until we can answer questions raised in this volume. We should do so wanting to cherish the good, the strong, the imaginative, and the social and political promise of youth creativity in the experiment of living for now and the future.

Works Cited

Austin, J. H. 2001. *Chase, Chance and Creativity: The Lucky Art of Novelty*. Cambridge, Mass.: MIT Press.

Bakhtin, J. J. 1986. *Speech Genres and other Late Essays*. Austin: University of Texas Press.

Bronfenbrenner, U. 1979. *The Ecology of Human Development: Experiments by Nature and Design*. Cambridge, Mass.: Harvard University Press.

Cross, W. E. Jr. 1991. *Shades of Black: Diversity in African-American Identity*. Philadelphia: Temple University Press.

Daiute, C., Z. Beykont, C. Higson-Smith, and L. Nucci. 2006. *International Perspectives on Youth Conflict and Development*. New York: Oxford University Press.

Elkington, John and Pamela Hartigan. 2008. *The Power of Unreasonable People: How Social Entrepreneurs Create Markets that Change the World*. Cambridge, Mass.: Harvard Business Press.

Heath, Shirley Brice. 2005. *Artshow 2 Grow*. Documentary film, DVD format.

Heath, Shirley Brice, Elke Boehncke, and Shelby Wolf. 2007. *Made for Each Other: Creative Arts and Sciences in the Secondary School*. London: Creative Partnerships.

Heath, Shirley Brice and Ken Robinson. 2004. "Making a Way: Youth Arts and Learning in International Perspective". In *Putting the Arts in the Picture*, edited by Nick Rabkin & Robin Redmond. Chicago: Columbia College, pp. 107-26.

Heath, Shirley Brice and Laura Smyth. 1999. *ArtShow: Youth and Community Development*. [A resource guide to accompany ArtShow, 2000, a documentary film.] Washington, D.C.: Partners for Liveable Communities.

Hetland, Lois, Ellen Winner, Shirley Veenema, and Kimberly Sheridan. 2007. *Studio Thinking: The Real Benefits of Visual Arts Education*. New York: Teachers College Press.

Matthews, John. 1999. *The Art of Childhood and Adolescence: The Construction of Meaning*. London: Falmer Press.

Perkins, David. 1994. *The Intelligent Eye: Learning to Think by Looking at Art*. Los Angeles: The J. Paul Getty Trust.

Rabin, Nick and Robin Redmond, eds. 2004. *Putting the Arts in the Picture*. Chicago: Columbia College.

Vygotsky, L. S. 1930. "The Socialist Alteration of Man". In *The Vygotsky Reader,* edited by R. Van Der Veer & J. Valsiner. 1994. Malden Mass.: Blackwell, pp. 175-84.

—. 1978. *Mind in Society*. Cambridge, Mass.: Harvard University Press.

CHAPTER ONE

RETHINKING THE ARTS AND YOUTH "AT RISK"

ANGELA O'BRIEN & KATE DONELAN

This book is a contribution to the lively international dialogue about creative and arts-based interventions for young people categorized as "at risk". The instrumental benefit of arts participation for disadvantaged and marginalized young people is an area of increasing interest worldwide. A body of research highlights the positive educational and social outcomes of arts programs within and outside the schooling system (Grumet 2004; Rabkin et al. 2004; Deasy 2002; Brice Heath 1999; Dreeszen et al. 1999; Fiske 1999). Studies in the USA, reported by the RAND Corporation, offer a systematic analysis of the intrinsic and instrumental benefits – cognitive, attitudinal and behavioral, health, social and economic – of young people's participation in creative arts activities (McCarthy et al. 2004; Stone et al. 1998, 1997; McArthur and Law 1996). British research including the UK National Advisory Committee on Creative and Cultural Education (2000) and *Creative Partnerships*, a large ongoing project between the British Arts Council and educational authorities, demonstrates the individual and community value of arts participation and enhanced learning across the whole curricula where the arts are privileged (Brice Heath and Wolf 2005, 2004). A number of studies reveal that out-of-school performing arts programs can provide rich learning contexts and a sense of agency for disadvantaged and "at risk" young people (Brice Heath 2000; Hughes and Wilson 2003). There is a strong argument for the development of methodological approaches that not only generate a useful evidence base to support arts interventions, but provide a depth of understanding of complex human interactions in potentially difficult research sites (Oakley 2007; Bamford 2006).

In Australia, there has been less systematic longitudinal research in this area, but a number of studies support the North American and British findings (O'Brien and Donelan 2007; Jones 2000; Marsden and Thiele 2000). Recent Australian Government initiatives have generated research into arts and education, the arts and wellbeing, and the arts and community (Hunter 2005; Bryce et al. 2004). A national study into *Art and Wellbeing* highlights the use of arts practice as a way of connecting people to support networks and community to achieve better health outcomes. Young people "at risk" and marginalized social groups are the focus of many case studies within this report, with researchers arguing that engagement in arts practice can promote confidence, resilience, communication skills and connectedness to others (Mills and Brown 2004; Thiele and Marsden 2003).

This book has its origins in the *Risky Business* research project (2002-05) – a major Australian study into the use of the creative arts as diversionary activities for youth "at risk". This four-year ethnographic study was designed to investigate the qualities and impact of effective arts programs with highly marginalized young people. The *Risky Business* project was conducted as a cross-disciplinary collaboration between the editors of this book, Angela O'Brien from Creative Arts and Kate Donelan from Arts Education, with doctoral student, Kiersten Coulter from Criminology, and industry partners from the fields of justice, health, the arts, human services and youth support services.

At a time when the arts are seen by many as a panacea for social disadvantage, we argue that it is important to interrogate key assumptions about the nature and purpose of work in this complex and difficult area. This book is designed both to profile the findings of recent research and to generate debate. Whilst many of the writers argue strongly for the value of creative diversionary programs they also raise questions about the claims made for the wide-ranging benefits of the arts for "at risk" young people, and the role of arts programs in reducing and preventing socially unacceptable and harmful behavior. Like many of the writers of these chapters, we welcome the increasing body of evidence demonstrating the positive aspects of engagement in creative arts activities for "at risk" young people. However, in what has evolved into something of a climate of advocacy for the pro-social benefits of the arts for vulnerable and disadvantaged communities, we see a need for a more critical discussion.

This book elaborates on the discussions about the efficacy of arts interventions for youth "at risk" that was a theme of the 2005 *Risky Business* Symposium held at the University of Melbourne. International presenters from youth studies, arts therapy, community and applied arts, education, criminology and juvenile justice engaged in a cross-disciplinary dialogue about the arts with young, socially marginalized people and examined the concept of "risk taking" in arts practice within an institutional and community context. Based on their work in a range of programs, artists and researchers spoke positively about the value of implementing arts programs for socially marginalized people, and the potential impact of alternative creative interventions on young people's future pathways. However, there was also debate about and critique of the categorization of young people as "at risk", the motivations of those using applied arts as an instrument of positive social change, and the ethical challenges of arts-based interventions.

Much of the research presented in these chapters occurs in an Australian context. Researchers draw on a range of theoretical perspectives and critical lenses to examine arts-based models of work with diverse groups of marginalized young people. Many of these authors provide contextualized accounts of arts activities, drawing on data that illuminates the ways in which particular young people have engaged with artists and with creative practices. The voices of the young people within these chapters reveal the constructive and re-constructive potential of the arts, showing that through the use of artistic processes and creative media young people can rebuild their sense of personal and social identity, shape and represent their views of the world, and re-imagine their future. The book also underlines the challenges inherent in using an applied arts approach with young "at risk" people. Many of these accounts of programs illustrate the problems faced by artists working with young people in custodial settings, drug rehabilitation, schools and community centers.

The first group of chapters opens up areas of critical debate about the use of the arts with disadvantaged and socially marginalized young people. The writers challenge the prevailing discourses informing current social, cultural and educational policy, including the problematizing of youth, the social efficacy of the arts, and cognitive behavioral models of rehabilitation for young offenders.

Helen Cahill questions the metaphors of "risk and rescue" within a social justice agenda. She discusses the differing perspectives on youth identity and agency that arise in the psychological and sociological research traditions and their relevance to arts projects which aim to empower "at risk" youth. She critiques the positioning of young people as passive victims or as "deviants" needing correction and argues instead that young people need to be seen as active and contributing cultural citizens. Examining the assumptions that can influence the architecture of work with young people, she notes that when youth are grouped around their "risk" status this can negatively impact upon program outcomes. Cahill offers a number of recommendations to guide the design of arts-based interventions, stressing the value of political, community or service-based modes of activity. She argues that arts programs should encourage young people to contest old stories and develop new narratives of self. Cahill challenges program leaders to examine the purpose of the arts intervention and the positioning of participants, and to ask whether the artworks "stereotype, demonize, glamorize or reinforce victim/oppressor stories". She discusses two drama programs that illustrate ways in which young people can take on meaningful roles with purpose and value within projects. She also highlights the importance of artists and teachers using theatrical conventions to provide narrative and aesthetic distance and protective framing for young people's personal material.

Martina Boese investigates the politics of achieving social inclusion through the arts in the light of recent critical perspectives about cultural activities as a vehicle for social change. She notes that in the present political context artists increasingly need to justify their work. Her chapter traces the path from community arts to more recent approaches to achieving social inclusion through culture. Boese examines some of the criticisms of these approaches, putting particular emphasis on training and employment initiatives within the emergent field of the "creative industries". She suggests that the use of the arts for social inclusion gained official recognition in the UK under Blair's New Labor Government and became the rationale for cultural investment. She identifies the global shift towards a policy agenda based on a neo-liberal discourse that promotes the arts for social and economic objectives. Her chapter asks whether this instrumental approach to the arts reduces rather than enhances their intrinsic value, and supports exploitative working conditions and unstable employment for those working in the arts. She draws on two empirical studies of arts interventions with disadvantaged youth in Vienna and Manchester to illustrate the importance of understanding culturally inclusive projects within their broader social, economic and political context. While she acknowledges criticisms of these projects she also argues for the potential of these types of projects to facilitate active citizenship.

Two chapters deal specifically with arts interventions with young offenders. Mark Brown is concerned with how young people stop offending and how the techniques, strategies and programs of arts-based interventions might play a role in reducing recidivism. Brown identifies key issues in theory and policy relevant to arts-based interventions and reviews some emerging findings that indicate an important role for this type of work in holistic, process-based interventions with young people "at risk" of offending. He outlines the policy context in Victoria, Australia following the implementation of the Juvenile Justice Reform Strategy, which draws on the same principles of risk assessment and risk management that guides adult rehabilitation in many western jurisdictions. He critiques the limitations of this deficit "risk-needs" model and sees the cognitive behavioral programs associated with it as "largely negative." He explains the "desistance model" where rehabilitation is understood as a "process of stopping" and the causes of offending are understood within the context of the psychological, historical, ideological and structural factors that have shaped an individual's social behavior. This model emphasizes positive and constructive work with young offenders who are positioned as active players in a process of change. Like Cahill, he stresses narrative identity as a key element in bringing about change through arts interventions. He argues that arts-based programs complement a desistance model as they provide a means for young offenders to construct a more positive and future- oriented sense of personal and social identity.

Kiersten Coulter draws on her work within the *Risky Business* project in two gender-specific custodial sites for young adults in Victoria, Australia. Coulter addresses the theoretical, conceptual and policy frameworks outlined by Brown and focuses particularly on the "desistance model". She argues that a significant gap in the criminological literature is the linking of the causes and consequences of offending and the development of risk factors with the processes and outcomes from arts-based research with offenders. She proposes that "intrinsic value", "narrative identity" and "responsivity", three concepts identified by Brown, are the means by which arts programs potentially contribute to the process of desistance from offending. Coulter's chapter seeks to answer a number of critical questions: can arts-based programs make a positive impact on young offenders and if so, what are the qualities of these programs, their expected outcomes and challenges? What kinds of arts programs can deliver outcomes that are theoretically and conceptually coherent? How are the outcomes linked to processes of desistance? She applies various intervention models outlined by Brown to her analysis of data from the *Risky Business* project. She draws on the words of young men and women who participated in the custodial drama and performance projects to provide evidence of a range of positive outcomes of these projects with young offenders within challenging settings. Coulter argues that arts-based programs form part of the solution on a pathway towards desistance from offending. She highlights the need for further research to identify the nature of the support necessary to address critical structural barriers, thus enabling arts-based programs for young offenders to be sustained and benefits to endure.

Dave Kelman focuses on *My Story/Our Stories*, his study of young people's enacted stories in two schools in the inner western suburbs of Melbourne. As the artistic director of a youth arts organization Kelman mentors and trains young emerging artists from diverse cultural backgrounds to work in teams with young people in school and community arts projects. In the drama projects that are the focus of this chapter the young participants, from economically and culturally marginalized communities, are "at risk" of disengaging from education and becoming involved in damaging behaviors. From his perspective as an artist-researcher, Kelman investigates how values, power, identities and narrative meanings are explored dialogically within the pedagogic space of the drama workshop. His account also examines the young people's resistance to involvement in processes that they perceive expose them to risk of ridicule from their peers. Like Cahill and Coulter, Kelman is interested in young people's narratives that are both constructive and re-constructive. He suggests that within these drama and performance projects the young people were involved in developing self-narratives of social agency. In devising and performing these plays the young people constructed meaningful moral frameworks and explored and challenged their own values. Kelman argues that at their most effective, these drama programs facilitated a dialogue between young people and their audiences through the performance of stories that were significant to themselves and their community.

John Hughes and Mat Howard present research that examines the positive role of the Shakespeare Globe Centre Australia's Youth Festival – specifically in providing "a refuge" for vulnerable and isolated gay male students. The Shakespeare Globe Centre Australia conducts a nationwide Festival that involves 20,000 students annually who perform excerpts from Shakespeare, compose music, create a dance piece or design a production. The Festival begins in schools, and selected students attend a regional event and a State Festival. Hughes and Howard highlight the impact of the Festival experience on the welfare of marginalized youth from regional Australia. A case study of a young, same-sex attracted regional participant is presented through the extended narrative voice of "Orsino" who provides a sustained reflection on the impact of the Festival. This chapter exemplifies how life history and narrative analysis can generate powerful insights into the lived experience of "at risk" young people. "Orsino's" account reveals how a vulnerable young man was able to build a more positive sense of his future through his engagement with the arts. This narrative is interpolated into Hughes and Howard's analysis of the ways in which participation in an extended theatre program can provide the means for marginalized school students to "re-imagine" themselves and reconstruct their lives.

Sharon Hogan draws on her study of *The Arts Pathways Initiative*, a Queensland Government program using contemporary art forms in an attempt to re-engage young people "at-risk" with formal education, training and employment programs. Hogan links the idea of adolescents as risk takers negotiating the complexities of social and cultural identity with the role of imagination and creativity in building resilience. She proposes that arts-based programs can offer young people a transitional and safe space for exploring identity, defining new social roles and building new pathways. However, based on her study of *The Arts Pathways Initiative* she argues that arts programs alone offer little benefit to "at risk" young people if they are short-term and unless adequate support structures and effective partnerships between educational institutions, youth service organizations and artists are in place. Significantly her analysis reveals that the young people in the program preferred a mediated arts experience where their personal lives were not the focus of the arts work. Hogan proposes that arts-based programs designed to re-engage young people should be run by artists and educators capable of building positive and respectful relationships, and that they should be flexible with multiple exit and entry points.

Bruce Burton reports on a ten-year action research project with John O'Toole investigating the implementation of DRACON, a drama-based education program in schools on bullying and conflict management. The project began in Queensland in collaboration with the international DRACON research program into conflict within schools, with partners in Sweden and Malaysia. Using a unique combination of drama and peer teaching, the program (also known as "Cooling Conflicts") has been conducted in more than eighty schools and continues to expand each year. Burton describes the structure of the program and argues that it provides a transformative educational experience, particularly for young people "at risk", including those who have experienced bullying behavior. The program employs a modified version of Boal's Forum Theatre involving participants in learning and enacting three stages of conflict and applying it to a simulated social situation. This interactive method also uses "hot seating" where participants take on roles designed to explore the various perspectives of those involved in a bullying or conflict incident. Burton reports a significant decline in bullying in at least one school in which the program has been conducted over an extended period of time. Burton argues that drama provides an effective vehicle for change in that it inherently addresses human relationships, conflict and power.

Anna Hickey-Moody considers disability within the paradigm of risk. She argues that within this paradigm signs such as intellectual disability are read as indicators of lack and disadvantage which, when connected, produce a deficiency of possibility. Her identification of a deficit model concurs with Brown's argument about the negative stereotyping of juvenile offenders. She suggests that dance theatre is a medium through which research can source positive images of young people with disabilities. Her chapter focuses on the Restless Dance Company's 2001 production of *Proximal*. She employs Deleuzian concepts of affect and sensation to examine the company's effectiveness in changing the way that bodies with intellectual disability are "thought". She suggests that the "aesthetic embodied labor of restless dancers" disrupts a deficit model of intellectual disability. Hickey-Moody argues that the work of the Restless Dance Company questions the nature of Cartesian assumptions about the relationship between mind and body, and draws upon what Deleuze and Guattari have called "the possible as an aesthetic category" (1996, 165). Through producing what they describe as "beings of sensation" these performers de-territorialize medical and sociological discourses of intellectual disability. There is a parallel here between the narrative reconstruction of identities proposed by Cahill, Brown and Kelman, and a reconfiguring of the way in which disabled performers in *Proximal* perceived themselves and were perceived by audiences through their dance.

Our own chapter draws extensively on our cross-disciplinary research project *Risky Business*. This ethnographic study across a number of community and custodial sites investigated the effectiveness of creative arts involvement as a diversionary intervention for highly marginalized young people. Over the four years of this study ten arts programs were conducted in urban and rural areas in South East Australia in association with youth support organizations and custodial centers. The *Risky Business* project has been analyzed in a recently published book (Donelan and O'Brien 2008) that outlines the arts programs, presents vignettes of young people, and discusses the research outcomes and policy recommendations. While we decided not to reproduce this information here, we felt it was important to offer some perspectives on such a significant body of material. We have chosen to reflect on our findings from *Risky Business* and interrogate them further, hopefully from a slightly more distanced stance. In our chapter we question how we might ensure that arts interventions with young people are ethically conceived and delivered.

Using our experiences within this research project we question the motivations of those of us working with "at risk" youth, and the ways in which we represent and respond to arts-based processes and products; we also critically scrutinize our selection of data, and our interpretations of instrumental and aesthetic outcomes. We notice that other contributors share our discomfort with some of the claims made for pro-social arts programs for youth, and we believe this signals a healthy commitment not to be seduced by socio-economic pressures into elevating the instrumental value of the arts and reducing their cultural and aesthetic qualities. We hope that this chapter will provoke readers to re-engage with some of the critical issues raised in the first group of chapters as they consider the other research projects presented in this book.

We have given the last word to Dr Peter O'Connor, the founder and artistic director of Everyday Theatre, an applied theatre company funded through the New Zealand Department of Child, Youth and Family Services as part of a national education campaign on child abuse, family violence and neglect. Everyday Theatre uses a dramatic process that invites young people to work together to explore social issues rather than presenting a predetermined message or previously scripted performance. In reflecting on this work O'Connor suggests that the success of the work of Everyday Theatre lies in its avoidance of the stance of "messenger or missionary"; instead it provides an uncontested space where young people can use the language of drama to explore and share their stories about the issues of abuse and family violence. In re-examining his work with young people and considering the positive and negative impacts of diversionary arts programs O'Connor shares his own memories of being a boy deemed to be "at risk". From a poor single parent family, O'Connor was exposed to the "church ladies" who brought food parcels containing what was "needed" not what was wanted. As he recounts his own life experiences he questions the potentially problematic relationship between arts workers and young people categorized as "at risk" and asks whether he is doing "more harm than good" in his current work with young people.

This and associated questions begin and end this book. Are arts interventions with youth "at risk" efficacious? How can we ensure the work we do with young people is socially and politically ethical? In undertaking this work are we, as Boese suggests, complicit in a neo-liberalist agenda to use the arts for their instrumental value in ensuring a "smooth world" (Hardt and Negri 2000)? Can we, as Cahill argues, position the young people with whom we work as potential adult citizens, rather than victims or the perennially marginalized?

At the conclusion of his chapter, O'Connor reflects on his conversations with Maori elders who recognized the capacity of the arts to awaken the life force, to allow us to become and know our true selves. Turner expresses this notion in other ways; he suggests that the arts can engender a liminoid space where true creativity can begin (1986). This is, as Nicholson (2005) suggests, the "gift" that engagement in the arts can offer – a chance to share, to communicate, to transform, to create and recreate at the personal, community, local and global levels.

Works Cited

Australia Council for the Arts. 2006. *Community Partnerships Scoping Study: Creative Communities.* Sydney: Australia Council for the Arts.

Bamford, Anne. 2006. *The Wow Factor: Global Research Compendium on the Impacts of Arts in Education*. New York: Waxman Munster.

Brice Heath, Shirley. 2005. *Dramatic Learning in the Primary School.* London: Creative Partnerships.

Brice Heath, Shirley, and Shelby Wolf. 2004. *Visual Learning in the Community School*. London: Creative Partnerships.

Brice Heath, Shirley. 2000. *Making Learning Work.* Retrieved from http://www.shirleybriceheath.com.

Brice Heath, Shirley, and A. Roach. 1999. "Imaginative Actuality, Learning in the Arts during the Non-school Hours". In E. Fiske, ed. *Champions of Change*. Washington, D.C.: Arts Education Partnerships/President's Committee on the Arts and Humanities. Retrieved from http://www.aep-arts.org.

Bryce, J., J. Mendelovits, A. Beavis, J. McQueen, and I. Adams. 2004. *Evaluation of School-based Arts Education Programmes in Australian Schools*. ACER. Retrieved from http://www.dest.gov.au/sectors/school_education/publications_resources/profiles/.

Deasy, Richard, J. ed. 2002. *Critical Links: Learning in the Arts and Student Academic and Social Development*. Washington, D.C.: Arts Education Partnerships.

Deleuze, G., and F. Guattari. 1996. *What is Philosophy?* London: Verso Publishers.

Donelan, Kate, and Angela O'Brien. 2008. *Creative Interventions for Marginalised Youth: The Risky Business Project.* Brisbane: Drama Australia.

Dreeszen, Craig, Arnie April, and Richard Deasy. 1999. *Learning Partnerships: Improving Learning in the Schools with Arts Partners in the Community*. Washington, D.C.: Arts Education Partnerships.

Fiske, Edward. ed. 1999. *Champions of Change: the Impact of the Arts on Learning*. Washington, D.C.: Arts Education Partnerships/Presidents' Committee on the Arts and Humanities. Retrieved from http://www.aep-arts.org.

Grumet, M. 2004. "No One Learns Alone". In N. Rabkin and R. Redmond, eds. *Putting the Arts in the Picture: Reframing Education in the 21st Century*. Chicago: Columbia College Press, 49-80.

Hardt, Michael and Antonio Negri. 2000. *Empire*. Cambridge, Massachusetts: Harvard.

Hughes, Jenny and Karen Wilson. 2003. "Playing a Part: A Study of the Impact of Youth Theatre on Young People's Personal and Social Development". *Research in Drama Education* 9 (1): 57-73.

Hunter, Mary Anne. 2005. *Education and the Arts: Research Overview, a Summary Report Prepared for the Australia Council for the Arts*. Sydney: Australia Council for the Arts.

Jones, A. 2000. *Visionary Images: A Model of Practice for Delivering Multiple Media Art Programs to Marginalized Young People*. Moonee Ponds: The Salvation Army Crossroads Network.

Marsden, Sally, and Martin Thiele. 2000. *Risking Art – Arts for Survival: Outlining the Role of the Arts in Services to Marginalised Young People*. Richmond, Melbourne: Jesuit Social Services.

McArthur, D., and S. Law. 1996. *The Arts and Prosocial Impact Study: A Review of Current Programs and Literature*. Santa Monica, California: The RAND Corporation.

McCarthy, K., E. Ondaatje, and A. Brooks. 2004. *Gifts of the Muse: Reframing the Debate about the Benefits of the Arts*. Santa Monica, California: The RAND Corporation.

Mills, D., and P. Brown. 2004. *Art and Wellbeing: A Guide to the Connections Between Community Cultural Development and Health, Ecologically Sustainable Development, Public Housing and Place, Rural Revitalisation, Community Strengthening, Active Citizenship, Social Inclusion and Cultural Diversity*. Sydney: Australia Council for the Arts. Retrieved from http://www.ozco.gov.au.

National Advisory Committee on Creative and Cultural Education. 2000. *All Our Futures: Creativity, Culture and Education*. London, UK: DfEE Publications.

Nicholson, Helen. 2005. *Applied Drama: The Gift of Theatre*. Hampshire: Palgrave Macmillan.

Oakley, K. 2007. *Educating for the Creative Workforce: Rethinking Arts and Education*. Sydney: Australian Research Council Centre of Excellence for Creative Industries and Innovation, QUT and Australia Council for the Arts. Retrieved from http://www.ozco.gov.au/news_and_hot_topics/media_releases/creative_education_for_workplace_report/.

O'Brien, Angela, and Kate Donelan. 2007. "*Risky Business*: Engaging Marginalised Young People in the Creative Arts". *The International Journal of the Arts in Society* 1 (6): 15-23. Retrieved from http://www.arts-journal.com.

Rabkin, N., and R. Redmond. eds. 2004. *Putting the Arts in the Picture: Reframing Education in the 21st Century*. Chicago, Illinois: Columbia College Press.

Stone, A., D. McArthur, S. Law, and J. Moini. 1998. *The Arts and Prosocial Impact Study: Program Characteristics and Prosocial Effects*. Santa Monica, California: The RAND Corporation.

—. 1997. *The Arts and Prosocial Impact Study: An Examination of Best Practices*. Santa Monica, California: The RAND Corporation.

Thiele, Martin, and Sally Marsden. 2003. *Engaging Art: The Artful Dodgers Studio: A Theoretical Model of Practice*. Richmond, Melbourne: Jesuit Social Services.

Turner, Victor. 1986. *The Anthropology of Performance*. New York: PAJ Publications.

CHAPTER TWO

RESISTING RISK AND RESCUE AS THE *RAISON D'ÊTRE* FOR ARTS INTERVENTIONS

HELEN CAHILL

In this chapter I discuss the differing perspectives on youth identity and agency that arise in the psychological and sociological research traditions and consider their relevance to arts projects that aim to empower "at risk" youth. I focus on the metaphors underpinning the differing stances we are likely to take depending on the way we conceptualize *who* "youth at risk" are, and the purpose of our work. I examine evaluations of targeted interventions for "at risk" youth, which show that being grouped for the purposes of the interventions is associated with increased negative outcomes for the participants. I discuss the underpinning assumptions that can influence the architecture of work with "at risk" youth, and note the potential for the way youth are positioned and grouped around their "risk" status to detract from program outcomes. I offer a number of recommendations to guide reflection about the artistic and relational architecture that informs approaches to working with youth, recommending an approach that encompasses an interdisciplinary rigor and civic orientation in the design of arts-based intervention programs.

The knowledge gap

It is easy to assume that an arts-based intervention project that has been designed to contribute to the development or wellbeing of youth deemed to be "at risk" would, in fact, do just that. Often the combination of artistic skill and a committed social justice agenda distinguishes such projects. But from another perspective, well-meaning folk arrive, provide an experience, and then leave. The community goes on. What has been left behind? Are those who have participated in the project less likely to engage in harmful behavior such as risky drug use, sexual risk-taking, offending, violence or truancy? The problem is when an arts-based intervention has taken place, we usually do not know, and we do not have the resources to follow-up with participants to assess short or long-term outcomes. What we get to do is to ask them about the experience, or observe as they encounter the experience.

Qualitative research is easier on a shoestring. Not only is it cheaper, we know it will deliver a sensitivity and depth of information that we could not hope to capture in a survey or through a psychological instrument used for pre- and post-testing. Consistently, participants in arts-based interventions speak with enthusiasm of the experience, of how it contributes to their sense of self. We feel good. Apparently they feel better. So what else do we need to know?

For a start, we need to acknowledge that there is a range of research dedicated to evaluating interventions for high-risk youth. One such tradition exists in the psychological field, where the dominant methodology is quantitative, and investment is made in employing closely matched intervention and control groups and utilizing psychological instruments to assess health status and behavior. On occasions a longitudinal approach is taken to assess the impact of the intervention in both the short and long-term. In this medicalized tradition, it is important to ascertain that the intervention has done no harm, as well as to ask whether it has accomplished its objectives.

Another relevant field, arising from a different research tradition, is that of the sociology of youth. Here research is primarily qualitative and theoretical. Emphasis is placed on considering the multiplicity of social factors affecting the ways in which young people construct their sense of self, including class, gender, sexual preference, ethnicity, location, culture, family and education (Dwyer and Wyn 2001).

Both traditions have important research to offer those using the arts to provide interventions for "at risk" youth. However, to embrace knowledge generated in both these broad traditions, one must first take a respectful stance towards the "cultures" of research and the language and terms used in these very different fields. I seek to do just that. I review recent research in the psychological tradition investigating high quality interventions for "at risk" youth, and turn to the sociological tradition to examine the assumptions made in this field.

Interventions that harm

There has been significant interest in recent times in using longitudinal approaches to researching the effectiveness of interventions for high-risk youth. Dishion (1999) used randomized controlled trials to evaluate two robustly developed and well-resourced, interactive lifeskills education programs for high-risk adolescents. This research showed that those who received the interventions were more likely to engage in problem behaviors and to experience negative life outcomes than those with similarly indicated needs who had not been assigned to the intervention. This was most concerning. To fail to make a difference is disappointing, but is often expected in work with high-risk youth; after all, they may have accumulated multiple risk factors over their lifecourse in contrast to which the intervention is puny. It is quite different, however, to find that participating in the "helping" program could lead to *increased* harm, and that those who had been assigned to the control group were better off.

Dishion (ibid) developed a theory to explain this iatrogenic effect, which he termed the theory of peer contagion or "deviancy training". It is worth examining this theory, as a number of subsequent studies, both by Dishion and others, have engaged with this theory, and it raises complex issues for those using arts-based approaches to working with youth (Gifford-Smith et al. 2005; Hyunsan, Hallfors and Sanchez 2005; Leve and Chamberlain 2005; Dishion 2004; Dishion, McCord and Poulin 1999).

Dishion's theory of "deviancy training" arises from a study of videotaped conversations between boys and a chosen friend (Dishion, McCord and Poulin 1999). The boys were given the tasks of planning a peer activity, dealing with a peer problem and with a family problem. Dishion observed that some pairs engaged in a lot of "rule-breaking talk" together with positive reactions (e.g. laughter) to such talk. Other pairs engaged in normative talk or did not reinforce rule-breaking talk with laughter or attention. The rule-breaking-to-laugh pattern (termed "deviancy training") was associated with later delinquency over a subsequent two-year period. Those pairs who engaged in "deviancy training" were more likely to move on to drug and alcohol use, self-reported deviancy and violence, relationship problems and sexual promiscuity and adult convictions than those who did not. From this, Dishion theorized that the reinforcement processes within the peer group are powerful and subtle, being provided in the form of reinforcement through laughter, social attention and interest. He posited that intensity of reinforcement from peers might outweigh the adult role model or leadership provided in the interventions. He argued that teens need normative education because those who are in the high-risk group have a different benchmark as to what constitutes acceptable, expected or "normal" behavior.

Following Dishion's study, other researchers have also made similar findings about the negative impacts of programs which group high-risk adolescents (Gifford-Smith et al. 2005; Hyunsan, Hallfors and Sanchez 2005; Leve and Chamberlain 2005). Despite evidence that youth "at risk" are likely to become more involved in risky or delinquent behavior if grouped together for the purposes of an intervention, most interventions for these youth continue to group them (Gifford-Smith et al. 2005; Hyunsan, Hallfors and Sanchez 2005). Hartup (2005) argues it is not well understood just why the negative effects happen, and that there has been very little study into the dynamics of how young people influence each other. Prinstein and Wang (2005) set out to examine the role that young people's perceptions of peers' behaviors may play as part of the mechanism for "peer contagion". Their study demonstrated that adolescents, particularly those who engage in high-risk behaviors, overestimate the level to which their close friends engage in risky behaviors. This can raise the threshold of the behavior that they believe is normative. The authors theorize that alongside positive reinforcement or "deviancy training" as posited by Dishion, peer modeling, peer demands (pressure), or adolescents' beliefs that emulation of peers' attitudes or behaviors may earn them social rewards, or a better place in the hierarchy, may also form part of the mechanism. They argue (as do Dishion 2005, 1999 and Hyunsan 2005) that in health promotion interventions, it is important to dispel these misconceptions and conduct normative education.

A similar hypothesis has been developed in the field of drug education research (classroom intervention programs designed for delivery to the entire cohort of students, rather than for delivery to targeted groups with indicated needs). It is now well-identified that normative messages are an essential component of effective drug education programs, and that programs which inadvertently glamorize or normalize risky drug use are associated with an increased likelihood that those who participate in the programs will adopt risky drug use patterns (Cahill 2006a; Midford 2000; Tobler and Stratton 1997; Dusenbury and Falco 1995; Dielman 1994). This suggests that the need for normative education is not restricted to "at risk" groups.

This body of research raises a number of issues for those who group high-needs youth for the purposes of arts-based interventions. Is it possible that these programs may also have these effects? The programs researched in the above studies demonstrated positive responses immediately post-program, and hence it was only through the longitudinal approach that other effects were noted. A way to approach this question (in lieu of the possibility of conducting similar matched control longitudinal research studies) is to consider some of the pertinent questions that are left unexplored by the theory of peer "contagion". Each of these questions employs different theoretical models to explain the negative effects of targeted interventions. The explanatory model used to define the problem will influence the choice of "solution" brought to bear. Some of the questions worth considering include:

- What was being "taught" in the hidden curriculum of the programs? Were the participants positioned as needy, bad, sad, mad or "failing" in some way? Foucault (1980) points out that processes of segregation and categorization inform identity formation. Thus, if marked out as needy or failing, people will come to understand themselves this way, and then enact their label. Is it possible to target or segregate without a negative labeling or that a positive categorization (such as the label "artist") might override the effect of segregation?
- Where do the ideas come from that lead to adolescents overestimating the levels of their peers' engagement in risky behaviors? Post-structural theorists argue that we learn various storylines or positions, absorbing them as part of the cultural discourse that we inherit. The positions we are assigned and adopt influence what we see as possible in terms of our actions and thus moderate who we can be (Davies 1994). Is it possible then that some programs may expand the sense of possibility that one holds for oneself whilst others might curtail it? Is it possible that some unlearning might need to occur to dismantle disempowering stories about the self, others and the world at large?
- Might the psychologized and classroom-based modes of learning reinforce a sense of shame or failure as problems become personalized? It may be that participants might benefit from political, practical or service-based modes of activity, doing their learning within a project that has a purpose that is larger than the self. Emancipatory theorists argue that empowerment and change is built through engagement in collective action (Freire 1994, 1985). It may be the experience of contribution and service that builds a sense of purpose, dignity and hope for a better future.

A number of explanatory models have been developed to deal with questions of agency, identity and positioning that are implicit in the questions above. As can be seen, these conceptual models reside in different bodies of literature, each of which may be useful to those engaged in developing or researching arts interventions for "at risk" youth.

As the scope of this chapter limits the discussion of these fields, I will briefly discuss a range of literature that I find particularly helpful in prompting reflective thinking when working with arts-based approaches and young people. I will refer first to the resilience literature with its concepts of "risk" and "protection", and then move to the sociology literature to consider how our concepts of youth might shape the nature of the work we do with them. Then I will refer to the social capital literature to critique issues of bonding and belonging, and finally, to that of narrative therapy and poststructuralist theory to raise questions about positioning and discourse. Finally, I offer some practical reflective tools which draw together some of the key concepts in the literature.

Risk and resilience

The concept of risk and protection is at the heart of many interventions designed to enhance the resilience of "at risk" young people. The metaphor underlying the risk and resilience model is that of a balance or seesaw. On one end, we see the weight of the risk factors the young person has accumulated. On the other end is the pile of protective factors, the presence of which helps to ameliorate or outweigh the effect of the risk factors.

Risk factors and protective factors are identified as occurring at the four levels of community, family, school and the individual. Risk factors include poverty, cultural discrimination, traumatic life events, parental mental health or drug problems, family breakup, bullying, poor attachment to school, membership of a deviant peer group, school failure and social isolation. Protective factors include cultural identity and pride, good physical health, supportive parents, responsibilities at home, social competence, optimism, problem-solving skills, a sense of belonging to school and community, positive school climate, opportunities for success/recognition and a good relationship with at least one adult (Benard 2004; Beyers et al. 2004; McNeely, Nonnemaker and Blum 2002).

Those working within the resilience model aim to strengthen protective factors and reduce risk factors. This is assumed to tip the balance towards resilience or the capacity to cope with adversity and challenge (Benard 2004). The limitation of this model is that many risk factors have already occurred as events in the life of the individual, and the identified protective factors tend also to be descriptive. The model however does not shed light on the *means by which* one is likely to attain or enhance protective attributes, such as optimism, problem solving or a sense of autonomy, meaning or purpose.

When the assumptions inherent in this model are interrogated, some elements defined as risk factors (single parent status, living in poverty, illness of the parent or refugee status) may be the very experience which helped to generate compassion, a sense of social justice, and the capacity to endure, persist and strive for goals. In addition, an individual may see these factors as part of a personal narrative of success, for without adversity, success is no great triumph or accomplishment.

Concepts of youth

Who we think Youth are, and what we think they need, will affect the way we shape interventions and the way we position the young people within the project. If we consider Youth to be "in development", we are likely to think that they "need" educating. If we see Youth as "victims", we may think that they "need" to be helped or rescued, or teach them to blame the perpetrators. If we believe Youth to be "deviant", we are likely to see that they "need" correction or surveillance. If, however, we see Youth as "citizens", we may see that they can contribute (now).

Adolescents are commonly mythologized in media, literature and in political discourse, often stereotypically represented as victims, potential criminals or agents of social disorder (Kelly 2003; Giroux 2000; Bessant and Watts 1998; Wyn and White 1997). Giroux (2000) points out that this stereotyping of youth can affect young people's sense of who they are and undermine their sense of agency. It can also moderate the way in which adults work with youth, restricting what is thought to be possible. If youth are understood to be the "problem", it is unlikely that they will be positioned as the "solution". This can lead to education programs and interventions being designed to help, fix, inoculate, or boost young people. It is possible that this may lead to a way of working with youth that aggravates rather than alleviates problems. It may inspire problem-centric programs or reinforce norms and assumptions about what young people are capable of or can do. Inside such thinking, young people are likely to be positioned as recipients rather than citizens with a contribution to make. At very least, notions of their citizenship are likely to be held in abeyance for some future time when they will acquire adult or "well" status. This can lead to a focus on developing skills and knowledge for the future, rather than a focus on learning in contexts in which skills must be employed on real and current tasks.

Sociology is an important field for those working in arts interventions for youth. A number of key concepts can provide critical reference points. Beck (1992) for example, helps us to broaden our thinking about the term "risk", which is so universally employed in relation to troubled youth (Dwyer and Wyn 2001). Beck theorizes that the new reflexive modernity is a "risk society". No longer "patterned" into traditional family, social, gender and class and geographic structures, individuals must "construct" a life for themselves. This task of individualization described by Beck and Beck-Gernsheim (2002) is one of endless choice and a concomitant sense of risk, if only the risk of making the wrong choice.

> Your life becomes in principle a *risky venture*. A normal life story becomes a (seemingly) elective life, a risk biography, in the sense that everything (or nearly everything) is a matter for decision. (ibid, 48)

One outcome of living in this culture of choice is the likelihood of perceiving that one's failure must somehow be one's own fault. The "individualized society tells us *to seek biographical solutions to systemic contradictions*" (ibid, xxi). The individual is de-politicized and therefore less able to see that broader social and economic forces contribute to experiences of disadvantage and marginalization. Using Beck's concept of the "risk biography" it is possible to theorize that a range of intervention programs may carry meta-messages about individual-as-site-of-blame. It could be logical, for example, for a participant in a program to deduce that if program efforts to reduce their "problems" are focused on the development of their social skills, then it must be a deficit in these skills that is "causing" the problem.

Social capital – bonding and bridging

Another conceptual model that can be used to assist in reflection upon this issue is the notion of social capital. Social capital is a term used to refer to the levels of trust, reciprocity and availability of perceived or actual social, emotional or instrumental support within a community (Putnam 2000). One of the foremost social capital theorists, Putman (ibid) identifies bonding and bridging to be two key mechanisms in the building of social capital. "Bonding" refers to the links people have *within* their family or cultural group. "Bridging" refers to the capacity that people have to transact with others who are not members of their central reference group.

Using the concepts of bonding and bridging it is possible to identify that many intervention programs for high-risk youth are structured so as to enhance bonding, but not necessarily provide opportunities for bridging. This may occur for a number of reasons, some of them institutional. Bridging experiences are more difficult to structure as they are not supported by current institutional design. Our systems habitually sort and group young people into like cohorts, as if that was the "natural" and best way to contribute to their education and wellbeing. This leads to youth being somewhat segregated from society unless connected at the level of family or community. It may be that what some high-risk young people need is less segregation and more opportunities to connect in a real and functional way with the broader society of the workplace and community.

In addition, the dominant influence of the risk and resilience model, with its emphasis on "connectedness" as a key protective factor for young people, has made it easy for educators to seize on this as an "answer" (McNeely, Nonnemaker and Blum 2002). What can all too easily be overlooked, however, is that bonding to a high-risk group with few social and economic resources may carry levels of risk, as well as protection (Hunter 2004). The false binary created with the terms risk and protection sets them apart as opposites, and it becomes more likely that the complexity of something being *both* risky and protective will be missed.

Identity

Giddens (1991) argues that a person's identity is something that must be created and sustained and resides in their ability to keep a particular narrative going. Davies (1989) argues that we take up available positions within stories through which we make sense of our lives. Our production of our sense of identity therefore involves the learning of binary categories that include and exclude, for example, male/female or good/bad. We imaginatively position ourselves as if we belong in one category and not another. The categories have meanings allocated to them, which then are taken up and internalized. This involves a sense of belonging in the world in certain ways, and an emotional commitment to that membership along with a moral system organized around it.

Using Davies' conceptual model it can be theorized that participants in an intervention will already have been "cast" into certain positions. If their behavior is to change, they may need the opportunity to recast themselves and imagine other possible storylines to enact. If the intervention reinforces identification with existing positions, then transformation is unlikely. There is a point of tension here, with the concept of normalization advocated by the psychologists cited earlier. It can be argued that "normalization" will only work insofar as one identifies with the group that displays those norms. Thus, teaching "norms" may only work insofar as the individual ascribes to membership of the group that holds those norms.

Narrative

Is it not necessarily therapeutic to pay heightened attention to one's self, however many arts and education projects assume that the self is the natural object of focus. Rickwood (1995) reviews the outcomes for youth receiving therapy and shows that whereas some show benefit from professional therapeutic care, others show no effect or a negative effect. He argues that heightened self-attention can have negative consequences for adolescents, and that young people benefit from coping strategies that reduce their level of focus on their problems and from focusing on other activities.

White (White and Epston 1990), a pioneer of narrative therapy, draws on Foucault in reframing therapeutic work. He asserts that it is the story that people tell about their problems which contributes to the survival or the "career" of problems. The stories we tell about ourselves provide us with continuity and meaning in our lives. We live into them as well as out of them. This notion of story as underpinning identity is very different from the analogy of an underlying pathology or sickness that has traditionally informed psychological treatment.

White sets out to promote new forms of subjectivity through the practice of narrative therapy in which people create new possibilities for themselves by contesting the old stories that have held problems in place.

> These counter-practices open space for persons to re-author or constitute themselves, each other and their relationships, according to alternative stories or knowledge. (ibid, 75)

White sees the untold pieces that fall outside the dominant story as fertile ground for the generation of these alternative stories. He uses techniques of externalizing the problem, or separating the person from their story as the means through which to assist the person to "re-author" their life. Some of the untold pieces or small moments of "resistance" are picked up as material to use as the basis for a new story.

> As persons are separated from their stories, they are able to experience a sense of personal agency; as they break from their performance of their stories, they experience a capacity to intervene in their own lives and relationships. (ibid, 16)

Which story?

Fine et al. (2003) point out that researchers tend to be drawn to the exotic and tend not to invite or research the *mundane moments* of more common experience. Select stories can conceal as much as they reveal, and they may glamorize or pathologize. Fine charges those who research with oppressed groups to resist the urge to tell only the *bad stories*:

> Simple stories of victimisation, with no evidence of resistance, resilience, or agency, are seriously flawed and…deny the rich subjectivities of persons surviving... (ibid, 125)

While she is writing about the bias that occurs through the researcher's focus, it may equally be true that the protagonist of the story herself may similarly bias the retelling of her own story. Thus young people participating in arts projects may be equally likely to tell the victim stories of their own lives, and omit what White calls the "untold pieces" and the "unique outcomes", which are in fact the moments of resistance.

Informed by narrative therapy and attuned to the political nature of storytelling that Fine alerts us to, we can think critically about the practice in some arts-based interventions whereby youth "at risk" are invited to play out their defining story. We can question whether it is necessarily therapeutic to play and replay a victim story, as this may reinforce the story as defining one's identity. This is not to diminish the reality of the traumatic events that many have encountered, but rather to ask which version of the story is being told, and if it leaves room for a possible future in which the person is not defined by this aspect of their story. White suggests the importance of young people focusing on other aspects of their lived experience which fall outside the dominant story, and may never have been considered worthy of telling. These "untold pieces" or the moments of successful resistance or mundane coping do not as readily capture attention, but they are the basis from which to build additional stories about the past and new stories about the future.

Advice from the dramatists

A number of theorists have reflected upon the use of drama and theatre as a tool for empowerment. Some of their advice is useful for those using the arts to intervene in the lives of troubled youth. Neelands (1996) describes four key strands through which drama or theatre for empowerment is approached. He cites work in the *personal* domain, whereby theatre is seen as a resource for transforming one's sense of self;

work in the *cultural* domain that seeks to make obvious the influence of culture; work in the *communal* domain, whereby theatre becomes a vehicle for expressing the needs and concerns of the community; and work in the *social/political* domain, in which theatre becomes a forum to conduct radical dialogue and to rehearse for change.

These four categories are a useful way to think about the intent and nature of the arts project. They do not however stand in as a guarantee that the goal (empowerment) will be attained. O'Toole (1992) alerts us to the gap that can occur between intent and actuality. He uses the term "maverick meanings" to alert us to the fact that the meaning that emerges from a drama is "multiple and many-layered" and "not always controllable" (ibid, 43). "Official" or deliberate metaphors may be subverted by "unofficial" meanings, and a well-meaning drama may inadvertently glamorize a behavior it purports to stand against, for example, sexist stereotyping and the glorification of deviant behavior (231).

Others have pointed out that arts-based approaches can all too easily stereotype or problematize certain groups, simply through ways in which scenarios are cast and framed, and via the selection of dramatic perspectives explored or ignored (Gallagher 2006; Fletcher 1995; Nicholson 1995a, 1995b). O'Neill (1996) offers advice about how to avoid this tendency when working through drama. She suggests that naturalism constrains the exploration of the themes of the drama, and argues for use of the surreal, allegory, parody and other stylistic possibilities to ensure that students gain both perspective on the issue, and the necessary control over the dramatic elements. Considered use of form, genre, style and framing can assist the dramatist to ensure that sensitive issues are explored in a robust and respectful manner, whilst also providing a protective distancing for the participants (Cahill 2006b). In this, what may occur is the distancing from the story, which makes room for the authoring of new possibilities.

Positioning

It is not just the messages inherent in the artistic piece that can work against the empowering intent of the leaders. So too can the way in which the participants are positioned in the project itself. If they are cast as recipients, victims or perpetrators, then, regardless of the quality of the artistic process or products, they may be re-learning a fundamentally disabling lesson. If they are cast within the project itself in roles of meaning, purpose and value, then they are more likely to find the experience empowering (Cahill 2005).

To explore the idea of positioning, I provide two examples of projects in which attention has been paid to the way in which young people are positioned within the project itself. In both, they work as co-teachers and key informants, as well as artists in that they contribute to the education of adults through their participation in arts intervention.

The "Your Shoes, My Shoes" project

Your Shoes, My Shoes is a Big hArt project conducted in Moree, New South Wales (Cahill, Murphy and Hughes 2005). In this project young Aboriginal people use photo and video to develop tools to inform police about their lives and needs, and to teach police to respond appropriately to young people such as themselves. Within the project they learn media skills and then engage in reverse mentoring as they teach the skills to their police arts-buddy. They then accompany their buddy on a day of police work to gain some insight into the work police do. The visual products developed in the project then become tools that are used to contribute to further training workshops for police who have not participated in the mentorship program.

From this brief project description, it can be seen that in addition to learning new skills from the photographic artists, the young people are cast as contributors to their community, and take on roles of purpose and value. Their new skills are put to use and their products have a real audience, and the purpose is integrated into the project. The young people develop bridging relationships (with the police as well as the artists). The narrative focus of their visual work is tipped so as to fall on the contexts within which the young people live, rather than centering upon their narrative or life stories.

The "Drama at the Heart of Learning Partnerships" project

In the Drama at the Heart of Learning Partnerships project, classes of school students participate in drama workshops designed to assist teachers and doctors to learn how to communicate with youth about social health issues (Cahill 2006c, 2005). Participants cross the boundaries of their social and professional roles to work as co-investigators, actors, coaches and key informants. As actors they co-create with their adult partners the scenarios, which then become the focus for the investigation. As coaches they assist the teacher or doctors in training to develop their skills in communicating with adolescents. As key informants they provide a perspective on the ways in which a range of issues impact young people, with regard to health and learning.

Participants engage in both ethical and practical questions around how to manage a range of predicaments arising in fictional scenarios involving social problems such as racism, bullying, family pressures, mental health problems and substance use. The students do not play out their own stories, but rather work with the tertiary students to investigate scenarios known to be common, based on prevalence data.

A range of alter-ego and surrealist devices is used to assist participants to investigate how who you are "being" can affect what you are "seeing", or your cultural understanding of causes and meanings of your own and others' actions. This process facilitates an embodied and thus accessible exploration of the discourses shaping behavior and lays the groundwork for new possibilities, pathways and positions to be adopted (Cahill 2006b). The whole class participates and thus the students involved are neither targeted because of indicated needs, nor selected due to special aptitude or other elite status. Rather the involvement is part of their core program. The work is purposeful and valued, conducted within the curriculum and timetable, and designed with the assumption that everyone has something to contribute and something to gain.

Powerful roles

These two projects illustrate the shifts that are possible when young people are positioned to contribute to others through their projects. However, in order to reposition young people as "co-providers" rather than "consumers", as part of a "solution" rather than just the "problem", we must challenge existing discourses about the role of youth and, in particular, the assumptions that may come with the label "at risk". This requires an act of imagination on the part of the program developers, and a certain willingness on their part to risk working beyond the traditional modes of provider/recipient that underpin dominant models within health and education traditions.

In this final section, I offer some questions that are useful in guiding the program leaders when framing arts interventions for youth deemed to be "at risk". These questions embrace the notion of positioning that arises from the poststructuralist literature, and respond to the challenges posed in the psychological literature regarding the potential for negative peer influence. My intent is that these questions open possibilities rather than prescribe action. Action is best designed reflexively, attuned to the context and purpose, and cognizant of the human and physical resources available.

Purpose and positioning

- What is the broader social purpose of this project?
- What are the structures or institutions within which the project will be housed? How will they define or confine the purpose and nature of the work?
- How are the participants positioned? Who will question the assumptions made about the participants and the work?
- Who will question whether the art works stereotype, demonize, glamorize or reinforce victim/oppressor stories?

Social architecture

- Who will participate, when, where and for how long?
- Who will be included/excluded and what effect might that have?
- How will participation be recruited/mandated?
- What will be the start? What is the end?
- What opportunities for participation will be sustained after the intervention?
- What structures will house participants' interactions with each other (bonding) and others beyond the immediate community (bridging)?
- What roles and positions will be available for the participants?

Meaning-making

- Why was this material, story, image or approach chosen?
- What are the meta-messages that may be transmitted by the work?
- What has been silenced or omitted and what effect does this have?
- What meanings are likely to be made up about this work?
- How will the selected genre, form, focus and metaphors influence the meanings made?
- What aesthetic structures or stylistic devices will be used to invite poly-

vocality and multiplicity of perspective?

- What will this contribute to?

Interdisciplinarity

- How will we gather knowledge about the populations we seek to serve, the social health issues or themes we seek to address and the institutions, services or settings within which we are working?
- How will we be informed by prior research and thinking, including traditions outside of our own disciplinary heritage?
- How will we know what difference we have made?

Program integrity

One of the challenges in the use of arts interventions to promote wellbeing resides in aligning practice to theory, so that the process works in alignment with the purpose. The program cannot be seen to have integrity if it inadvertently subverts its own goals. Given that the experiences gained in association with a program can transmit negative messages about the identity or storyline of the participants, it is important to structure powerful roles for young people engaged in the arts work. One way to do this is to ensure that, rather than being defined as therapeutic in nature, the arts project is designed to make a civic contribution. This will locate the artists in powerful roles that connect them socially and politically to the broader community. The real opportunity in arts-based work with young people who have been disadvantaged, marginalized or silenced may be to equip them to take up their own rewriting of the personal, social and political scripts that will shape their individual and shared futures.

Works Cited

Beck, Ulrich, and Elizabeth Beck-Gernsheim. 2002. *Individualization. Institutionalized Individualism and its Social and Political Consequences*. London: Sage.

—. 1992. *Risk Society: Towards a New Modernity*. London: Sage.

Benard, Bonnie. 2004. *Resiliency: What We Have Learned.* San Francisco: WestEd.

Bessant, J., and R. Watts. 1998. "History, Mythmaking and Young People in Time of Change." *Family Matters* 49: 5-10.

Beyers, Jennifer, John Toumbourou, Richard Catalano, Michael Arthur and David Hawkins. 2004. "A Cross-national Comparison of Risk and Protective Factors for Adolescent Substance Use: The United States and Australia." *Journal of Adolescent Health* 35 (1): 3-16.

Cahill, Helen. 2006a. "Devising Classroom Drug Education Programs." In *Drug Education in Schools: Searching for the Silver Bullet*, edited by R. Midford and G. Munro. Camberwell: Pearson.

—. 2006b. "Sensitive Issues: Supportive Structures." *NJ (Drama Australia Journal)* 30 (1): 7-22.

—. 2006c. "Research Acts: Using the Drama Workshop as a Site for Conducting Participatory Action Research." *Drama Australia (NJ)* 30 (2): 61-72.

—. 2005. "Profound Learning: Drama Partnerships between Adolescents and Tertiary Students." *Drama Australia (NJ)* 29 (2): 59-72.

Cahill, Helen, Bernadette Murphy and Alex Hughes. 2005. *Promising Programs: A Review of Drug Prevention Interventions to Assist Young People in Transitional Pathways*. Canberra: Department of Health and Ageing.

Davies, Bronwyn. 1994. *Post-structuralist Theory and Classroom Practice*. Geelong: Deakin University Press.

—. 1989. "The Discursive Production of the Male/Female Dualism in School Settings." *Oxford Review of Education.* 15 (3): 229-41.

Dielman, T. E. 1994. "School-based Research on the Prevention of Adolescent Alcohol Use and Misuse: Methodological Issues and Advances." *Journal of Research on Adolescence* 4: 271-93.

Dishion, Thomas, J., J. McCord, and F. Poulin. 1999. "When Interventions Harm - Peer Groups and Problem Behaviour." *American Psychologist* 54 (9): 755-64.

Dishion, Thomas, J., Sarah E. Nelson, Charlotte E. Winter, and Bernadette M. Bullock. 2004. "Adolescent Friendship as a Dynamic System: Entropy and Deviance in the Etiology and Course of Male Antisocial Behavior." *Journal of Abnormal Child Psychology* 32 (6): 651-63.

Dusenbury, L., and M. Falco. 1995. "Eleven Components of Effective Drug Abuse Prevention Curricula." *Journal of School Health* 65 (10): 420-5.

Dwyer, Peter, and J. Wyn. 2001. *Youth, Education and Risk, Facing the Future*. London and New York: Routledge.

Fine, Michelle, Lois Weiss, Susan Weseen, and Loonmun Wong. 2003. "For Whom? Qualitative Research, Representations, and Social

Responsibilities." In *The Landscape of Qualitative Research: Theories and Issues, 2nd Edition*, edited by N. K. Denzin and Y. S. Lincoln. Thousand Oaks: Sage.

Fletcher, Helen. 1995. "Retrieving the Mother/Other from the Myths and Margins of O'Neill's 'Seal Wife' Drama." *NADIE (NJ)* 19 (2): 25-38.

Foucault, Michel. 1980. *Power/Knowledge. Selected Interviews and Other Writings 1972-1977*, edited by C. Gordon. Brighton, Sussex: The Harvester Press.

Freire, Paulo. 1994. *Pedagogy of Hope: Reliving Pedagogy of the Oppressed*. New York: Continuum.

—. 1985. *The Politics of Education: Culture, Power and Liberation*, translated by H. Giroux. London: Macmillan.

Gallagher, Kathleen. 2006. "(Post) Critical Ethnography in Drama Research." In *Research Methodologies for Drama Education*, edited by J. Ackroyd. Stoke on Trent: Trentham Books.

Giddens, Anthony. 1991. *Modernity and Self-Identity: Self and Society in the Late Modern Age.* Cambridge: Polity.

Gifford-Smith, Mary, Kenneth A. Dodge, Thomas J. Dishion and Joan McCord. 2005. "Peer Influence in Children and Adolescents: Crossing the Bridge from Developmental to Intervention Science." *Journal of Abnormal Child Psychology* 33 (3): 255-65.

Giroux, Henry A. 2000. *Stealing Innocence: Youth, Corporate Power and the Politics of Culture.* New York: St Martins Press.

Hartup, Williard W. 2005. "Peer Interaction: What Causes What?" *Journal of Abnormal Child Psychology* 33 (3): 387-8.

Hunter, Boyd. 2006. *Taming the Social Capital Hydra? Indigenous Poverty, Social Capital Theory and Measurement. Discussion Paper 261.* Centre for Aboriginal Economic Policy 2004. Retrieved January 30 2006, www.anu.edu.au/caepr/.

Hyunsan, Cho, D.D. Hallfors and V. Sanchez. 2005. "Evaluation of a High School Peer Group Intervention for At-Risk Youth." *Journal of Abnormal Child Psychology* 33 (3): 363-73.

Kelly, Peter. 2003. "Growing Up as Risky Business? Risks, Surveillance and the Institutionalized Mistrust of Youth." *Journal of Youth Studies* 6 (2): 165-80.

Leve, Leslie D., and P. Chamberlain. 2005. "Association with Delinquent Peers: Intervention Effects for Youth in the Juvenile Justice System." *Journal of Abnormal Child Psychology* 33 (3): 339-47.

McNeely, C.A., J.M. Nonnemaker, and R.W. Blum. 2002. "Promoting School Connectedness: Evidence from the National Longitudinal Study of Adolescent Health." *Journal of School Health* 72 (4): 138-46.

Midford, Richard. 2000. "Does Drug Education Work?" *Drug and Alcohol Review* 4: 441-6.

Neelands, Jonothan. 1996. "Agendas of Change, Renewal and Difference." In *Drama, Culture and Empowerment: The IDEA Dialogues*, edited by J. O'Toole and K. Donelan. Brisbane: IDEA Publications.

Nicholson, Helen. 1995a. "Drama Education, Gender and Identity." *Forum of Education* 50 (2): 28-37.

—. 1995b. "Genre, Gender and Play: Feminist Theory and Drama Education." *NJ, Drama Australia Journal* 19 (2): 15-24.

O'Neill, Cecily. 1996. "Alienation and Empowerment." In *Drama, Culture and Empowerment*, edited by J. O'Toole and K. Donelan. Brisbane: IDEA Publications.

O'Toole, John. 1992. *The Process of Drama: Negotiating Art and Meaning*. London: Routledge.

Prinstein, Mitchell J., and Shirley S. Wang. 2005. "False Consensus and Adolescent Peer Contagion: Examining Discrepancies between Perceptions and Actual Reported Levels of Friend's Deviant and Health Risk Behaviours." *Journal of Abnormal Child Psychology* 33 (3): 293-306.

Putnam, Robert. 2000. *Bowling Alone. The Collapse and Revival of American Community*. New York: Simon and Schuster.

Rickwood, D.J. 1995. "The Effectiveness of Seeking Help for Coping with Personal Problems in Late Adolescence." *Journal of Youth and Adolescence* 24 (6): 685-703.

Tobler, N, and H. Stratton. 1997. "Effectiveness of School-based Drug Prevention Programs: A Meta-analysis of the Research." *Journal of Primary Prevention* 18: 71-128.

White, Michael and David Epston. 1990. *Narrative Means to Therapeutic Ends*. Adelaide: Norton.

Wyn, J., and R. White. 1997. *Rethinking Youth*. Sydney: Allen & Unwin.

CHAPTER THREE

THE POLITICS AND POLICIES OF ACHIEVING SOCIAL INCLUSION THROUGH CULTURE

MARTINA BOESE

The arts have been viewed as a vehicle of social change for some time now. This perspective has never been uncontested, but it is timely to review some of the more recent critical perspectives in relation to this view. In the present political context artists are increasingly under pressure to make their work pay for itself, and many artists are involved in initiatives that aim to fight social exclusion or to further social inclusion. Different politics and policies shape these initiatives. To understand their significance, it is useful to consider the rationale of those who are engaged in "making culture work" to achieve social inclusion. I will attempt to further such an understanding of the politics and policies of achieving social inclusion through culture, based on the analysis of empirical examples in the UK and Austria.

In the first section, I will briefly review different approaches to the use of culture for the purpose of social inclusion. I will then address a number of reservations that have been raised against such use of culture. Particular attention will be paid to critical views of the more recent trend of promoting employment in the creative industries. The following section will discuss two initiatives that address disadvantaged young people through cultural activities in Vienna and Manchester. In the final discussion, I will contextualize these project rationales and challenge their categorization as vehicles of neoliberal policies.

From community arts to creative industries: development strategies

At first sight, the arts and social inclusion are an unlikely pair. The consumption of culture has indeed long served as a marker of social difference between the educated bourgeoisie and the "uncivilized" masses (Bourdieu 1987), and even now, the arts have not lost their association with elitism altogether. However, the arts have also been attributed with a "civilizing" potential, which governments have called upon at various times in different political contexts (Bennett 1998). Culture appeared in social democratic political discourses around "extension" and "access" in the early twentieth century in Britain (McGuigan 2004) and beyond, long before it entered the European Union-driven "social inclusion" and the British "social exclusion" agenda. The central idea was the appropriation of culture from its domination by a privileged elite and its extension or opening to the masses.

The emergence of community arts on cultural policy agendas epitomized the cultural democracy movement of the 1970s. Various social and political movements, from feminism to anti-racism, formed the context of the social democratic demand for increased access to and participation in the arts – captured in the internationally popular slogan "Arts for all". Community arts initiatives aimed at engaging those outside of the privileged social realm in the production of culture (Hawkins 1993). The domain of community arts has traditionally embraced a wide range of cultural forms and practices, unified by a focus on the creative process and relationships, rather than its end product. Many examples of community arts have focused on the therapeutic benefits of art making; others have been closely linked with activism, using the creative process as a vehicle for developing and disseminating ideas, thus facilitating participatory democracy. Whichever form, a unifying element has certainly been their contribution to widening the circle of people expressing themselves through artistic means (Matarasso 2005, 1997).

More recently the pairing of culture and the arts with "social in/exclusion" has become associated with another political discourse characteristic of neoliberalism. Concepts like the "creative class", the "cultural or creative industries"[1] and "cultural planning"[2] (Stevenson

[1] This is not the space to review ongoing debates on the definition of this term and its precursor, the "cultural industries" (see e.g. Hesmondhalgh 2002). The British Department for Culture, Media and Sport has included the following fields in its Creative Industries Mapping Documents (DCMS 1998): advertising, architecture,

2004) typify this discourse. At its core is the understanding of social exclusion as economic exclusion. The new focus on social exclusion in the UK emerged in the late 1990s, from the "New Labour" government's concern with the regeneration of poor neighborhoods and the National Strategy for Neighbourhood Renewal. Culture – understood as "a whole way of life" (Williams 1971, 1958) – has been considered as a crucial factor in urban regeneration processes since the early 1980s (Landry 1996; Myerscough 1988). The target of social change in these developments was and still is usually a neighborhood that is viewed as deprived, and the objective of the urban regeneration process is to turn this spatially constructed community around to give it a sustainable future. The development of culture-led urban regeneration emerged along with a growing recognition of popular culture as an economically beneficial factor. The cultural industries were celebrated for creating employment, rejuvenating city centers and attracting tourists, as well as corporate investment. The new support for the cultural industries carried a democratizing element, with the view that they symbolized the majority's cultural consumption (e.g. television, film, popular music) as opposed to publicly funded recipient art forms (O'Connor 2000).

Culture-based urban regeneration initiatives spread across Europe in the 1980s (Bianchini and Parkinson 1993). However, urban redevelopment benefited city managers and urban planners more than the socially disadvantaged citizenry. The focus on economic growth, rather than social factors, failed to bring about the expected urban renaissance and evoked increasing criticism (Bianchini 1999; Fisher and Owen 1991). By the mid-1990s a shift occurred towards social, rather than economic considerations in the UK. Cultural industries, such as the music industry, were promoted not only to re-image cities and attract capital investment, they were furthermore considered as "vital for the social and economic wellbeing of community and place" (Fleming 1999), and a tool to "manage urban change" (Healey et. al. 1995), which explains their prominent role in

---

arts and antique markets, crafts, design, designer fashion, film, interactive leisure software, music, television and radio, performing arts, publishing, software. While early studies still referred to the "arts and the cultural industries", others used the notion of the "cultural sector" including the "traditional arts" as well as commercial cultural activities (O'Connor 1999).

[2] Cultural planning is a place-based approach to cultural policy making which aims at social, economic and urban, as well as creative outcomes, and "variously involves establishing cultural precincts, nurturing creative activity, and re-evaluating public life and civic identity" (Stevenson 2004, 119).

cultural planning processes. Following Stevenson's recent analysis of the logic of cultural planning:

> (S)ocial inclusion is achieved through economic development which is achieved by fostering the creative industries (which in practice largely refer to "the arts", but discursively embraces the popular and multicultural) in a way that "includes" the marginal and rejuvenates degenerative urban spaces. Through their participation in the economy, the marginal will thus be integrated into society as "full" citizens, and redeveloped urban space will become the public sphere wherein citizenship is expressed and social inclusion affirmed. (Stevenson 2004, 128)

Under Blair's New Labour government, the potential of the arts to contribute to social inclusion gained official recognition, and became indeed the rationale for investment in culture. However, contrary to the support for community arts, which was framed in terms of social justice, the more recent agenda of supporting the cultural or creative industries is informed by the concept of social inclusion, which is framed in terms of economic participation (Stevenson 2004). This shift from a social democratic agenda of "Arts for all" towards a policy agenda that promotes the arts to achieve social and economic objectives has been international, possibly headed by New Labour in the UK.

By the late 1990s critical commentary on this instrumental approach appeared in the UK:

> (M)uch has come to be expected of creativity and culture in cities today. Culture is supposed to overcome social exclusion and poverty by empowering individuals and neighbourhoods and by democratising and enlivening urban ways of living. Creativity is held up as a means of generating new ideas, new solutions and new ways of working on seemingly intractable social problems. Yet, despite this, the bottom line is that together culture and creativity are supposed to foster economic growth. It is a tall order. (Foord 1998, 38)

In the course of the depicted policy developments many artists or cultural practitioners have taken on the role of commissioned "cultural workers", purveyors of creativity that deliver their skills to those affected by social exclusion: communities, neighborhoods or putting it bluntly, local economies. By looking at this role and the implications of the depicted change, I will now turn to critical perspectives on the use of the arts within the context of a social inclusion agenda.

Critical perspectives towards a "social inclusion through the arts" agenda

This section will address five partly interrelated directions of criticism. Firstly, several authors have raised concerns about the increasing economic pressures on artists in the depicted political context. Governments' earlier mentioned recognition of a mismatch between arts funding and the cultural consumption of the population majority, alongside an ideological shift away from the concept of the "public good", had dire consequences for the arts in countries such as the UK, the US and Australia. It led to cuts in arts funding and increased pressure on the arts sector to emphasize its economic viability. Employment creation, cultural tourism and cultural export are typical examples of arguments for the economic benefits of the arts (Caust 2003). These notions were raised in the hope that speaking the same language as the government would help the sector to preserve existing levels of cultural expenditure (Belfiore 2002).

Secondly, the recognition of the social benefit of the arts by the government and their incorporation in urban and neighborhood renewal agendas exerts pressure on artists to engage in "socially useful" art activities. This shows a failure to acknowledge the intrinsic value of the arts and reduces them to instruments of a social policy agenda (ibid).

A third strand of critique concerns political implications of the use of the arts. It emerged in critical commentary on "Third way"[3] policies, as well as in the theory of social interventionist art. Its prime concern is the relationship of arts projects with the state and other systems of regulation and social control. More precisely, this critique is concerned with the utilization, or co-option of artists, cultural workers and community workers by the state or other bodies equipped with regulatory authority. It is grounded in an understanding of the arts as a medium of counter-culturaland counter-hegemonic transformation, and is against a conception of the arts as a tool of civilization, domestication and social control (Stevenson 2004).

[3] The Third Way is the particular ideological direction of "New Labour" under (the then) PM Blair in the UK, which has been described as "a compromise – a hybrid position that seeks, variously, to transcend or bridge the divide between the traditional Left and the neo-liberal Right", thus "challeng(ing) many of the core social and political assumptions and values of the traditional Left, including those associated with the role of the state, the nature of democracy and the goal of social justice" (Stevenson 2004, 126).

Examples of counter-hegemonic approaches to "utilizing" the arts as a medium of social intervention can be found worldwide under different labels. These include participatory art, intervention art, political art, art in the social field and more recently, "new genre public art", a label used in the US for art in the public interest, in collaboration with representatives of different public spheres and interest groups (Rollig and Sturm 2002; Babias und Könneke 1998). Resistance against being submitted to a social policy agenda is characteristic of many artistic interventions in this context. While these might overlap with such policy agendas, they occur outside of a delivery-upon-contract relationship.

Towards the end of the 1990s, art forms under the umbrella of "socially interventionist art" underwent criticism for having superseded political interventionist art practice by becoming "social work art 'in the public interest' to mean policy: administration, engineering and possibly technocratic handling of social problems. Public art becomes a privatist version of public welfare" (Marchart 1998). According to radical democracy theorists, who have forwarded this critique, these art initiatives fail to politicize by taking on a pacifying role.

A fourth direction of criticism, which is fundamentally different from the previously depicted ones, challenges the very assumption that social inclusion can be achieved through participation in the arts. It is based on the difficulty of measuring outcomes of such participation. If the achievement of social inclusion is indeed sustainable, outcomes have to be measurable in the long-term. As with other social interventions, a reliable measurement tool would demand the consideration of external factors and isolate these from the effects of the arts initiative. Furthermore, the universal claim about the social impact of participation in the arts fails to acknowledge the existence of differences between kinds of participatory arts activities, communities and cultural contexts in which they are placed (Merli 2002).

Fifthly, another criticism in relation to the effectiveness of community arts pertains to its potential to reach the most isolated and socially disadvantaged community members. A recent review of such initiatives in Australia and overseas has highlighted the critical importance of their conceptual design and implementation. A division of arts' projects along class and ethnic lines can, for example, enforce the division between these groups, rather than act as a social bridge (Barraket 2005).

The issue of limited potential and selective benefit has also been raised in relation to culture-led urban regeneration programs. One of their limitations lies in their intermediaries, such as arts consultants, who influence the recognition and legitimization of cultural practices by ascribing cultural value and potential economic value to particular cultural events, artifacts and experiences (Foord 1999). Based on her analysis of the London-based Hidden Art Initiative, Foord coined the term "economic normalization" for the outcomes of locking culture and creativity into economic regeneration. The values and practices of the market determine which cultural practices and artifacts are included in the regeneration process (ibid, 60). Other studies of culture-led urban regeneration projects have pointed to the danger of excluding particular social groups, or even the local population altogether, due to the focus on corporate-cultural needs (Talbot and Boese 2007; Chatterton and Hollands 2002; Blake and Jeffery 2000).

Social inclusion through participation in the creative economy: a risky business

A central argument in the association of the creative industries with a social inclusion agenda pertains to the alleged employment effects of local industries development. The hope for newly emerging employment opportunities in sectors, such as the music and new media industry, was particularly prevalent in cities that suffered from high unemployment rates in the aftermath of economic restructuring in the early 1980s (O'Connor and Wynne 1996).

Young people are typical target groups of cultural industry projects within the social inclusion paradigm. They are targeted to engage in their local neighborhoods through so-called cultural hubs, to train in creative skills, and importantly, to integrate in the local economy as "creative entrepreneurs". Young people are not only an important group of participants in contemporary cultural practices, they also contribute actively to these practices based on their intimate familiarity with and knowledge of different cultural codes, which has been referred to as "subcultural capital" (Thornton 1995). It is hence not surprising that the creative industries have come to be viewed by some as the ideal work environment for young people and thus a fit remedy for youth unemployment, especially in cities.

The growing body of research on employment in the creative economy suggests, however, a harsher picture than the widespread romanticization of a "blur between work and pleasure", and between the realms of consumption and production. Most accounts speak of exploitative working conditions and unstable employment in the creative industries. McRobbie (2002) for example, observed that the reality of working in the creative sector is not as inclusive of the social margins as many might think, based on the informal and fluid nature of creative work environments. It might be relatively easy to slip into "creative" jobs at the lower end of the scale (as a DJ or flyer designer) where nobody asks for formal training or qualifications. Yet to find employment in the creative industries demands network resources and the skill of using them to one's advantage. Furthermore, practitioners need to be willing to accept short-term and underpaid contracts in a highly competitive industry where everybody can be quickly replaced, and to be ready for self-exploitation in a field without a history of industrial relations and the merits of trade unions (Hesmondhalgh 2002). Different studies have documented that groups that have traditionally been disadvantaged in other segments of the labor market, for example, women and ethnically defined minorities, meet similar barriers in the creative sector (e.g. Boese 2003b; Richards and Milestone 2000).

Where does this leave initiatives that aim at the social inclusion of young unemployed people through fostering creativity and developing skills that are actually useful in the creative labor market? Are they merely variants of the "work for the dole" scheme in the cultural field? In other words are they "cultural workfare" tools, aimed at no more than getting young unemployed people off the unemployment statistics, and thus offering another example of shortsighted neoliberal thinking?

Examples from Manchester and Vienna

The following discussion is based on two separate pieces of research: my doctoral research project on racism and exclusion in Manchester's club culture economy, and a recently completed comparative research project funded by the EU on cultural diversity policies and transnational migration in seven capital cities in Europe (Meinhof and Triandafyllidou 2006).

Example I: DJ Academy and talent shows in Manchester

The Manchester-based project DJ Academy was set up in 2000 by two longtime practitioners in Manchester's music industry, who had met in the corridors of Manchester Town Hall when trying to gain funding for a DJ training project. The DJ/promoter/band manager and the musician/manager of a recording studio decided to collaborate on a European funding bid, to be matched by the city council.

The DJ Academy formed an extension to an already existing course at the recording studio called "Music and Open Learning Division" and operated within the New Deal scheme for musicians.

As one of its two founders wanted to counteract racist exclusion in the music industry, the DJ Academy aimed at a 50 percent share of participants from so-called "ethnic minorities". The demand for places in the DJ Academy quickly exceeded the supply of places. The recruitment of participants occurred partly through the project managers' personal networks in various local communities and partly through New Deal advisors, since the project was also run as a New Deal (match-funded) initiative, and therefore addressed young, unemployed people.

The course objective was above all to provide its participants with industry-relevant skills, as well as a formal recognition of these skills on course completion. Most importantly, the DJ Academy also provided its young trainees with personal contacts, and thus a crucial entry point into the highly networked music industry. By providing a pathway out of unemployment and into the creative sector, the DJ Academy project clearly offered an interesting opportunity to its target group.

One of the project founders and managers depicted his approach to the course design:

> I don't know how to make somebody the best scratcher in the world, the best mixer in the world academically. But I know how you can make a living out of it! And so the course will be done like that. And then all the people that I've got informing our course, they're employed in it as well! It'll probably have big academic holes in it but at least all the DJs they stick on the course will be able to go: "I know how they'll be able to survive; they wanna do some club nights. But the thing is if they're crap DJs, then I'd be telling them to save up whatever money they can and buy a taxi and become a taxi driver." [4]

This statement clearly shows that the principal purpose of the DJ Academy was preparation for employment, rather than providing access to cultural expression.

Local talent shows were another bottom-up attempt to promote access to the music sector in Manchester that targeted socially disadvantaged youth. The aim was to give young people from the area the space and opportunity to perform their act in front of an audience that exceeded their friends and families and included talent scouts. These talent scouts would be able to promote them and put them in touch with recording studios and other industry players. Such events took place amongst others in one of Manchester's socially disadvantaged and most criminalized and stigmatized inner city neighborhoods. They were funded by local government via a

[4] I conducted this interview on January 28, 2000.

local support organization, organized by some local industry practitioners, among them, a music producer. The shows proved to be very successful in terms of opening up further opportunities in the music sector to some of their participants. Besides this most directly targeted effect of the talent shows, they also offered the social benefit of offering participants an alternative to illegal pastimes, as one of the organizers explained in an interview:

> The shows helped to spot the talent, which helped us give an alternative to the lifestyle that was prevalent in the area! So you know, it's easier to put money to a project which diverted the kids attention from thinking, I can get a big car if I sell drugsthan to say: well, if I develop my talents and become a pop artist or a pop star or a musician, I can get a big car! And there is a big difference! And if he hasn't got that diversion, then the only odd thing he's gonna look at is: well, I want a big car. The other sections of society are looking down at me because I've got nothing.[5]

Like in the DJ Academy, the objective of this initiative is to provide pathways into employment in the creative industries.

Example II: *DEZENTRALE MEDIEN* in Vienna

The Vienna-based group, *Dezentrale Medien*, is comprised of four artists, two of whom are migrants, who work with mainly migrant young people, through art and new media technology. A central motivation of their work is to address questions of social exclusion and access to education and training in the fields of art and new media, particularly for minority groups who are socio-economically or in other ways socially disadvantaged.

It is not their principal aim to offer young people new media skills, although they also do that. Above all, they want to instigate a socio-political dialogue about the participants' living realities and experiences, and to explore issues that matter to these participants in a visual, artistic way. Their emphasis is on process and teamwork and they consider the personal interaction of the teenagers over a long period as an important outcome. The teenagers view their voluntary participation over several months initially mainly as an opportunity to get free Internet access and a basic course in new media. But the fact that they design and create something that is not judged or evaluated in terms of "right' or 'wrong", "good" or "bad" is a new experience to many of them. The exchange of

[5] I conducted this interview on March 10, 2000.

experience and images about current affairs and the city they live in promotes the feeling of solidarity among the teenagers and helps them to put their problems in perspective. One of their projects was the building of a virtual house, in which eleven young people designed their ideal living space. The starting point for this project was the young people's migration to Vienna and their life in Vienna, including their living, working and education situations. The participants learned to design a webpage, a typical skill in demand in the creative industries. However, the principal objective was to provide the participants with a space to reflect on and exchange their experiences as well as express them in a creative way.

Over the last ten years, a number of comparable initiatives and projects have emerged in the "third sector" (alternatively called the "community" or "not-for-profit" sector) in Austria. They use different art and media forms to explore different social and political issues with young people, who are viewed as "at risk" groups (e.g. due to their residential neighborhood or their belonging to a certain social group). These projects are often collaborations between artists, intellectuals and youth workers associated with a politically activist left field. The distinctive element of *Dezentrale Medien* and similar projects, that separates them from the earlier Manchester-based examples, is their more explicit focus on political issues such as exclusion, racism and marginalization, often in the context of current affairs. While these initiatives provide their participants undoubtedly with creative skills, often in the field of new media, their aim is not to improve the participants' employability. Their objective is to encourage young people to participate, yet the participation they have in mind is socio-political rather than economic. Reflection on the processes occurring in the project, including power relationships between cultural workers and participants, forms an important part of this approach.

In summary, the analysis of these different examples shows both basic similarities and significant differences. What unites them is their common aim to tackle the social exclusion of disadvantaged young people through the use of creative activities whereby participants gain specific creative skills. What distinguishes them is their respective socio-political orientation and politics of inclusion. In the Manchester-based examples, the focus is on inclusion in the economic sense; empowerment means promoting participants' ability to enter the labor market at a higher end. In the Vienna-based examples, the focus is on inclusion in the political sense; empowerment means facilitating ways in which participants can express themselves as citizens.

Putting initiative in context

The wider context of the described examples, namely the shift to an economic paradigm in social inclusion policies, has been described in the first section of this chapter. However, the more specific social and political context of these projects also deserves more attention.

In Manchester, the creative industries support proclaimed by the Department for Culture, Media and Sport at the national level found its local expression in a Cultural Production Strategy for Manchester commissioned by the City Council and the establishment of a Cultural Industries Development Service (CIDS) in 1999. CIDS was created to assist the development of independent cultural and creative business in Manchester. Its principal objectives were to "raise the profile of the cultural sector" in Manchester and surroundings, and to "provide a voice and strategic forum for the creative industries by acting as a sectoral lead body" (CIDS profile), improving internal cohesion and self-awareness, as well as acting as a port of call for information about the sector. The funding for CIDS stemmed partly from the European Regional Development Fund through an application by the Manchester City Council (Fleming 1999; O'Connor 1999).

While this emergence of interest and support for locally produced culture appeared to pursue a democratizing agenda, it failed to include many people at the margins of the local cultural economy, for example, many cultural practitioners of African-Caribbean descent. A more general history of criminalization of "black music" and black music practitioners, and more specifically, a local history of violence in night clubs were conflated into the stigmatization of black people[6] as risky participants in Manchester's pop cultural economy, whether as cultural producers (DJs or promoters) or cultural consumers ("punters" at night clubs) (Boese 2005). Furthermore, newly established local governance tools, such as the Local Area Partnerships including different stakeholders in the night-time economy, did not necessarily pursue a focus on social inclusion. The shift of responsibilities for the safety and wellbeing of participants in cultural venues, from the metropolitan police force to cultural businesses, led the latter to prioritize their vested interest in "staying in business". This facilitated, in turn, a widespread practice of "preventive discrimination" rather than an agenda of cultural democratization, the origin of creative industries support in the 1980s (Talbot and Boese 2007; Boese 2003b).

[6] The term "black people" has been adopted from the practitioners who informed this research and denotes people of African-Caribbean descent.

Considering this context, both initiatives, the DJ Academy and the talent shows, seem perfectly suited to address a local framework of exclusion, which has frustrated many cultural practitioners. Viewing the hopes and aspirations of materially deprived and socially discriminated against young people, a pathway out of risky illegal activities and into a locally and nationally celebrated "creative industries" sector clearly provides a social inclusion strategy.

To understand better the rationale of the Vienna-based example, it is pertinent to consider the role of the third sector in the changing political climate in Austria. A crucial aspect of this change is the shift towards neoliberalism under the conservative People's Party and the right-wing Freedom Party that entered government in 2000. This change in power signaled a retreat of the state from arts funding together with a shift to promoting creative industries. Another characteristic of the cultural policy orientation of this government was its support of traditional folk culture, while critical cultural institutions came under threat due to funding cuts.

In Austria, many cultural initiatives in the third sector began in the early 1970s in a phase of cultural democratization alongside an expansion of the welfare state under the social democratic government. The catchphrases, "culture for all", "access to arts education" and "opening up of society" incorporated some of the aims of the workers movement at the beginning of the twentieth century. A Cultural Services Office (ÖKS) was established to help break down the barriers to participation in cultural life, by bringing artists and creators of culture to schools, adult education institutions, companies and cultural centers (Ellmeier, Baumgartner and Perchinig 2000). Many non-profit and non-governmental cultural initiatives advocated not only for a more inclusive cultural policy, but also for a more inclusive society. While some of these organizations and projects locate themselves today primarily as cultural projects, others present themselves as social projects that use art above all as a medium to convey socio-political content.

Since the shift to the political Right at federal government level in 2000, the funding of several established and well-networked community initiatives that had engaged immigrant youth through cultural projects for several years (often funded within a budget dedicated to youth at a city level) has been cut. Some of these initiatives were "invited" to reschedule their agenda into either specializing on training particular skills, for example, new media skills, thereby making them economically more useful. Others focused on the integration of recent immigrants through, for example, German language courses, instead of aiming them at broader social and civic empowerment. The entry of the conservative right coalition at federal government level politicized many agents in the cultural field, and facilitated alliances between artists and cultural initiatives, third sector organizations across the board (from youth culture projects to minority groups) and political activists. Anti-racism and anti-exclusionism formed an important political agenda that united many of these previously disparate groups (Boese, Busch and Dragicevic-Sesic 2006).

Initiatives such as *Dezentrale Medien* are indeed very conscious of the risk of being instrumentalized by a public sector governed by neoliberal ideals. Their strategy to politicize disadvantaged youth, rather than to act as a pacifying agency, is consistent with the position of many other third sector agencies in Austria that engage in social interventionist practices.

Concluding remarks

I have attempted to depict strategies of engaging through cultural participation as a highly contextual practice, which needs to be viewed in connection with surrounding policy developments and political discourse. Funding frameworks obviously have a strong influence on how these initiatives are shaped and how their objectives are worded, which helps to explain some of the similarities between projects in very different contexts. However, the way in which cultural workers go about the "inclusion" and "empowerment" elements of their work with young people informs other influential factors, which include their understanding or vision of the role of these initiatives in a wider societal context, and their understanding of the arts and of culture as an aesthetically, politically, socially or economically relevant practice.

The empirical examples discussed in this chapter appear to fit well into the different stages of the "social inclusion through the arts" agenda mentioned in an earlier section. The Vienna-based example, with its focus on politics, seems closer to the community arts approach, while the Manchester-based DJ Academy, with its focus on the economy, looks clearly like a child of the cultural regeneration era. However, looking at these examples in more depth, this categorization would not do them justice. Rather than dismissing the DJ Academy as a utilitarian, neoliberal workfare tool, I would highlight its grounding in experiences of racism and exclusion. It addresses the lack of public provision for industry specific support that other social groups can access through the Cultural Industries Development Service. Rather than calling it irresponsible, because it "lures" young marginalized people into a risky field of employment, I would highlight its provision of training to unemployed young people, which promotes self-confidence and self-development, a typical outcome of community arts (Matarasso 1997). Likewise, it would be easy to dismiss the Vienna-based *Dezentrale Medien* as "stuck in the past" and oblivious to economic pressures on young, socially excluded people. Yet its focus on new media as a means of expression equips its participants with skills that improve their employability. Both initiatives offer their participants more than the obvious, employment skills in the Manchester case, and socio-political awareness and self-expression in the Vienna case. In both cases, the social and cultural background of the involved workers informs their practice in the project, whether it is the experience of racism in the music industry in Manchester or the migratory experience in Vienna.

A recently completed research project in Austria, titled ART WORKS, funded through the EU funding scheme EQUAL, explored and documented the employment opportunities for artists in the social services sector. Many artists, cultural workers and activists in Vienna, who have, over the years, engaged in projects aimed at the emancipation, empowerment or social inclusion of disadvantaged groups, viewed this research project with considerable suspicion. This suspicion has grown from their fear of losing a field of practice they consider as one of political transformation, to the hegemonic move to "economic normalization" (Foord 1998). This fear might be well founded. What is needed however in order to adequately evaluate changes in the field of achieving social inclusion through the arts is sensitivity for the political contexts of different initiatives. This might allow us to see that the provision of training and pathways into employment in the cultural field also has the potential to provide participants with resources such as cultural and social capital, which allows them to partake as citizens, and develop civic skills in ways they might not have without these initiatives. And it might help to identify where politics is needed. At the same time, Matarasso's caveat at the end of his contested study on the social usefulness of participation in the arts, *Use or Ornament?*, has not lost its currency:

> (I)t is necessary to stress that participation in the arts is not being advocated as a form of, still less an alternative to, social policy. The current problems of British society will not be solved if we all learn to make large objects out of papier-maché, play the accordion or sing Gilbert and Sullivan. Nor will British culture be improved by being sold into bonded labour to a social policy master. (Matarasso 1997, 85)

Works Cited

Babias, M., and A. Könneke, ed. 1998. *Die Kunst des Öffentlichen.* Projekte/Ideen/Stadtplanungsprozesse im politischen/sozialen/ öffentlichen Raum. Amsterdam, Dresden: Verlag der Kunst.

Barraket, J. 2005. *Putting People into the Picture. The Role of the Arts in Social Inclusion.* Social Policy Working Paper 4, Brotherhood of St Laurence and Centre for Public Policy.

Belfiore, E. 2002. "Art as a Means of Alleviating Social Exclusion: Does it Really Work? A Critique of Instrumental Cultural Policies and Social Impact Studies in the UK." *International Journal of Cultural Policy* 8 (1): 91-106.

Bennett, T. 1998. *Culture – A Reformer's Science.* London: Thousand Oaks and New Delhi: Sage.

Bianchini, F., and M. Parkinson. 1993. *Cultural Policy and Urban Regeneration: The West European Experience.* Manchester: Manchester University Press.

Bianchini, F. 1999. "Cultural Planning for Urban Sustainability." In *City and Culture: Cultural Processes and Urban Sustainability*, edited by L. Nyström. Swedish Urban Environment Council.

Blake, A., and G. Jeffery. 2000. "Strengthening Local Musical Cultures in the 'Global City'. Music, Representation and Cultural Policy in Newham and Eastleigh." Paper presented at City Cultures and Urban Change Conference, September, Manchester Metropolitan University.

Boese, M. 2005. "Difference and Exclusion at Work in the Club Culture Economy." *International Journal of Cultural Studies* 8 (4): 427-43.

. 2003a. "'Race' and class in the 'post-subculturalist' economy." In *The Post-Subcultures Reader*, edited by D. Muggleton & R. Weinzierl, 167-80. New York, Oxford: Berg.

—. 2003b. "'Black music' in Manchester: 'Diversity' and Exclusion in a City's Club Culture Industry." PhD dissertation, Manchester Metropolitan University.

Boese, M., B. Busch, and M. Dragicevic-Sesic. 2006. "Despite and Beyond Cultural Policy: Third and Fourth Sector Practices and Strategies." In *Transcultural Europe: Cultural Policy in a Changing Europe*, edited by U. Meinhof & A. Triandafyllidou. Basingstoke: Palgrave Macmillan.

Bourdieu, P. 1987. *Distinction – A Social Critique of the Judgement of Taste.* London: Routledge.

Caust, J. 2003. "Putting the 'Art' Back into Arts Policy Making: How Arts Policy has been 'Captured' by the Economists and the Marketers." *The International Journal of Cultural Policy* 9 (1): 51-63.

Chatterton, P., and R. Hollands. 2002 "Theorising Urban Playscapes: Producing, Regulating and Consuming Youthful Nightlife City Spaces." *Urban Studies* 39 (1): 95-116.

Department for Culture, Media and Sport (DCMS). 1998. *Creative Industries Mapping Document*. Retrieved May 10 2007, http://www.culture.gov.uk/Reference_library/Publications/archive_1998/Creative_Industries_Mapping_Document_1998.html.

Ellmeier, A., G. Baumgartner, and B. Perchinig. 2000. *Cultural Policy and Cultural Diversity.* Report prepared by Österreichische Kulturdokumentation. Strasbourg: Council of Europe.

Fisher, M., and U. Owen. eds. 1991. *Whose Cities?* London: Penguin.

Fleming, T. 1999. *Local Cultural Industries Support Services in the UK: Towards a Model of Best Practice*. ICISS Report. Manchester: Manchester Institute for Popular Culture.

Florida, R. 2002. *The Rise of the Creative Class and how it's Transforming Work, Leisure, Community and Everyday Life*. New York: Basic Books.

Foord, J. 1998. "Creative Hackney. Reflections on Hidden Art™." *Rising East* 3 (2): 38-66.

Hawkins, G. 1993. *From Nimbin to Mardi Gras: Constructing Community Arts*. St. Leonards: Allen & Unwin.

Healey, P., S. Cameron, S. Davoudi, S. Graham, and A. Madani-Pour. eds. 1995. *Managing Cities. The New Urban Context.* Chichester: Wiley.

Hesmondhalgh, D. 2002. *The Cultural Industries.* London: Sage.

Landry, C., L. Greene, F. Matarasso, and F. Bianchini. 1996. *The Art of Regeneration: Urban Renewal through Cultural Activity.* Stroud: Comedia.

Marchart, O. 1998. "Art, Space and the Public Sphere(s): Some Basic Observations on the Difficult Relation of Public Art, Urbanism and Political Theory." Retrieved January 30 2006, http://www.eipcp.net/diskurs/d07/text/marchart_prepublic_en.html.

Matarasso, F. 2005. "Art for Our Sake: The Artistic Importance of Community Arts" (Lecture in Whitby, April 28, 2005.) Retrieved May 9 2007, http://homepage.mac.com/WebObjects/FileSharing.woa/wa/Art_for_Our_Sake.pdf.pdf/zip.zip?a=downloadFile&user=matarasso&path=/Public/Lectures/Art%20for%20Our%20Sake.pdf.

—. 1997. *Use or Ornament? The Social Impact of Participation in the Arts.* Stroud: Comedia.

McGuigan, J. 2004. *Rethinking Cultural Policy.* Maidenhead: Open University Press.

McRobbie, A. 2002. "Clubs to Companies: Notes on the Decline of Political Culture in Speeded Up Creative Worlds." *Cultural Studies* 16 (4): 516-31.

Meinhof, U., and A. Triandafyllidou. eds. 2006. *Transcultural Europe: Cultural Policy in a Changing Europe.* Basingstoke: Macmillan.

Merli, P. 2002. "Evaluating the Social Impact of Participation in Arts Activities: A Critical Review of Francois Matarasso's Use or Ornament?" *International Journal of Cultural Policy* 8 (1): 107-18.

Mörsch, C. 2003. "Socially Engaged Economies. Leben von und mit künstlerischen Beteiligungsprojekten und Kunstvermittlung in England". *Kurswechsel* 4: 62-74.

Myerscough, J. 1988. *The Economic Importance of the Arts.* London: Policy Studies Institute.

O'Connor, J. 2000. "The Definition of 'Cultural Industries'". *The European Journal of Arts Education* 2 (3): 15-27.

—. 1999. *The Cultural Production Sector in Manchester Research and Strategy*. Manchester: Manchester Institute for Popular Culture.

O'Connor, J., and D. Wynne. eds. 1996. *From the Margins to the Centre: Cultural Production and Consumption in the Post-Industrial City.* Aldershot: Arena.

Richards, N., and K. Milestone. 2000. "What Difference Does it Make? Women's Pop Cultural Production and Consumption in Manchester." *Sociological Research Online*, 5 (1). Retrieved May 9 2007, http://www.socresonline.org.uk/5/1/richards.html.

Rollig, S., and E. Sturm. eds. 2002. *Dürfen die das? Kunst als sozialer Raum*. Vienna: Turia + Kant.

Sholette, G. 2002. "Some call it Art: From Imaginary Autonomy to Autonomous Collectivity." In *Dürfen die das? Kunst als sozialer Raum*, edited by S. Rollig & E. Sturm. Vienna: Turia + Kant.

Stevenson, D. 2004. "'Civic Gold' Rush: Cultural Planning and the Politics of the Third Way." *International Journal of Cultural Policy* 10, (1): 119-31.

Talbot, D., and M. Boese. 2007. "Racism, Criminalisation and the Development of Night-time Economies: Two Case Studies in London and Manchester." *Ethnic & Racial Studies* 30 (1): 95-118.

Thornton, S. 1995. *Club Cultures. Music, Media and Subcultural Capital.* New England: Wesleyan University Press.

Williams, R. 1971/1958. *Culture and Society*. London: Penguin.

CHAPTER FOUR

THE ROAD LESS TRAVELED: ARTS-BASED PROGRAMS IN YOUTH CORRECTIONS

MARK BROWN

Criminal behavior is so widespread amongst youth in western societies that criminologists now regard it as an established feature of modern life. An influential life course model of offending proposed by Moffitt (1993), for instance, describes offending as normative and gives explicit attention to the processes by which some young people actually manage not to offend at all. Yet most of the offending that criminologists such as Moffitt refer to is both trivial in nature and relatively short-lived. Indeed, Moffitt distinguishes between what she terms "adolescent limited" offenders – those who begin offending relatively late, have an established repertoire of social and academic skills, and who desist when it no longer seems to give value – and a much smaller cohort whom she terms "lifecourse persistent", who begin early, are more serious and continue their offending through adulthood.

This chapter is concerned with how people stop offending and how the techniques, strategies and programs of arts-based intervention might play a role in the stopping process. One of the unfortunate features of the criminological and psychological literature on offending behavior, however, is that it is only very poorly integrated, meaning that knowledge gained within different "approaches" – lifecourse, criminal career, desistance, "what works" /risk-need – tends to be relatively contained, and to have little influence outside that area. So too is this literature divided between approaches that aim toward theoretical coherence – such as the life course and desistance schemes – and others like the criminal career or "what works" approaches that are largely empirically driven. My aim in this chapter is not to provide a comprehensive overview of this complex, and some might say chaotic field, but to identify key issues in theory and policy relevant to arts-based interventions – these issues to date have received little attention in this literature – and to review some emerging findings that point toward an important role for this type of work in holistic, evidence-based intervention with young people at risk of offending. The chapter has three parts. Part I briefly reviews and places in context the policy environment in Victoria, Australia, where the *Risky Business* research took place. This environment, not unlike many others in Australia and elsewhere, is driven by a subscription to the risk-need model first popularized by Canadian researchers (Andrews and Bonta 1998) in the adult correctional environment, and now embedded within what is termed the "what works" framework. Part II will provide a critique of this *type* of policy framework, illustrating its technical and conceptual limitations, plus the great limits placed upon its effectiveness by its structural inability to draw upon and integrate findings from the other approaches mentioned above. One of these, the desistance approach, will be used as a case in point. Part III will then take a more detailed look at two notions that have re-emerged as acceptance of risk-need programming has begun to wane: first, that of positive work with offenders, and second, the idea of narrative as a key ingredient in processes of self-change.

I. Policy context: The Victorian Juvenile Justice Rehabilitation Review

A *Juvenile Justice Reform Strategy* has shaped current policy on youth offending in the state of Victoria (Minister for Community Services 2000). Policy and practice developed in respect of young people under the *Reform Strategy* is guided by an aim "to prevent low risk young people from entering the Juvenile Justice system, to rehabilitate more serious young offenders, and to support young offenders after release from custodial care to establish a non-offending lifestyle." (ibid, 1) The detailed framework supporting the *Reform Strategy*'s rehabilitation component was established when the Victoria Department of Human Services adopted as policy the findings of the *Victorian Juvenile Justice Rehabilitation Review* (Day, Howells and Rickwood 2003). What the *Rehabilitation Review* proposed was that youth rehabilitation in Victoria should be underpinned by the same principles of risk assessment and risk management that have come to guide adult rehabilitation policy in many western jurisdictions.

These principles have been advanced under a banner, perhaps mischievously termed, the "what works" approach (McGuire 1995). The approach identifies five principles of "effective" intervention with youthful and adult offenders, and proposes that these principles should guide rehabilitation intervention. Empirical research underpins the five main principles and this forms both a key strength and a key weakness of the approach. Before describing how this is so, however, it is worthwhile briefly outlining the five principles themselves. First is the *risk principle*, which proposes that: (i) interventions with high risk offenders produce greater impacts on subsequent offending than with low risk offenders; (ii) intensive interventions with low risk offenders may be counterproductive (increasing offending); and thus (iii) intensity of intervention should be matched to risk level. Risk itself is marked by a number of established statistically derived "risk factors" which may be divided into those that are static, or unable to be changed (such as age at first conviction), and those that are dynamic and thus may be manipulated (such as attitudes, associates or employability). A second principle, the *needs principle*, proposes that dynamic risk factors should be understood as "criminogenic needs" and should be the target of intervention programs. How they are targeted is determined by the *responsivity principle*, which recognizes that people learn and respond differently, and so proposes that interventions should take account of factors such as age, gender, ethnicity and so on, all of which can affect individuals' capacity to engage effectively with intervention programs. The quality of these programs is secured by an *integrity principle*, which proposes that programs should be delivered in exactly the way they were intended, so that effectiveness is not diluted by poor implementation or failure to comply with key theoretical principles. Finally, a *professional discretion principle* recognizes that the preceding principles should not be implemented in a mechanistic or overly programmatic way, but should be guided by the professional judgment of those implementing the framework.

The question of precisely what intervention programs should do is answered by meta-analytic research. This is a methodology that allows data from multiple studies to be pooled, and thus permits conclusions to be drawn across the entire group in a statistically meaningful way. Although few meta-analyses of interventions with juveniles have been conducted, the *Rehabilitation Review* was able to identify three, giving the authors confidence that the broad conclusions of research on adults may be equally valid in the context of youth offending and rehabilitation. Programs should: (i) be directed at medium and high risk offenders and targeted at criminogenic needs; (ii) be structured and multi-modal in approach; (iii) include both behavioral and cognitive components; (iv) aim to engender high levels of response from the person; (v) be either community based, or if custodial, be linked with a post-program community intervention; and (vi) maintain treatment integrity and be conducted by trained professionals

(Day et al. 2003, 36). It is perhaps not difficult to see how arts-based interventions might find it difficult to claim a place within this policy framework, principally because their mode of intervention is not cognitive-behavioral and program staff are not trained in the psychological principles of the "what works" doctrine. This said, however, there is nothing in the policy to prohibit any number of other approaches being undertaken with offenders.

But that would be to misunderstand the purpose of the "what works" approach, which is not simply to promote cognitive-behavioral interventions on defined targets, but also to limit the range of possible intervention targets and exclude approaches it does not sanction. Thus, many of the typical targets of arts-based interventions (self-esteem, or dealing with personal turmoil, for example) have been defined as "non-criminogenic and "discretionary". It is important to note at this point that the term "non-criminogenic" does *not* mean that these factors are unrelated to offending. What it does mean is that there is no *extant* literature linking work on these targets to reduced offending, or linking intervention of this type to improved responsivity in "approved" programs. Thus, the critical definition of a target as "criminogenic" and important, or "non-criminogenic" and therefore discretionary, is bound by no known rule or psychological theory, but instead by the vagaries of decision making about correctional programming and investment in program evaluation. So it is important to note that many "non-criminogenic" targets may in fact be entirely valid and that non cognitive-behavioral approaches also have value, and there is an increasing body of literature to suggest just that, as will be shown below.

II. Current status of the "what works" policy model

Despite pessimism in some areas, opportunities for arts-based interventions with offending or "at risk" young people have in fact probably never been stronger. The reasons for this lie in a confluence of three forces. The first is a significant confusion and incoherence within the "what works" model itself around the pivotal notion of "criminogenic need". The second force is increasing dissatisfaction among practitioners with a singular reliance upon "what works" cognitive-behavioral programs, combined with increasing evidence of minimal or even negative impacts when these programs are rolled out more widely. The third force is the increasing recognition that "stopping offending" is less an event than a process, and that the "what works" *treatment–rehabilitation* model may be less appropriate than some form of the *process of desistance* model that is currently taking shape within criminology. Together, these constitute a threat to the risk-need/"what works" policy paradigm at all levels, from its empirical claims through to its theoretical and conceptual adequacy. This chapter is not the place for a thoroughgoing review of these problems, but I will attempt briefly to sketch their contours and then, in the following section, point to two areas of advance directly supportive of arts-based programming.

Defining offender "need"

Together with Tony Ward (Ward and Brown 2004, 2003; see also Ward and Stewart 2003) I have sought to draw out some of the logical and theoretical difficulties inherent in the criminogenic/non-criminogenic needs distinction, part of which also has to do with labeling of risk and need factors. In our view, the main failings of the "what works" paradigm's risk-need model lie in two areas. First, it simply makes no sense to re-label statistically derived risk factors as needs. The term need has well recognized meaning: it connotes an essential element of life and both common knowledge and psychological theory alike have long sought to describe these basic building blocks of individual and social existence. So to label lack of stable employment, or prevalence of crime conducing attitudes as needs, is both wholly inappropriate and confusing. Tony Ward and I have instead suggested that statistically derived, dynamic risk factors (the "what works" paradigm's criminogenic needs) should be demoted from their current position as primary intervention targets. Instead they should be connected with a comprehensive theory or account of their relationship to the fundamental needs that shape human life and conduct; the needs for autonomy, relatedness and competence. Of course, opening up these broad human needs as targets of attention would also open up a space in which a variety of complementary intervention types could be brought to bear upon the problem.

Secondly, however, we also contest the implication contained in "what works" principles that so-called criminogenic needs such as (un)employment, anti-social attitudes and anti-social associates provide any guidance at all as to the *nature* of the problems faced by the offender. As we put it: "the current crop of empirically derived criminogenic needs are for the most part little more than range riders – they tell you that there is a problem but they do not tell you what to do or how to go about it" (Ward and Brown 2003, 352). Thus, programs that seek to target, for instance, pro-crime attitudes, do so in a conceptual and theoretical vacuum, since there is nothing underpinning the "what works" model that would link these sorts of attitudes to the fundamental needs that animate human thought and action. In the section below, reference will be made to the extraordinarily low completion rate of "what works" programs in the United Kingdom. Perhaps the failure of offenders to engage with and complete these programs stems from this fundamental mismatch between the forces that shape behavior and the left-of-field targets of "what works" interventions; in other words, maybe they just do not make sense to the offenders themselves. The "what works" approach of setting negative goals (things to get rid of) and attempting to suppress offender characteristics or capacities (such as bad attitudes or friends) also runs in the face of established principles of intervention. Moreover, the approach treats each "need" as a discrete, manipulable unit, offering no theory to connect such needs together in a holistic explanation of human behavior. Again, a broader and more sophisticated understanding of need, its dimensions and the opportunities for a variety of *coordinated* approaches to bear upon these needs, would seem to offer a very positive way forward.

Cognitive-behavioral therapy ascendant?

In a recent review of probation work with offenders, the head of Oxford University's probation studies unit noted that:

> [a]lthough the elements of the What Works agenda are sometimes listed as if set in stone, the authority of this so-called "agenda" remains open to question and rigorous evaluation. (Burnett 2004, 172)

One aspect of the problem, she suggested, was that UK policy makers had latched too quickly and uncritically on to the conclusions of meta-analyses of program effectiveness, often playing down even the cautions of those who had conducted them. She has not been alone in expressing worry over the "what works" program, particularly in the United Kingdom, where this policy prescription was adopted early. In a UK review of the "what works" policy framework Gorman, O'Byrne and Parton (2006) suggest that a key draw card for the risk-based approach has been the protection it offers risk averse bureaucracies. "The caution that has arguably typified [the UK Probation Service's] retreat into a procedural and pragmatic defensiveness when assessing and managing risks", they argue, "contrasts sharply with the unbridled and uncritical enthusiasm with which it has embraced the circumspect and questionable findings of meta-analytic reviews on recidivism." (15). Moreover, they note that the policy uptake has been distorted in important ways, focusing on risk and criminogenic need targets, whilst downplaying the important (and expensive) caveats implied in the *responsivity* principle, in favor of large homogenized program roll-outs. They go on to review a number of UK studies that identify two key problems with the "what works" cognitive-behavioral model. The first is a tendency for initial positive results of programs (i.e. lower reoffending rates among those who complete the program in the order of 10% to 15%) to either fade or disappear completely once the program is rolled out service-wide. This seems entirely predictable, given the difficulty of securing and coordinating high quality, psychologically sophisticated and motivated professional staff across a whole service (which was of course recognized, and so enshrined in the *integrity* principle). The second problem identified by Gorman et al. is a high attrition rate within programs. They cite National Probation Directorate figures showing that in 2004 more than one-fifth of probation areas in England and Wales achieved less than half their target completions. Indeed, examination of the tables to which they refer (National Probation Service 2004) shows that across England and Wales as a whole, just 35% of offenders ordered to undertake an accredited "what works" program actually completed the program. Of course, it is difficult to know how many actually began the program at all, but it does suggest an enormous rate of attrition.

What might be the impact of that attrition, of partial completion of a program? Gorman et al. do not go down that path, but a recent UK study, the largest ever reported in the international literature, does. Palmer, McGuire, Hounsome et al. (2007) followed 6,479 offenders, 4,089 of whom had been referred to a community-based "what works" program. Predictably, not all of those referred to a program completed it, leaving three groups in the study: 1,311 completers, 2,778 non-completers and a comparison group of 2,390 offenders. The completion rate of 32% was just below the 2004 national average of 35% described earlier, and so broadly in line with expectation (low as that may be). Reconviction varied markedly by group, with completers doing best overall (54% reconvicted), followed by the comparison group (60%) and then the non-completing group (76% reconvicted). Thus, on the face of it, completing the program improved outcomes by just 6% over doing nothing, and not completing made matters much worse. Yet this may be misleading due to, among other things, a selection effect: lower risk offenders may have been more likely to turn up in the control group, thus accounting for the minimal "impact" (6%) of the intensive treatment program. Once the key variables that might affect reoffending (age, risk, offence type and length of follow-up) were controlled for in a multivariate analysis, reconviction data showed that completers were actually 33% less likely to be reconvicted than the comparison group for whom nothing was done, but non-completers were 86% *more* likely to be reconvicted than counterparts in comparison groups. Palmer et al. argue that such findings are "in line with the 'What Works' literature" and note that the programs "are designed to be effective only if they are completed, as stipulated in the accreditation criteria relating to 'dosage'" (10).

In the face of such worrying findings, the cheerful optimism with which they are incorporated and naturalized becomes itself a disturbing feature of the "what works" paradigm. This study by Palmer et al. can be regarded as a capstone study, broadly reconfirming findings of smaller studies undertaken in the United Kingdom and Canada. Three main conclusions may be drawn: first, that high-dosage, intensive and well-implemented programs can reduce offending; but, secondly, that all evidence seems to indicate system-wide implementation of such high-integrity programs to be nigh on impossible. There might be little problem with this but for the third finding, that non-completion, for reasons that have evaded the grasp of Palmer et al. and the many other researchers they cite, is associated with much higher rates of reoffending than if nothing were done at all. The only broad conclusion Palmer et al. were able to offer was that some aspect of offender preparation, offender motivation or offender readiness is lacking among non-completers. And when these ill-prepared offenders meet the exigencies of a "what works" program, the effects are largely negative – both for themselves and for society at large.

Rehabilitation vs. desistance

The "what works" framework sits squarely within the classical medical disease model. The four conceptual elements around which it revolves are disease (criminogenic needs to be eliminated); treatment (allocation to, ideally, a cognitive-behavioral program); dose (notionally ≥100 hours = completion; otherwise, non-completion); and cure or rehabilitation (no further offending; otherwise, reconviction). Additional principles such as *risk* and *integrity* govern the distribution and application of elements within the framework. As Palmer et al. noted, the "what works" model's combination of assessment, treatment selection and treatment dose are aimed to produce what they term a "completers effect" (10), and failure particularly to achieve target dosage, will, as we are told about courses of antibiotics, both fail to cure the disease and possibly also aggravate its symptoms. Criminologists trained in the sociological tradition have long regarded this individual disease model as woefully inadequate and pernicious, a position that "what works" architects have termed "knowledge destruction" (Andrews and Wormith 1989). Yet their basic point, that offending cannot be de-contextualized and all responsibility for it sheeted home to individual deficits, is broadly in line with modern psychology, even if the sociologists and psychologists might differ as to the relative weight to be accorded internal and external factors.

The eminent American psychologist Craig Haney, whose career began when working on the Stanford Prison Experiment, noted the irony of individualistic psychologists propounding programs that were out of step with modern psychology that has moved increasingly toward greater contextualization of action, placing an even greater weight on the power of situational factors (2005, cited in Carlen and Tombs 2006). As a measure of the distance between the "what works" individualistic medical model and current thought, it is worth considering Haney and Philip Zimbardo's conclusion that:

> [v]irtually all sophisticated contemporary accounts of social behaviour now acknowledge the empirical and theoretical significance of situation, context and structure.

They go on to add that:

> [i]n academic circles at least, the problems of crime and violence – formerly viewed in almost exclusively individualistic terms – are now understood through multilevel analyses that grant equal if not primary significance to situational, community and structural variables. (Haney and Zimbardo 1998, 720)

Indeed, Haney (2002) suggests that psychological research and theory would point our attention toward what he terms "criminogenic social contexts" (33) rather than criminogenic needs residing in the offender. The strength and direction of research here completely undermines the rhetoric of "choice" and "responsibility" underpinning conceptions of both the rational legal actor and the diseased body of the offender as it is constructed within the "what works" agenda. "By demonstrating the various ways in which deviant behavior arises from a psychologically potent combination of traumatic social histories and criminogenic social circumstances" he argues, "this literature casts doubt on the normative framework used to structure existing doctrines of responsibility" (34).

The reconfiguration of thinking proposed here by Haney is currently taking place in the developing field of theory and research around the idea of desistance. Desistance may be thought of as both an end state (when something has stopped) and as a process leading to that state (Mulvey et al. 2004). While the former is that which we strive towards, it is the latter, the idea of a process of stopping, that is capturing much of the current attention and research effort. The desistance model aims to take account of those five key domains identified by Haney – psychological, historical, situational, local and structural – that each impinge upon and shape the behavior of all people at all times. Proponents of desistance often cite the process of recovery from alcoholism as an analogy: it does not occur overnight, it will have a wide variety of variables influencing the final outcome which, itself, is always a contingent and often-difficult state, and so on. I would encourage a further analogy, which is of the process of education. One reason is that there are clear similarities between becoming educated and stopping offending: a student is not miraculously "educated" by exposure to a course at school or university, for instance. But a more important reason for using this analogy is the contrast between what is expected of and granted to students, and the structure of expectations surrounding young people involved in crime.

This was no better revealed than in a recent Menzies Oration to the graduating class of 2005 at the University of Melbourne. Professor James Wilkinson, director of the Derek Bok Centre for Teaching and Learning at Harvard University argued that elite students are commonly given too little opportunity to experiment with ideas and strategies, and accorded too little space for stumbles and failures in the process of their education. "Students need an atmosphere in which they can stumble occasionally and not pay a penalty," he argued. The process of education, he suggested, is one in which students need to be able to "return to a question again and again, searching for answers that get more solid with each iteration" so that they may "ultimately relish the messiness and inefficiency that are the handmaidens of creativity" (2006, 10). That sort of thinking should, I believe, also animate the desistance project. If it is felt that the brightest and most privileged students in the land are shunted through their education in a way that impedes, rather than expands, their capacity for trial and error experimentation, and so success, what might we say of those who end up in prison or community-based corrections? What model of change underpins our new idea of desistance and what principles guide this project? In fact, the shape of this project is rather too wide ranging to sustain review here (see Maruna and Immarigeon 2004; Maruna 2001; *Youth Violence and Juvenile Justice* 2004; Barry 2006). In the next section, I will try to draw out two aspects of it that seem directly to connect with arts-based programs for young people who have been involved in criminal behavior.

III. Theorizing arts-based interventions

Arts-based interventions struggle to claim space within an environment of policy and practice framed by the "what works" doctrine. Yet even as the over-reach and over-sell of highly intensive and specialized psychological programs comes to be recognized, a new generation of criminologists and more sociologically astute psychologists has begun to elaborate the dimensions of "desistance" and the much more limited role that a deficits-based "what works" approach should probably take within the justice system. Two important features of the emerging desistance model from the perspective of arts-based intervention are its focus on constructive, positive or strengths-based work with young people, and the renewed interest and importance given to narrative in the behavioral change process.

From deficits to strengths

> Constructive work with offenders will be articulated as a complex and dynamic process of intervention which is more artistic than technicist, more creative than procedural, more collaborative than instrumental. (Gorman, O'Byrne and Parton 2006, 21)

A new focus on young people's strengths – what is good about the young person, what they have to offer themselves, others and the community, what there is in their lives to be proud of and to capitalize upon – makes a welcome change. It is part of a wider movement occurring right across the social and behavioral sciences, sometimes called constructive work (Gorman et al. 2006), other times positive psychology (Morrison et al. 2006) or strengths-based intervention (Maruna and LeBel 2003). It returns attention to a number of long-established psychological principles of behavior change that seem, under the risk-management regime of "what works" thinking, to have inexplicably been set aside. These include the principle that behavior change is more effectively achieved when individuals are recruited into a process of achieving positive approach goals rather than negative avoidance goals, and that the goal of interventions is to work with, or alongside, the offenders rather than upon them.

Perhaps the key difference, however, lies in the structure of presumptions upon which "what works" and constructive or strengths-based approaches rest. Proponents of the "what works" approach place enormous emphasis on it being evidence-based, but they elide the important choices and presumptions their approach entails. The evidence to which they refer is essentially two tiered: first, is a voluminous archive dating back to at least the 1950s, showing strong predictable associations between what are now termed "risk factors" and offending behavior; second, is a much more limited set of findings that, in the words of Maruna and LeBel (ibid, 95):

> supports the notion that rehabilitative interventions can marginally reduce recidivism rates when treatment is correctly matched to a client's criminogenic needs.

The key presumption in the "what works" approach is thus that the correct response to (a) well-established correlates of offending is (b) to focus upon and extinguish them (e.g. eliminate pro-crime attitudes; get rid of pro-crime associates). Positive or strengths-based approaches query this presumption and they do it in two ways, one rather stronger than the other approach. In neither case, however, is there any debate or disagreement that research consistently identifies a set of social and psychological variables associated with offending: debate instead turns on what should be done with this knowledge. In the weaker version of the argument against the "what works" approach, proponents of a constructive approach such as Michelle Hayles (2006) object that it makes no sense to expect "in such a context of personal deficiency" (73) that offenders should be able to cease their pattern of conduct without much greater attention to what should replace it. This, I would argue, is a weaker argument because it either under-estimates or misrepresents what cognitive-behavioral programs actually do: no "what works" proponent is suggesting that bad attitudes should be replaced by no attitudes, so providing alternatives is indeed a central and legitimate part of that approach.

Ward and Stewart (2003) make a stronger argument in the context of their "good lives" model of offender rehabilitation. They propose that if the concept of offender need is to be taken seriously, then needs must be "embedded in a model of human wellbeing and a view of human nature" (126). They align themselves with what they term the "enhancement approach", common within clinical psychology, but curiously absent in the risk-driven discourse of corrections. Under an enhancement approach, public safety will be achieved not by attempting to suppress a handful of statistically derived risk factors (the so-called "criminogenic needs") but by assisting offenders to solve problems that have blocked or frustrated their attempts to secure the basic human goods of autonomy, relatedness and competence. These they term basic or categorical needs and they distinguish them from the risk factors that form the focus of the "what works" approach by noting that the latter (e.g. anti-social associates) are merely the outcome of thwarted attempts to secure basic needs. As such, it makes no sense to concentrate upon suppressing them. Rather, they suggest, an enhancement approach will focus on "providing offenders with the necessary conditions (e.g. skills, values, opportunities, social supports, etc.) for meeting their needs in more adaptive ways" (126).

Strengths-based approaches thus attempt to shift the focus of intervention with offenders and to recruit offenders as active players in the change process. The approach is, as Maruna and LeBel (2003) note, anti-pathologizing, and that in itself, is a significant factor in securing and capitalizing upon offenders' motivation to make things different. Strengths-based approaches have been promoted across a wide spectrum of correctional interventions, ranging from the more social work-oriented perspectives of the contributors to Gorman et al.'s (2006) *Constructive Work with Offenders* to the intensive clinical psychological approach of Tony Ward and his collaborators (e.g. Ward and Garton 2006). The implications for arts-based interventions are that there now exists a significant body of work pointing toward not simply the desirability, but the necessity that attention should be given to a whole range of offence-related factors displaced and diminished by the rhetorical strategies of "what works" proponents (e.g. through labels such as "non-criminogenic needs" and "discretionary targets"). Included in this group of offence-related factors demanding renewed attention are personal and social-contextual factors related to offending. They include the offender's embeddedness in a social system and his or her relationship to others and institutions; aspects of personal functioning, including factors that affect engagement with the process of change, such as personal distress, self-esteem and the like; goals or desires that animate the person, including the elements of what it would be to lead a fulfilling life; and the need to construct a narrative sense of self and personal identity. Fergus McNeill (2003, cited in Gorman et al. 2006) suggests the elements of a desistance focused practice model should include three key objectives:

> developing personal maturity, changing social bonds associated with certain life transitions, and the individual subjective narrative constructions which offenders build around these key events. (20)

Indeed, it is the latter, narrative identity, which is emerging as a key element of contemporary desistance research, and which has particularly strong resonances with the objectives and approaches of arts-based intervention.

Narrative identity and behavior change

> Narrative identities, for offenders and for all people, are constituted from the pursuit and achievement of personal goals. (Ward and Marshall 2006, 1)

Narrative has re-emerged within criminology as a powerful concept structuring research, such as in the use of methods of narrative and discourse analysis, and new ways of conceptualizing the behavior change process. It marks a return of phenomenological and hermeneutic theory and method to a domain that had been stripped bare of meanings and social constructions by the radical behaviorist principles of "what works" psychology and correctional managerialism (Brown 2005). In part, the attraction of narrative to understanding and activating the process of desistance from crime is simple: few accounts given by offenders of the ways and reasons they gave up crime include treatment among the important factors in their success. Instead, it is aspects of personal maturation and self-awareness, transitions from one stage of life to another, and growing responsibility in the forms of relationships, work or parenthood that figure prominently. Importantly also, however, these narratives have been shown directly to contradict some of the foundational assumptions of cognitive-behavioral theory. One of these is that offenders should accept personal responsibility for their crimes, recognizing that they have done ill, and adopt realistic plans for their future. In fact, Shadd Maruna (2001) found that those who successfully desist from crime often employ quite unrealistic expectations of control over their future, while at the same time downplaying, denying or ignoring their responsibility for past actions. The function of these seems to be to provide a kind of springboard of motivation and self-assurance that provides a trajectory out of criminal behavior and its social mores. Paradoxically, then, it was the persisters in Maruna's study, those who failed to escape their patterns of criminal conduct, who best fitted the cognitive-behavioral ideal. These people integrated the seriousness of their past conduct and the bleak reality of their future prospects into what Maruna termed "condemnation scripts", realistic perhaps but ultimately unhelpful to the process of life change.

While Shadd Maruna's (ibid) study was small and localized, its effects have been wide reaching in two ways. First, it has prompted a resurgence of interest in the use and importance of narrative in behavior change. Second, as an echo of Craig Haney's work discussed above, it has triggered a series of efforts to examine critically the widening gulf between what is "done with offenders" and the principles of modern social psychology. The latter has served to reinforce many of the broad findings of Maruna's study. In two recent review papers, for instance, Maruna and colleagues have examined the sociological theory of neutralization (Maruna and Copes 2005) and the cognitive-behavioral principle of cognitive distortion (Maruna and Mann 2006), both central to understanding the way people construct accounts of their lives past and future. The findings show that, like the students of Harvard University who are deemed to need more opportunity to experiment and court failure, there seem to be two standards afoot in the community. While key texts on offender rehabilitation continue to fetishize personal responsibility and the need for offenders to attribute their behavior to stable internal causes, the same does not apply elsewhere. Indeed, Maruna and Mann (ibid) use a range of examples to illustrate the ways in which this occurs. They note that blame shifting has been found to be "both healthy and beneficial" in most psychological studies and cite Schlenker et al.'s (2001) summary finding that the extant psychological literature:

> recommend[s] that people who fail or otherwise encounter difficulties in life should be taught to shift causal responsibility away from core components of the self, thereby making excuses to shield them from emotional and interpersonal costs. (162)

The point here is not to exculpate offending (and socially offensive) behavior, but to shift the focus of rehabilitative efforts away from the past and toward developing in those who have transgressed a sense of responsibility for what is to come in the future. Maruna and Mann distinguish between what they term passive responsibility, or taking responsibility for what one has done in the past, and active responsibility, "the virtue of putting things right for the future" (167). The latter is solution focused, and narrative accounts of who a person is, what they have experienced and what skills and assistance they can marshal to change things for the future, are thus increasingly being recognized as key to the desistance process (see also Byrne and Trew 2005; Farrall 2004; Gadd and Farrall 2004; Nellis 2002). One approach proposed by Ward and Marshall (2006) has been to draw these insights from desistance research into the framework of Tony Ward's "good lives" model. Recall that Ward proposes that the well-known correlates of offending, or risk factors as they have more recently become known, simply reflect the result of frustrated attempts by offenders to meet basic human needs, such as the need for relatedness or for autonomy. Ward and Marshall propose that if offenders are to find a way out of offending, a number of changes need to take place. These include the formulation of a definite plan for life – "the good life plan" – and an explicit recognition of what goods are sought, the skills necessary to achieve and limit them to the person's current skills and capabilities. Ward and Marshall propose that change in behavior needs to be linked to "a more adaptive narrative identity" (2), a notion that reflects their view that offending behavior is a maladaptive response to internal and external demands and stressors in an individual's life. Offending will disappear, they suggest, when individuals can meet their own needs and the demands of the world more effectively. To achieve this, they suggest, offenders require assistance in four areas:

> acquisition of accurate knowledge of the social and physical world, development of a robust understanding of their own values and standards, the ability to pursue their own personal good in specific environments, and being able to utilize the resources they require to overcome routine obstacles in the pursuit of that good. (2006, 10)

The value of this approach to thinking about arts-based intervention seems to be at least twofold. First, although Ward and Marshall's proposal is couched within a discussion of intensive psychological therapeutic work with offenders, there seems little reason why its general strengths and individual enhancement approach could not be adapted for arts-based interventions. Each of the four focal strategies listed above, of education, examination of values, sense of self and utilization of resources in the face of life's routine obstacles fit easily within some of the projects discussed elsewhere in this volume. Second, while arts-based interventions have tended to focus on (and be defined by) their medium of engagement – the arts – they have been far less clear about the theoretical underpinnings and justification for their efforts. The Ward and Marshall approach asks those who work with offenders to "specify the aims of [intervention], provide a justification of these aims in terms of its core assumptions about etiology and the values underpinning the approach, identify…targets, and outline how treatment should proceed in light of these assumptions and goals" (4). The "good lives" approach and the literature on narrative identity and desistance might usefully structure thinking in arts-based intervention, providing a clearer approach into engagement with offenders, and a clearer sense of what that engagement might reasonably achieve.

Conclusion

Arts-based programs are relatively rare within the correctional system, whether adult or juvenile. The purpose of this chapter has been to explain and critique the policy context within which offender rehabilitation programs in many Australian and Anglo-American jurisdictions operate. I have labeled arts-based interventions the "road less traveled", but I hope that this chapter has shown why that might readily and perhaps also quite quickly change. Correctional policy, like that in many other spheres of government, is subject to fads and fashions, and the "what works" doctrine discussed here is, perhaps, a case in point. Part of its appeal to policy makers has been its simple structure and its appeal to a kind of empirical high ground. Yet as this chapter has shown, it in many ways reflects an outdated view of the psychological discipline upon which it rests, and contemporary thinking in psychology, sociology and criminology long ago debunked some of its sacred articles of faith. The challenge for those who advocate a greater role for arts-based programs in the correctional system will be to harness this research to make a clear policy case for change. This should not be difficult. To begin, the recent work discussed here provides strong evidence for the importance of intervention targets which are policy based on the "what works" approach. This tends to push to one side: the social contexts of offending; the complex and, perhaps, diffuse familial and social networks within which trauma has been experienced, and wherein offending behavior developed and has been maintained; the crucial role of difficult factors like self-esteem and personal identity, and so on. Moreover, the evidence base now exists for a new, forward-looking, approach to change. Victorian-era principles of individual choice and passive responsibility that have been used as a stick with which to browbeat offenders should make way for an active engagement of offenders in their own(ed) change process and the construction of imaginative goal- and value-focused strategies of change.

Works Cited

Andrews, D.A., and J. Bonta. 1998. *The Psychology of Criminal Conduct* (2nd ed.). Cincinatti, Ohio: Anderson Publishing.

Andrews, D.A., and J.S. Wormith. 1989. "Personality and Crime: Knowledge Destruction and Construction in Criminology." *Justice Quarterly* 6: 289-309.

Barry, M. 2006. Youth Offending in Transition: The Search for Social Recognition. London: Routledge.

Brown, M. 2005. "Corrections." In *Australian Crime and Criminal Justice*, edited by D. Chappell and P. Wilson. Sydney: Butterworths.

Burnett, R. 2004. "To Reoffend or not Reoffend: The Ambivalence of Convicted Property Offenders." In *After Crime and Punishment: Pathways to Offender Re-integration*, edited by S. Maruna and R. Immarigeon. Devon: Willan Publishing.

Byrne, C.F., and K.F. Trew. 2005. "Crime Orientations, Social Relations and Involvement in Crime: Patterns Emerging from Offenders' Accounts." *The Howard Journal* 44: 185-205.

Carlen, P., and J. Tombs. 2006. "Reconfigurations of Penality: The Ongoing Case of the Women's Imprisonment and Reintegration Industries." *Theoretical Criminology* 10: 337-60.

Day, A., K. Howells and D. Rickwood. 2003. *The Victorian Juvenile Justice Rehabilitation Review*. Melbourne: Department of Human Services.

Farrall, S. 2004. "Social Capital and Offender Reintegration: Making Probation Desistance Focused." In *After Crime and Punishment: Pathways to Offender Reintegration*, edited by S. Maruna and R. Immarigeon. Devon: Willan Publishing.

Gadd, D., and S. Farrall. 2004. "Criminal Careers, Desistance and Subjectivity: Interpreting Men's Narratives of Change." *Theoretical Criminology* 8: 123-56.

Gorman, K., M. Gregory, M. Hayles & N. Parton, eds. 2006. *Constructive Work with Offenders*. London: Jessica Kingsley Publishers.

Gorman, K., P. O'Byrne, and N. Parton. 2006. "Constructive Work with Offenders: Setting the Scene." In *Constructive Work with Offenders* edited by K. Gorman, M. Gregory, M. Hayles, and N. Parton. London: Jessica Kingsley Publishers.

Haney, C. 2002. "Making Law Modern: Toward a Contextual Model of Justice." *Psychology, Public Policy and Law* 8: 3-63.

Haney, C., and P. Zimbardo. 1998. "The Past and Future of US Prison Policy: Twenty-five Years after the Stanford Prison Experiment." *American Psychologist* 53: 709-27.

Hayles, M. 2006. "Construcing Safety: A Collaborative Approach to Managing Risk and Building Responsibility." In *Constructive Work with Offenders*, edited by K. Gorman, M. Gregory, M. Hayles & N. Parton. London: Jessica Kingsley Publishers.

Maruna, S. 2001. *Making Good: How Ex-Convicts Reform and Rebuild their Lives.* Washington DC: American Psychological Association Books.

Maruna, S., and R. Immarigeon, eds. 2004. *After Crime and Punishment: Pathways to Offender Reintegration.* Cullompton, Devon: Willan Publishing.

Maruna, S., and H. Copes. 2005. "What Have We Learned in Five Decades of Neutralisation Research?" *Crime and Justice: A Review of Research* 32: 221-320.

Maruna, S., and R.E. Mann. 2006. "A Fundamental Attribution Error? Rethinking Cognitive Distortion." *Legal and Criminological Psychology* 11: 155-77.

McGuire, J., ed. 1995. *What Works: Reducing Reoffending: Guidelines from Research and Practice.* New York: Wiley.

Minister of Community Services. 2000. *A Balanced Approach to Juvenile Justice in Victoria*. Melbourne: Author.

Moffitt, T.E. 1993. "Adolescence-limited and Life-course-persistent Antisocial Behavior: A Developmental Taxonomy." *Psychological Review* 100: 674-701.

Morrison, G.M., M. Brown, B. D'Incau, S.L. O'Farrell and M.J. Furlong. 2006. "Understanding Resilience in Educational Trajectories: Implications for Protective Possibilities." *Psychology in the Schools* 43: 19-31.

Nellis, M. 2002. "Pros and Cons: Offender Auto/biographies, Penal Reform and Probation Training." *The Howard Journal* 41: 434-68.

Palmer, E., J. McGuire, J. Hounsome, R. M. Hatcher, C. A. Bilby & C. Hollin. 2007. "Offending Behaviour Programmes in the Community: The Effects on Reconviction of Three Programmes with Adult Male Offenders." *Legal and Criminological Psychology* 12 (2): 251-64.

Ward, T., and C. Stewart. 2003. "Criminogenic Needs and Human Needs: A Theoretical Model." *Psychology, Crime and Law* 9: 125-43.

Ward, T., and M. Brown. 2004. "The Good Lives Model and Conceptual Issues in Offender Rehabilitation." *Psychology, Crime and Law* 10: 243-57.

—. 2003. "The Risk-need Model of Offender Rehabilitation: A Critical Analysis." In *Sexual Deviance: Issues and Controversies*, edited by T. Ward, D.R. Laws & S.H. Hudson. Thousand Oaks, CA: Sage.

Ward, T., and T. Garton. 2006. "Rehabilitation, Etiology and Self-regulation: The Good Lives Model of Sexual Offender Treatment." *Aggression and Violent Behavior* 11: 77-94.

Ward, T., and B. Marshall. 2006. "Narrative Identity and Offender Rehabilitation." *International Journal of Offender Therapy and Comparative Criminology* 10: 1-20.

Wilkinson J. 2006. "Undergraduate Education: What Good is it? An International Perspective." Menzies Oration on Higher Education, University of Melbourne.
http://www.unimelb.edu.au/speeches/menziesoration.html

Youth Violence and Juvenile Justice 2004, 2 (3): whole issue.

CHAPTER FIVE

"THROUGH THE MAZE, FINDING THE HOOK, WALKING A TIGHTROPE": THE ART OF POSITIVE WORK WITH YOUNG OFFENDERS IN CUSTODY

KIERSTEN COULTER

> …these are hard young women to engage…it can be really really hard to get that initial catch…It's a bit like negotiating your way through the maze…get the hook and …you can work with them…It's like walking a tightrope. (Female Worker #16, Young Women's Centre)

The exploration of theoretical and conceptual models to underpin explanations of the impact of arts-based programs has been sadly neglected, especially in the criminal justice area where, despite a worldwide proliferation of interest and initiatives, few attempts have been made to link outcomes with criminological theories of offending and rehabilitation (Hughes 2004). Theoretical coherence—so important to our understanding of the impact of interventions—requires clear links between the causes and consequences of offending, the method and purpose of intervention, and possible outcomes (Ward and Maruna 2007). Given firstly, the recent emergence of various theoretical approaches into the debates on programs in juvenile justice; secondly, the lack of theoretical coherence; and thirdly, the lack of "research in the real world on programs", it is argued that: "research at this stage should be focused on theoretical development" (Burnett and Maruna 2006, 86). That is to say, "why and how something should work rather than what works" (ibid). It is this general approach that has influenced my research and for which qualitative methods are so applicable.

This chapter draws on the theoretical, conceptual and policy frameworks discussed in Brown's chapter (this volume, Chapter Four). The details will not be reiterated here. The approaches he outlines are the "what works" or Risk, Need, Responsivity Model (RNR) (Andrews and Bonta 2003), and positive or strengths-based models including the Good Lives (GLM) and Desistance Models (Ward and Maruna 2007; Maruna 2003). Within his theoretical discussion, Brown (this volume, Chapter Four) emphasizes at least three concepts for consideration. Firstly, he suggests that arts-based programs have intrinsic value, providing a program model that may address some of the key targets for development identified by proponents of constructive or positive work with offenders. Key targets for programs will include a focus on the "personal and social-contextual factors related to offending" (ibid) and the development of a skills base to equip offenders in the pursuit of their needs and the demands of the world they inhabit. Secondly, he discusses the role played in the change process by the offender's personal narrative(s) and the potential arts-based programs offer for the (re)construction of that narrative as a critical part of the process of desisting from offending. Thirdly, he suggests strengths-based art programs, may improve participants' "responsivity" to mandated programs, including programs operating under the "what works" rubric. Using these theoretical models and drawing on empirical evidence, I explore the concepts of intrinsic value, narrative identity and increased responsivity, as evidenced in an ethnographic study of arts-based programs at two gender-specific (one male, one female) custodial sites, to investigate the contribution such programs may make to desistance from offending. The study, based in Victoria, Australia, was part of the *Risky Business (RB)* program of research that is detailed elsewhere in this volume. As the criminologist in the team, I set up similar programs in the custodial centers with identical linked workshops in the community for participants transitioning out of custody or post-release.

The *Risky Business* custodial study

The participants

Relative to the population, Victoria detains the lowest number of juveniles in custodial centers of any state in Australia. Custodial sentences are reserved for only the most serious, chronic and high-risk offenders, when no other sentence is appropriate (Harris and Muller 2001). The women's centre for all juveniles aged between ten and seventeen, also has a significant population aged eighteen to twenty (average daily population

~ twelve). The men's centre is restricted to young men aged seventeen to under twenty-one (average daily population ~ sixty–seventy). Victoria has a dual track system, enabling adjudicated young adults (under twenty-one) to serve their sentence in a juvenile facility.

These young people present with a range of concerns and "risks" that, in many respects, do not distinguish them from similar populations elsewhere (e.g. high level poly-drug use; significant health concerns; learning difficulties; sexual exploitation; poor educational achievement; repeated contact with all areas of the justice system). Each centre reflects considerable cultural and linguistic diversity.

The programs

Interdisciplinary programs were offered to all young men and women in the two custodial sites, focused on producing a self-devised theatre work. There were three six-month programs for young women and one for young men. Artists ran weekly workshops offering writing, music, dance, improvization/performance and visual arts paralleled in the community for those in transition. Young people had the opportunity to participate in custody, through their transitional phase and post-release. Goal-focused workshops culminated every six months in community-based theatre performances. Young people in custody accessed a supervised day leave program to join the community group in the final production. Audiences included family, relatives and friends, juvenile justice workers, community service providers and their clients and secondary school students.

Young people's experiences were placed at the centre of the creative process and all the material was chosen, written, developed and performed by them. The model was underpinned by an emphasis on personal expression and creativity rather than therapy. Participation was by choice, and while a strong commitment was encouraged, this was flexible. Juvenile justice workers were excluded from workshops to enable young people the greatest possible freedom of expression in the creative process.

Three principal artists ran each program; one was common to both sites. They share a broad range and depth of arts-based skill, training and experience; most have carried out arts programs in custodial environments before; have shared histories of drug use; and three of the artists have been in prison. One of the artists on the young women's program is also a psychologist and drug and alcohol counselor.

The research

Seventy young people participated in the programs. The young women were aged between fourteen and twenty-three: average age, eighteen; and the young men were aged between seventeen and twenty-two: average age, nineteen. A total of 197 semi-structured interviews were conducted across time periods (at least the beginning, middle and end) with seventy participants (forty-one young women and twenty-nine young men); thirty-five custodial and community-based youth workers, management and health staff; and the five principal artists. Follow-up interviews were conducted between six months and two years after completing the program. Field notes were collected from extensive researcher participant observation. There were considerable additional data sources including artists' notes, material produced in workshops, video recordings, notes on informal discussions and a de-identified database giving background and offending profiles of all young people in the potential sample. Hyper research electronic software was used as an aid in establishing themes, codes and collating material. Research subjects are identified using simple codes explained in Note 1 at the end of the chapter.

I. Intrinsic value

The intrinsic value of arts-based learning as "fundamental to education" has been reflected in school-based educational research (Bamford 2006, 19) and in community-based programs, where researchers have established a number of unique intrinsic characteristics leading them to conclude that arts-based programs represent "especially powerful developmental sites" (Heath and Soep 1998, 9). Can these learning environments be used to engage young offenders in ways that are conceptually linked to understandings of pathways into, and desistance from, offending, and do they reliably assist in the production of important outcomes related to current theories of rehabilitation?

Commonly reported outcomes from largely non-custodial studies have included problem solving, negotiating, teamwork, social and communication skills, motivation, positive behavioral changes, improved self-esteem, engagement with learning and goal setting (Bamford 2006; Hughes 2004; Jermyn 2004, 2001; Mills and Brown 2004; Deasy 2002; Hillman 2001; Fiske 2000; Heath and Soep 1998; Walters 1997). This list is by no means comprehensive.

Importantly, these outcomes were reproduced in each of the RB custodial sites (Coulter 2006). Space prevents the presentation of the substantial evidence, but detailed accounts of these and of enhanced self-concept and self-belief, increased confidence, the sense of being skilled, capable and valued, goal setting and future planning, positive attitudes and behavioral changes constitute just some of the intrinsic values and outcomes. They were significant in this context in at least two broad areas; firstly, in the potential of the arts to engage the target group and secondly, the process of participation in the arts appears to elicit outcomes identified in strengths-based models of offender rehabilitation as important to the desistance process. As predicted in these models, effecting change in these areas appears to have a positive impact on skills development within some of the key areas of criminogenic need.

Engagement

Running programs in custodial institutions is a complex process. The interaction between the nature of the closed institution, and the skills and needs of the clients, produces young people frequently characterized as lacking motivation to participate in "change" programs (Losel 1995) and described by staff as difficult to engage (Alder and Hunter 1999; Alder and Baines, 1996). Programs in custodial settings are less likely to be effective and face greater challenges than similar programs run in the community (Sealock, Gottfredson and Gallagher 1997; Wellisch, Anglin and Prendergast 1993). One of the clear challenges is attracting and sustaining engagement. Critics of the RNR model argue that the characteristic focus on deficits (things to suppress or get rid of) and risk reduction, presents considerable challenges in this regard (Ward and Marshall 2006; Brown 2008). The GLM suggests that offender engagement in programs should be motivated by positive approach goals identified and desired by the offender (Ward and Maruna 2007).

Engagement requires interest, investment, motivation and commitment. The programs attracted unexpectedly high levels of engagement, participation and commitment, with most eligible custodial participants completing the program. Many young people transitioned to the post-release group and continued participation in more than one program. Participants said they were attracted to the arts and creative programs because of their active, participatory nature. Young women described the arts program as "…better than any other session we have to do here. Any other program" (FP#3, 21) and they saw themselves as "…doing something constructive…" (FP#2, 19). The young men said, "For some people the whole day is not enough. When it's finished [we] want some more." (MP#11, 19)

Workers reported much higher rates of participation and commitment in RB than in many other programs, describing young people as "very excited, very drawn in and very committed to it" (FW#8, YWC). Young people who were described as particularly resistant to engaging with programs, or who workers felt would not engage with the performing arts, did so.

> …getting someone like [name of client] to commit to that, I thought, was fantastic. Because she hates learning. (FW#1, YWC)

Skill development

Beyond engagement, the experiences of being skilled at something, feeling proud and receiving praise were regarded by staff as unique both for the young people and within programs.

> …the quality of the performance blew everybody away…seeing the guys do something that they were so proud of…a lot of our guys don't get that. That's a huge confidence boost… (MW#6, YMC)

All young people in the study could identify the acquisition of particular skills and felt validated and proud of themselves—a new experience for most of them.

> …in my whole life, right, I haven't had people come to me and say you know, you're good at this and good at that. People reject us because we are the way we are. And it just felt good to hear people say, "oh you're a good dancer, keep it up." It felt good, totally. (FP#24, 16)

These kinds of experiences are closely related within the GLM to the goods of competence, offering experiences of mastery, and a sense of self as a skilled individual with valued, acknowledged and recognized abilities. On reading the transcripts of their largely negative and limited formal educational experiences, it is clear this marks a significant shift in self-perception.

Approach goals as motivation

The GLM, rather than emphasizing deficits, posits that motivation and skills enhancement will be encouraged by approach goals geared to the personal choices, interests and needs of offenders (Ward and Maruna 2007). The RB data lends support to these assumptions. Participants identified a number of motivating approach goals, including the desire to tell their story in a public forum; develop a relationship with the facilitators; develop a better understanding of themselves and express their feelings; be creative; have some fun; get a leave from the centre; and improve their chances of parole. Eliciting a strong commitment to the desired approach goals appeared to sustain motivation when challenges faced within the program began to bite.

> …as soon as it becomes a little bit too hard, they think this is a little bit uncomfortable and I don't know whether I want to do this…I was really pleased by their level of commitment…I was surprised by…what they gave up to do that. My history tells me if they are enjoying something they are going to commit to it. (MW#9, YWC)

Goods and criminogenic needs

A number of "intrinsic" outcomes carry a particular significance. A lack of problem solving skills and the inability to work through the associated processes are frequently linked with offenders' anti-social behavior. The RNR highlights impulsivity, poor emotional regulation and a lack of problem solving skills as key criminogenic needs (Andrews and Bonta 2003). The GLM recognizes these as difficulties that indicate a deeper level of need to be addressed along with requisite skills enhancement.

> The criminogenic need of impulsivity points to problems in achieving the good of autonomy…the person concerned experiences difficulty in formulating and carrying out a plan successfully…because he…has little experience of effective decision-making (Ward and Maruna 2007, 150).

The inherent problem solving nature of arts-based programs, especially theatre-based initiatives, is well documented in some of the research literature already cited. There were multiple sites for problem-solving challenges documented in RB field notes; heightened in the custodial context because of the lack of skills/knowledge of participants (e.g. little knowledge of the performing arts, poor literacy), and because of the complex nature of the context (e.g. heightened emotionality, interpersonal conflict, inconsistency of attendance, high mobility, custodial disciplinary practices and frequent interruptions). The pressured performance week accelerated the need to implement problem solving practices, requiring participants to see, reflect, negotiate, cooperate, compromise and act, while at the same time dealing with frequently heightened emotional states. One of the artists gave a glimpse into this world early in the workshop process.

> Somebody like [MP#18] can see that something can be done in the world although there are obstacles because he thought…how am I gonna do this, how can I be part of a play when I can't read or write…there are huge obstacles that they have to overcome every day… (FA#2, YMP & YWP)

Most of the "intrinsic" values and outcomes identified in the RB programs have intrinsic links with goods identified in the GLM and, more generally, as targets in strengths-based models (e.g. self-esteem is encompassed within the goods of quality of life-health, agency and inner peace). These goods, in turn, have intrinsic value. They motivate and animate human life and behavior. It has been possible to show that these carry a key importance for engaging with offenders, and may enhance the likelihood of a progression toward desistance theoretically and conceptually linked to understandings about the causes of offending and the processes of desistance.

Intrinsic but contingent?

Are these intrinsic values and outcomes a given or contingent? At both sites there was a drama program running concurrently with RB. This was not well received: "I don't like [that] drama. I hate it…all this airy fairy stuff" (FP#14, 18); "it pissed me off…I hated it…It was nothing compared to this [RB] drama" (MP#11, 19). This led me to question the apparent universality of many of the positive outcomes. A process evaluation revealed a critical nexus between the nature of the artists and the processes and structure of the program. The skills, background and experience of the artists was foremost in engaging with and motivating the target group. As past offenders and drug users they had immediate "street cred". Participants desired their friendship and saw them as inspirational role models: "if he/she can do it, then so can I".

The artists found their histories assisted them in understanding and managing the challenges posed by the institutional environment and the young people. The nature of the artists' interaction is reflected in the feedback from young people and included the level of choice, control, equality, respect, lack of judgment, understanding and caring they experienced. Young people and workers also praised the level of artistic skill, the development of valued product and the artists' ability to impart knowledge in non-judgmental ways.

In different ways, the participants at each site posed multiple challenges to engaging with and committing to the program. Hence the artists regularly faced inconsistency and particularly (but not exclusively) with young women, resistance and occasionally tantrums, even with committed participants. They worked with this resistance and each developed a kitbag of responses to turn it around. It was not as simple as the love of arts-based programs leading to high participation; it was the artists' knowledge of, and skill and willingness to work with the challenges that made a significant difference.

That the programs had an internal discipline was very clearly revealed in the data. Others have referred to this as the "habits of mind" instilled by the arts process (Heath and Soep 1998, 15); as a criminologist observing the artists at work with offenders, I observed informal social controls on multiple levels resulting in pro-social modeling and skills enhancement with a positive impact on behavior, attitude and engagement. These structures were flexible, and each artist had their own distinct methods for engaging with young people and managing challenging situations. They were highly skilled, displaying multiple roles of friend, mentor, sibling, parent, counselor, teacher, rule enforcer, negotiator and artist.

Valued structural and process factors identified included program/artist flexibility, high ratio of artists to participants (1:3), a number of art disciplines offering different entry points, exclusion of statutory staff, focus on participants' creativity and desires, and time spent in the program coupled with the commitment and provision of adequate resources from within the centre. The latter turned out to be critical in sustaining commitment, the depth and nature of engagement and in maximizing program and participant potential.

The young men's program ran once a week all day (six to eight hours), as a fully integrated unit of their Technical and Further Education (TAFE) programs. Participation was encouraged by awarding both course-related and temporary leave points (leading to a day leave). By contrast, the young women's program was placed within recreational non-TAFE time, and the workshops were just two hours per week. Given the complexity and competing agendas that exist within the custodial environment, the model for the young men's program assisted in ensuring that at least some program time was available to the greatest number of participants with minimum intrusion. Of even greater significance was the time and flexibility it afforded artists and participants in the development of work and a commitment that once established, carried the participants through rehearsal during the week when the artists were absent.

> …a hugely different capacity of working with the boys…we had a whole day to rehearse the scenes, and we had a chance to build on it. (FA#2, YWP & YMP)

This level of commitment was much more challenging to achieve with the young women for a number of reasons, but the extra time combined with the greater institutional centrality given to the young men's program vis-à-vis their core programs was significant. It was also important, given the nature of the environment, to have a program manager at each site; this ensured quality of service delivery. While the responsivity principle of the RNR model seeks to address program design and facilitator qualities, it remains somewhat vague on detail. The GLM has outlined the general approach for programs and detailed the nature of the interaction between facilitators and offenders (Ward and Maruna 2007). These are largely consistent with what has been described here.

II. Narrative identity

> TAFE is…all about the future…Drama is where you get to explore yourself and get yourself together… If you don't know about yourself first how are you going to focus on a computer and a book? (MP#24, 19)

Shadd Maruna (2003) reinvigorated interest in narrative work with offenders, identifying distinct qualities in the narratives of those who desisted from offending and those who persisted: "…individuals need to establish an alternative, coherent, and pro-social self-identity in order to justify and maintain their desistance from crime" (Ward and Maruna 2007, 86). Desisters constructed "a narrative that made sense of their earlier crimes and experiences of adversity and created a bridge between their undesirable lives with new ways of living". They were more likely to live their lives according to a "redemption script, where negative past experiences were reinterpreted as providing a pathway…to the forging of a new identity and more authentic ways of living" (ibid). Persisters were more likely to fit the ideal promoted by the RNR model, accepting responsibility for their crimes and the "bleak reality of their future prospects" (Brown, this volume, Chapter Four) with a narrative that reflected a "condemnation script".

There are at least three broad categories in which the RB data is able to offer guidance on the contribution of arts-based programs to the (re)formation of participants' narrative identity. The first is a change in self-belief about their capabilities. The second is the understanding and integration of identity forming past experiences and the third relates to the emergence of the "new me" (Ward and Maruna 2007) and the impact this has on participants' sense of worth and connectedness to the "straight" world.

The achievers' narrative

Change in personal narrative to do with abilities and skills was shown to be closely linked with the intrinsic values of arts process and outcomes. A change was evident in all participants from "I can't do this" to "I can do this, I do have skills, I can learn, I can write," and so on. The experience lifted their self-esteem and made them "feel proud", "confident" and "good about" their "achievements".

Participants, who were resistant to learning and struggling with important basic skills (e.g. reading, writing) underwent enduring attitudinal change with requisite skills enhancement that led to the adoption of newly developed skills as life tools; it refocused their direction and opened up future pathways. One brief case study from each site will illustrate the nature and diversity of this journey.

(FP#1, 16), a serious repeat offender with an intellectual disability, was described by workers as one of the most disadvantaged young women in the State and hard to engage in programs. She was distracted and deliberately disruptive in early RB workshops. In her first interview she said she was interested in art (drawing, music) but described her other skills as "causing trouble, doing crime..." She left school in Year 7 because "[I] couldn't do my work properly…couldn't concentrate…" and said "I hate reading…[it's] too hard" and "…I can't spell so I hate my writing…". Her attitude to the educational programs on site was clear: "…What the fuck is this stupid work, fuck ya. No, I'm not doing that…"

In her second interview she described the RB program: "…I like it…it's fun, it's interesting, it teaches you…it gives you that chance to try and be someone you always wanted to be." She described her feelings while participating.

> You'll feel happy! You'll go I can't believe I did that…for the first time in my life…you get excited, you get that confidence and you want to do it again!

There were profound changes in her attitude as she became committed and able to concentrate for long periods. Trust developed in her relationship with two artists and, uncharacteristically, she began sharing, writing and performing aspects of her life. Her Juvenile Justice (JJ) worker, reflecting on her progress, described an event where she bowled up to interstate visitors.

> ...she did the whole performance, totally in front of two strangers...with a confidence that a kid with that amount of damage had had in her life...she wanted people to hear and see what she had to say... (MW#9, YWC)

She was enjoying participating in a TAFE program on release. I asked her if there were any lasting things that RB had changed for her. She said: "yeah to write...like [artist name] told me to write my feelings down in a book...ever since I've done that and it helps me..."

Not all participants faced extreme skill deficits. There is scope within the GLM to recognize that everyone is an individual with likes and dislikes shaped by life experience. Nourishing and catering for diverse needs and individuality was important to keeping young people engaged. Each participant's journey and achievements through the program were shaped by context, needs, originating skills and experience. Through a combination of tragic refugee experiences, addiction to heroin and entry into crime in Australia, (MP#10, 19) had lost his sense of what he was good at and wanted from life. He was experiencing severe depression in custody, accompanied by a sense of hopelessness. Reflecting on the RB program he said:

> ...an experience that will last a lifetime...if I...pursue a career and make something out of myself, this drama was the thing that set me towards that. It made me really think about what I wanted to do and what I was good at...it made me feel special. It gave me hope. Like I can do something...I'm really interested in reading and writing...When I was younger I was thinking about writing but once I got into trouble and I came here [to the custodial centre] I forgot about that, but then when I wrote my monologue and...song...it reminded me...I like writing and I think I'm pretty good at it. And now I'm thinking about...my future. (MP#10, 19)

Life journey narrative

Moving from a narrative appreciation for their skills base, the second broad category explores the development of a greater understanding of their life journey and behavior. Both the GLM and the RNR rely heavily on counseling approaches. The assumption that this will be engaging and effective may be problematic.

Counselors at both sites said that engaging clients was challenging and a "nightmare". Many young people said: "I hate counseling" (FP#16, 14), or simply and emphatically stated: "I don't talk to counselors" (FP#7, 19). Given these challenges, all staff interviewed was surprised by the achievements of the RB program.

> …the main struggle you have is…engagement, motivating them to look at their lives,…and be committed to…change…That's what we've seen with the young women [in the RB program]. (MW#4, YWC)

Young people sought out the program specifically as a means of exploring themselves and expressing their concerns.

> …it's just helped me deal with my shit. And it's helped me to understand a bit more, about me… (FP#2, 19)

> Drama is always like a counselling session to us…we talk about our offences and we reflect on it and act it out…we find ways of going around a situation… (MP#24, 19)

Many young people explored a much greater range and depth of personal concerns than workers had witnessed in most other programs. The diverse experiences expressed through their artwork were identified as the basis for participants' offending and drug use. Their learning how to express themselves and their feelings in a pro-social environment led to reports of behavioral changes, including reduced levels of anger, pro-social and empathetic attitudes to others, changes in attitude about substance use, and an ability to express their feelings in appropriate ways and seek help. Positive behavior changes were observed to persist outside and beyond the program.

> I'm learning how to express myself in a different way. How to deal with old issues…Rather than trying to forget my past and go shoot up heroin, I'm actually expressing what happened. Like in a good surrounding…like I'm dealing with it rather than pushing it to the back of my mind and forgetting it… (FP#2, 19)

The GLM predicts that assisting offenders with pro-social ways of achieving desired goods through skills enhancement, while at the same time addressing underlying concerns and barriers, will lead to a diminution or even elimination of some criminogenic needs without the need to target them specifically. Evidence from this research lends empirical weight in key areas such as substance use, empathy, and anger/emotional management and regulation.

> I never really talked about my stories…at the performance…I let people know what happens to me…I'm so much better…more relaxed…I've got me own little routine, my anger doesn't even come out…it's improved heaps…everyone says that to me… (FP#24, 16)

> …I learnt how to express myself in there; it helps me deal with my anger problems too. It does really… I just think about things…what I wrote…about when I'm feeling angry, how to make myself happy…it…helps me relieve some stress… (MP#20, 19)

This young man had participated in "a lot" of anger management programs during his eleven sentences. He said they "had not really helped".

Some of the outcomes are particularly important in relation to offending. Substance use – a key criminogenic need – was a significant concern across both sites. It was explained in many performance pieces as a coping mechanism for emotional distress, which had its basis in a variety of personal life challenges. Many responses to drug use, such as cognitive behavioral therapeutic (CBT) approaches, pharmacotherapy and detox programs, do not directly address this underlying distress. While the RNR largely regards distress, anxiety and depression as discretionary targets, strengths-based models seek to address them as integral to the change process. The RB data suggests this is of key importance. An examination of the connection between the seeking of at least three primary goods (inner-peace, life-health and relatedness), the means for achieving these, young people's emotional and mental distress and drug use, could greatly assist in addressing this critical criminogenic need. That is, drug use can be viewed as a (mal)adaptive response to seeking these goods. Examining their own trajectory into drug use through the non-threatening pathways provided in the arts program enabled participants to gain "knowledge of why they use drugs…if you know why…then hopefully you have conquered your reason to want it" (FW#17, YWC).

They were equally influenced by the journey of others. The collective experience led to important shifts in perception about working in groups, and there was a clear narrative change in how they related to each other with a shift in the point of reference from criminal peers to collective achievers.

> To be honest I have never worked with a pack of girls, like some of them girls…there was something special about it. We had a couple of blues but it felt real different and it just felt to get involved with them girls. Just having fun with them and participating in it. It was good. (FP#16, 14)

A consequential spin-off at both sites was the emergence of an uncharacteristically empathetic self and supportive group dynamics were observed by staff operating on the unit.

> [FP #7]...Very considered. An empathy. It was just so wonderful to be around. She's doing stuff for other girls and they are noticing it and talking about it and she's just continuing on… (MW#2, YWC)

Re-authoring and taking control of their story/narrative seemed to give most participants a sense of control over their lives and an ability to identify for themselves what changes they may need to make.

> …we've got issues and problems. Drama helps you with those things…Like discover what you want, it makes you want it…We are going there [RB] out of our own will because we like it and we are learning things about ourselves that we can change… (MP#24, 19)

Redemption or condemnation narrative?

The third aspect of narrative identity change occurred when the newfound understanding of formative life experiences and what they were now capable of (the "new me"), was both symbolically "presented" and reflected out to the "straight" world through performance. Young people's most desired approach goal through telling their story, their way, was to change the way they were perceived as "bad people". It was a destigmatizing process, likely to be important to future desistance and integration (Burnett and Maruna 2006). Within the RB program it was an iterative process, reinforcing the life change; "publicly saying that is very different from private counseling. That public affirmation, that really is meaningful for them…" (MW#3, YMC). Young people said they felt the experience of being applauded and valued for their work "was amazing".

> …obviously the life we got from the applause at the end of every performance. The lift from the clapping thing was amazing. And that I will always carry with me…It definitely seemed like they [the audiences] were much more enlightened in a sense. To me it felt like as if they had opened their eyes. And because of the emotions involved, you can tell that it really has touched them… (MP#28, 20)

Participants articulated a sense of control over their lives and the image that others have of them, including workers. This is essential to operating as an autonomous and empowered individual and is an integrative, rather than fragmenting process, enabling young people to take from their past experience and move with it into the future, seeing their experiences as valuable, not as aspects of themselves to be ashamed of or to hide.

The performance pieces, almost without exception, reflected "redemption" scripts. More importantly, it is evident that all participants took away a redemption narrative and felt they had been able to present a positive "redemptive" image.

> Most people don't know what that life is about. And I think it's important to put across that message…To understand that we are still people and we make mistakes…We're not evil or something. (FP#7, 19)

> Yeah, we still say how proud we are, having us on the Centre and we've made [custodial facility] look good too. Not everyone here are [sic.] bad…People who do things in institutions like this can still change… (MP#24, 20)

Working with narrative identity – a risky business?

These narrative identity outcomes were largely dependent on specific approaches in the RB program; firstly, allowing young people the creative freedom to shape and present their own work and life-story; and secondly, having a public forum in which the outcome is reviewed. For both contextual and participant originating reasons, these carry significant elements of risk: firstly, the impact of the inevitable tensions present when strengths-based opportunities operate within a risk-based/management policy environment; secondly, the nature of the narrative; and thirdly, challenges posed by gender differences.

The tensions between risk-based management policies and the leaps of faith necessary to fulfill the program aims, not only meant that the program operated under the constant tension that a single incident could have repercussions for all programs involving custodial day leaves, but these tensions threatened to disrupt the fragile "new me". This was realized in a number of ways, including denial or withdrawal of access to leaves (and therefore to some or all rehearsals/performances), leaves granted at the last minute so that young people were inadequately prepared for performances and denial/withdrawal of access because of behavioral incidents (which meant the program became implicated in punishment). Most of these alleged "incidents", as described by workers, were relatively minor. When participants were subject to these kinds of policies or even just the threat of them, they were reminded they were offenders and disempowered. When leaves were denied or withdrawn, it became very difficult for the artists to motivate ongoing participation because young people could not see the point. The program became a representation of every other life experience; you put in all the effort and you get none of the rewards.

It was difficult for the artists to obtain clear information about why some of these decisions were made and they were never part of the process. These collisions and the fragility of the gains made were all the more prominent because of the personal nature and investment in the material. This alone meant that there were tensions within individuals as the performance drew closer and some behavioral issues were inevitable. While artists were quite capable of dealing with these on their watch, if they erupted on the unit between workshops/rehearsals/performances, the way the behavior was understood and addressed was out of their hands. These concerns impacted the extent to which the potential benefits for an individual could be realized and enduring or significantly diminished.

While in four years of continuous operation there has been no serious incident, it is arguable that the program faces increasingly stringent risk assessment processes and it is harder to obtain leaves for participants. Even in actuarial terms this makes little sense. There is insufficient room in blanket, risk management procedures to consider individual programs or cases. When making assessments on the level of risk, the impact of the powerful informal social controls that exist, combined with the level of individual and collective commitment to the program and the facilitators, may receive insufficient consideration. The risk-benefit analysis is skewed toward minimizing perceived community risk, not maximizing benefit or giving adequate attention to the potential harm such risk-based approaches may deliver in the context of strengths-based programs. While to some extent these tensions as inevitable, integrating the artists into the discussion on risk management, and reviewing management and punishment procedures in the light of the RB findings, could be fruitful.

Secondly, participants did not necessarily produce a narrative in line with the aims and objectives of the program or the custodial centre and this had a counter productive rehabilitative/narrative potential. This occurred once at the young men's site under the guidance of the artist with no experience in this context. Two rival groups were vying for control of the program and over each other. One of the groups produced a scene placing the ringleader at the head of his drug trafficking gang, demonstrating his support base to the other group. The warning was clear. Far from challenging any of the young men in this group to explore their underlying narrative identity, it was confirming and fuelling the existing one, with real potential for violence. While the young men had stated strongly that their approach goal for participating in the RB program/performance was to shift and inform the negative public perception of young offenders through their personal stories, on this occasion they did not produce material to this end. The two more experienced artists were able to turn this situation around over several weeks, and the rival group dynamics were completely disrupted so that there was just one cohesive group. This highlights the skilful work of the artists. While young people perceived the end product as all their work and their stories, the artists played a vital role in directing how the content was elicited and realized. This was equally true when participants shared deeply affecting material in ways that laid both them, and potentially their families, wide open and vulnerable. The artists worked with them, through an ethical and open process that enabled them to say what they wanted to say, but at the same time, protected them from potential repercussions. This is not easy work.

The third challenge underscores this even more. Young men and women took different risks and faced different challenges within the process. Finding ways of enabling young men to fulfill their main approach goal was challenging. They found discussing personal information and emotions difficult and the artists developed a whole range of approaches to address the challenges they faced as facilitators in realizing the script. The majority of young men were easy to work with on the floor in the physical realization of performance. This display was empowering and highly energized. By contrast, young women eagerly sought out the program to discuss problems and with somewhat alarming ease, plunged into deeply affecting and emotional spaces, producing a rich tapestry of written material to work with. For the majority of young women, painfully self-conscious about their bodies, or disconnected from the physical self through trauma, the awareness and physicalization necessary to realize a performance, was clearly at times excruciating. This was the point at which artists faced the greatest resistance from the young women, and they were very sensitive to just how challenging the journey to performance was.

> …for a lot of these young women, [it] is about disconnecting through trauma, to manage to get through…it brings such an awareness and self-consciousness…when you can't really even look in the mirror [it's] incredibly daunting…with the boys that confidence did show out more…being out there and puffing your shoulders and looking confident is how those boys have survived in the world. Equally, how the girls have shut down and close and don't be seen is how they have survived. (FW#3, YWC)

The artists used quite different approaches throughout the process at each site. Without this it seems unlikely that a program at either site would have been completed or resulted in the kinds of outcomes that have been discussed. Strengths-based models seek to address diversity, including gender differences, by acknowledging the importance of individual context and experience as part of the development of the rehabilitative good life plan (Ward and Maruna 2007). The RNR mentions gender as potentially important within the responsivity principle but is vague on the detail of what this means in practice. Andrews and Bonta (2003) have also suggested there is little evidence to support the need for significantly different approaches or content when delivering programs to women. The experience of this research suggests the assumption is deeply flawed and needs interrogation (see also Shaw and Hannah-Moffat 2004; Worrall 2002).

III. Responsivity and desistance

While there is substantial evidence for responsivity, understood as a broad principle covering attitudes and behavior, receptiveness and participation, there is inadequate space remaining to unpack these concepts here. The following is a brief summary of the main findings. Significant positive changes were reported in participants, in the way they conducted themselves in the centers and in their skills, confidence and willingness to engage more fully with a much broader set of workers and programs. Workers assisting young people in preparation for release said participants were much more competent and confident in relating and expressing themselves and in identifying their needs to the workers. Workers also said they had a much more rounded picture of what the young people were capable of, and an enhanced client worker relationship based on greater understanding.

Counseling staff said that hitherto unknown concerns came to light through the process of participation. This enabled important matters to be identified and then addressed. They were particularly enthusiastic about the potential of having the arts program run alongside their counseling and cognitive behavioral programs, identifying the example of the violence program that paralleled the arts program at the young men's site. They observed young men struggling in the violence program, and yet able to access and address fundamental concerns in the arts program. Counselors at both sites concluded that different media complement different things in different individuals. They also identified participants who, previously unwilling to engage in counseling, were able to identify areas in their lives that they knew needed attention and to seek the help of counselors voluntarily.

Other workers and young people reported a greater receptiveness to educational programs in some very resistant young people and adoption of the skills learned (e.g. public speaking, social and communication skills and confidence) in other programs and settings, such as employment.

A few of the highest risk young people did eventually return to custody, but were reported by workers to uncharacteristically complete their parole, to be more compliant and engaged with services, and to desist from re-offending for a longer period.

While the outcomes reported here are important in promoting the desistance process, they need to be supported once young people are released (as well as while they are in custody). Ward and Marshall (2006, 28) emphasize the need for basic social supports that help an offender to realize and sustain a "good lives plan"; "because identity construction is essentially an interpersonal and dynamic process it is necessary to ensure offenders' social environments are capable of reinforcing and sustaining their rehabilitation (good lives) plans". The life trajectory of some RB participants post-release begs the question: how do we achieve this goal? Narrative change and development was observed in RB participants to be a dynamic and ongoing process that persisted post-release and beyond the program. By this time some of them were living in particularly difficult circumstances and in some cases, with little or no support, either financial or personal. This is a critical concern.

The barriers to ongoing engagement with RB post-release (and other initiatives) go to the heart of structural concerns associated with inclusion, equality, access to resources and social justice. These challenges go far beyond the possibilities offered by engagement in arts programs, and yet they are at the heart of capitalizing on program benefits and consolidating new lives.

Structural challenges conspired against most participants, whether it was employment in mindless, repetitive jobs with no future, or an inability to secure and maintain adequate housing or employment, a lack of sufficient money to continue studying, or returning to the margins of racialized communities, an inability to obtain Australian residency, or to maintain a methadone program on a low income. Often these scenarios were complicated by loneliness, a reconnection with offending peers, and a not infrequent return to some level of substance use to numb out their bleak reality.

Addressing significant structural barriers requires a paradigm shift in assessing the impact of government policies and the provision of services to marginalized young people, including offenders. It requires a shift in political will, and the attitudes and participation of media and community in constructing and maintaining the barriers that enable marginalization and resource impoverishment to persist. These concerns require careful consideration by researchers to identify the policy changes and the specific nature of supports and resources that promote and sustain transitions and long-term change.

Conclusion

The question frequently asked about arts-based programs (or any other programs for offenders), is whether they stop offending. The answer, I suspect, is about pathways. Desistance from offending is not an event but a process and it can take years. We do not learn all we need to in one program, or at one time. Offenders progress towards desistance. One or more episodes of reoffending indicates neither that the program, nor the offender have failed or that they have not progressed. The evidence that these arts-based programs offered choices in pathways and education toward desistance is substantial. Perhaps the best answers will come from these young people in the years to come as they reflect back on that RB time when they felt good about themselves.

The potential benefits of arts-based programs to young offenders in custody will be realized within policy environments that respect their value and place them in appropriately targeted multi-service environments. While arts-based programs are not a panacea, and it is clear there are still gaps to be filled, this chapter has presented strong evidence that they can form part of the solution on the pathway toward desistance from offending. This emerges from a strong epistemological and conceptual base that helps makes sense of why they work, when they work.

Note

1. Research subjects are identified using simple codes: M (male) or F (female); P (participant) or W (worker) or A (artist) followed by a discrete number identifier (#n). A young person's age completes their code (e.g. MP#3, 18). Workers are further identified by YWC or YMC respectively for young women's or young men's custodial centers (e.g. FW#5, YMC). Artists are identified by YWP or YMP respectively for young women or young men's programs (e.g. FA#2, YWP).

Works Cited

Alder, C., and N. Hunter. 1999. "Young Women in the Juvenile Justice System." In *Findings 1: Young Women's Offending & Findings 2: Not*

Worse, Just Different? Canberra, Australia: Criminology Research Council (March).

Alder, C., and M. Baines. 1996. *...and when she was bad? Working with Young Women in Juvenile Justice & Related Areas.* Hobart, Tasmania: National Clearinghouse for Youth Studies.

Andrews, D. A., and J. Bonta. 2003. *The Psychology of Criminal Conduct* (3rd ed.) Cincinnati, Ohio: Anderson Publishing Company.

Bamford, A. 2006. *The Wow Factor: Global Research Compendium on the Impact of the Arts in Education.* Munster, Germany: Waxman.

Brown, M. 2008. "The Road Less Travelled: Arts-based Programs in Youth Corrections." In *The Arts and Youth "At Risk": Local and Global Challenges* edited by A. O'Brien & K. Donelan. Newcastle upon Tyne: Cambridge Scholars Publishing.

Burnett, R., and S. Maruna. 2006. "The Kindness of Prisoners: Strengths-based Resettlement in Theory and in Action." *Criminology & Criminal Justice,* 8: 83-106.

Coulter, K. 2006. "The Arts: A Program Model in the "Rehabilitation" of Young Offenders in Custody." Risky Business Working Papers (unpublished). Risky Business Project Custodial Case Studies 1 and 2. Melbourne, Australia: University of Melbourne, School of Political Science, Criminology and Sociology.

Deasy, R. ed. 2002. *Critical Links: Learning in the Arts and Student Academic and Social Development.* Washington, D.C.: Arts Education Partnership and the National Endowment for the Arts. Retrieved, http://www.aep-arts.org

Fiske, E. B. 2000. *Champions of Change – The Impact of the Arts on Learning.* Washington, D.C.: Arts Education Partnership and The President's Committee on the Arts and the Humanities. Retrieved, http://www.aep-arts.org

Harris, R., and D. Muller. 2001. "Recidivism among Juvenile Justice Clients 1997-2001, DHS, Victoria." Melbourne, Victoria: Juvenile Justice Section, Community Care Division, Victorian Department of Human Services.

Heath, S. B. and E. Soep. 1998. "Youth Development and the Arts in Non-school Hours." *Grant makers in the Arts*, 9 (1) Spring: 9-32.

Hillman, G. 2001. *Arts Programs for Juvenile Offenders in Detention and Corrections – A Guide to Promising Practices*. USA: US Department of Justice, Office of Juvenile Justice and Delinquency Prevention, and the National Endowment for the Arts.

Hughes, J. 2004. "'Doing the Arts Justice' – A Review of Research Literature, Practice and Theory." In *The Unit for the Arts and*

Offenders edited by A. Miles & A. McLewin (unpublished). UK: Centre for Applied Theatre Research, Research into Arts and Criminal Justice Think Tank, Arts Council of England & partners.

Jermyn, H. 2004. "The art of inclusion." Research report 35 prepared for the Arts Council of England. Retrieved, http://www.artscouncil.org.uk/

—. 2001. "The Arts and Social Exclusion." Review prepared for the Arts Council of England. Retrieved, http://www.artscouncil.org.uk/

Lösel, F. 1995. "The Efficacy of Correctional Treatment: A Review and Synthesis of Meta-evaluations." In *What Works: Reducing Reoffending, Guidelines from Research and Practice*, edited by J. McGuire, 79-111. West Sussex, UK: Wiley.

Maruna, S. 2003. *Making Good – How Ex-Convicts Reform and Rebuild Their Lives*. Washington, D.C.: American Psychological Association.

Mills, D., and P. Brown. 2004. *Art and Wellbeing.* Sydney, NSW: The Australia Council for the Arts.

Sealock, M. D., D. C. Gottfredson, and C. A. Gallagher. 1997. "Drug Treatment for Juvenile Offenders: Some Good and Bad News." *Journal of Research in Crime and Delinquency* 34: 210-36.

Shaw, M., and K. Hannah-Moffat. 2004. "How Cognitive Skills Forgot about Gender and Diversity." In *What Matters in Probation*, edited by G. Mair, 90-121. Portland, Oregon: Willan Publishing.

Walters, R. 1997. "Big hArt: The Theatrical Side of Youth Crime Prevention." *Youth Studies Australia* 16: 22-6.

Ward, T., and S. Maruna. 2007. *Rehabilitation, Key Ideas in Criminology Series*. London: Routledge.

Ward, T., and B. Marshall. 2007. "Narrative Identity and Offender Rehabilitation." *International Journal of Offender Therapy and Comparative Criminology* 51: 279-97.

Wellisch, J., M.D. Anglin, and M. L. Prendergast. 1993. "Treatment Strategies for Drug-Abusing Women Offenders." In *Drug Treatment and Criminal Justice* edited by J. A. Inciardi, 5-29. California: Sage Publications.

Worrall, A. 2002. "Rendering Women Punishable: The Making of a Penal Crisis." In *Women and Punishment – The Struggle for Justice* edited by P. Carlen, 47-66. Portland, Oregon: Willan Publishing.

CHAPTER SIX

NARRATIVE, DIALOGUE AND RESISTANCE: MAKING MEANING THROUGH DRAMA WITH YOUNG PEOPLE "AT RISK"

DAVE KELMAN

Introduction

This chapter is based on research I undertook in 2004, as part of an extensive study funded by Vic Health (Kelman, O'Brien and Donelan 2005), that examined young people's stories told through performance to their own communities. This research project involved over one hundred young people from four different schools. I have chosen to focus on two groups of young people who were most obviously "at risk". "At risk" is a broad term and many young people fall into this category in the course of their adolescence (Mackenzie and Chamberlain 2002), but it is strongly linked to social exclusion (Jermyn 2001), a process of social, economic and cultural marginalization that creates profound feelings of alienation and associated problems (Cunneen and White 1995).

Research sites and methodology

This chapter explores projects at two different research sites. The first is a state school in inner Melbourne that has one of the highest proportions of both Education Maintenance Allowance (EMA)/Youth Maintenance Allowance (YMA) recipients, and language backgrounds other than English as a percentage of enrolments in the state. The participants were a group of twelve young people who were recent arrivals, aged around fourteen years, and most had originated from the Horn of Africa. The second site is also a state school in inner Melbourne, but one that operates as an "alternative" to traditional mainstream schooling. Approximately 80 percent of students have a history of chronic truancy, learning difficulties and/or behavioral problems; these problems may have been further exacerbated by mental health issues, physical abuse, sexual abuse, substance use and/or involvement in crime. The participants were ten young people aged between thirteen and seventeen years who were predominantly Anglo-Celtic in ethnicity.

Projects with both these groups ran over twenty weeks, with a ninety-minute session per week during school hours, and a more intensive rehearsal period prior to performance. The data collected included interviews with young people at the mid-point and the end of the projects; interviews with teachers and community artists working on the projects; audience response data; and my own field notes and reflections on workshops. Interviews and logbooks were transcribed and analyzed in relation to research questions that concerned:

- The experience of the participants
- The content of their enacted stories
- The role of the teacher-artist

The projects were run by SCRAYP,[1] a community arts organization based at Footscray Community Arts Centre. SCRAYP is an organization that recruits and trains young emerging artists from diverse cultural backgrounds to work in teams with young people, mostly in schools. I was both the team leader of artists working with both these groups and the researcher collecting data as the projects developed. As a researcher, I was attempting to understand the young people's experience of the projects and the significance to them of their own enacted stories. As an artist, I was also engaged in reflective practice. Taylor considers reflective practice as being central to the craft of theatre making with young people:

> The artist's reflective conversation with himself, with the artwork, with the people and objects which inhabit that work, and with the audience, is what gives the craft its life. (1996, 29)

As a maker of theatre with young people I am constantly engaged in the interpretation and re-shaping of the working process. The more this process includes the voices of the young people, the richer the work will be, both as meaningful art making and as research. Winston (2006, 43)

[1] Schools Community Research Arts Youth Projects

makes a strong connection between creating a case study and those of process drama, talking about a form of research that "can chime with the forms of knowledge generated by the art of drama itself". He also makes the important point that a researcher needs to be responsive to data that does not necessarily support what s/he already thinks, and that this is essentially an "ethical issue".

Dialogue

The sort of "reflective conversations" that Taylor refers to above, were manifested throughout both the projects being considered here. These conversations are dialogues about meaning, ownership, power and identity. Unlike other dialogical processes, in these projects much of the dialogue between teacher-artists and the young people was conducted through process drama structures. Statements were made dramatically and were responded to, amended and developed within a fictional context using drama devices such as forum theatre, empty chair dialogues, depictions, teacher-in-role, etc. Rather than focusing on the devices themselves, which are commonly used and recorded in drama education literature (e.g. Neelands 1990), I want to focus on the nature of the dialogues that took place and their meaning and also briefly consider the nature of dialogical pedagogy. Paulo Freire offers this analysis of "meaningful" dialogue:

> Dialogue is meaningful precisely because the dialogical subjects, the agents in the dialogue, not only retain their identity, but actively defend it, and thus grow together. Precisely on this account the dialogue does not level them, does not even them out, reduce them to each other. Dialogue is...a sincere fundamental respect on the part of the subjects engaged in it, a respect that is violated or prevented from materializing by authoritarianism. Permissiveness does the same thing, in a different but equally deleterious way. (1998, 246)

Freire is writing about dialogue as a sort of balance of power between teacher and student that is based on mutual respect. The key to this relationship is where it is placed on the continuum between authoritarianism and permissiveness; if it is positioned too far in either direction then the dynamic interaction of values that Freire outlines cannot occur. The other key concept outlined here is the active defense of identity, with all the issues of culture and cultural values implied within it. The type of pedagogic space that I was trying to establish with the young people in these projects was a space where values and identity could be explored dialogically through story. The establishment of such a relatively sophisticated process requires that the participants have a certain level of social skill, and a degree of trust that they will not be manipulated into revealing aspects of themselves through such a dialogue that they do not wish to reveal. Although very different, both groups of young people in this study appeared to this teacher-artist, with over twenty-five years of experience of working with "at risk" young people, to have very low self-esteem, and the dynamics of both groups were often dysfunctional, involving frequent verbal abuse of other group members. In particular, the relationships between boys and girls in both groups were often very strained. Generating the required levels of trust with these groups of alienated young people, with irregular attendance and many other issues impacting their lives, was extremely challenging and not always successful.

Resistance

The concept of resistance provides a helpful means of understanding some of the behaviors of the young people involved in these projects. I am referring to a wide range of disruptive behaviors that made running a play-building process in a supportive and safe environment extremely difficult, and sometimes impossible. If such behavior is framed as "resistance" rather than simply "difficult behavior" then it becomes part of the dialogue of the process. When working with both these groups of young people, there was significant resistance that needed understanding and a response. In interviews, both groups later explained that one of the concerns underlying some of this behavior was an intense fear of being exposed to ridicule by their peers, something that most had previously experienced.

Henry Giroux (1983, 109) defines resistance as needing to have a "revealing function, one that contains a critique of domination". By this definition, to what extent could the disruptive behaviors of these young people, when engaged in the drama programs, be described as "resistance", as opposed to just difficult or disruptive behavior? One observation that suggests their behavior was, at least in part, resistance, was that when the material being explored allowed the young people to act high status roles – as perceived by them and their peers – the resistance/disruptive behavior stopped, or was significantly reduced. Therefore disruptive behavior was a mechanism by which young people exerted control over the nature of the material on which they were working, and ensured that their cultural capital was recognized and valued. As Giroux also points out, however, resistance is often contradictory.

> ….resistance may represent and express the repressive moments inscribed by the dominant culture rather than a message of protest against their existence. (1983, 103)

A whole range of oppressive behaviors, particularly the verbal oppression of weaker group members and sexist behaviors by boys towards girls, highlighted the contradictions to which Giroux refers. As well as being a mechanism by which young people asserted their identity and drew attention to their own marginalized status, this behavior also perpetuated forms of oppression in which they themselves were the oppressors. Rather than addressing such issues at length outside the fictional context being developed, I decided it was better to explore such issues within the drama. But resistance can manifest itself within as well as without the drama process. O'Toole (1992), in his analysis of the drama process, points out that the meanings of a drama narrative are contextual and often relate to issues within the group, and/or have a subversive meaning of which the teacher-artist may not be aware. This subversion of the drama process is often a form of resistance to being controlled and manipulated by an authoritarian teacher; but it can also be a way of taking advantage of a permissive teacher to create work that purposefully oppresses group members or members of the wider community. An understanding of resistance in all its forms, and a constant reading of the meanings being created in the dramatic fiction are therefore essential to the construction of a successful dialogical process.

Narrative

The play-building process used in these projects was centered on the negotiated construction of narrative. Perhaps the key feature of narrative is that meanings created through narrative are negotiable (Bruner 1990), and this negotiation formed the basis of the dialogue between artists and young people. Interviews with the young people in both projects indicated that the concept of a "message" within a story was relevant and meaningful for them, as it is for young people generally. This awareness of "messages" in stories is significant because as Bruner (ibid, 51) points out: "To tell a story is inescapably to take a moral stance, even if it is a moral stance against moral stances".

The types of messages that the two groups embraced were quite varied. The young people from the older, Anglo-Celtic group explicitly rejected the idea of a simple moral message in the play. Anything that smacked of didactics was strongly rejected, particularly if they saw it as having been initiated by the teacher-artists. This group was engaged in the making of moral statements through their work, but these messages were often ambiguous and subversive rather than simple and moralistic. It was important to the group that the story reflected their own values rather than those of the school or the artists. For example, the central character Tracey was presented as extremely aggressive and violent, but the group saw these attributes as positive because it was her means of surviving in a tough world. The younger, predominantly African group was much more accepting of the idea of a moral, didactic message in their work: for example, they wished to make a point about violence and fighting being wrong. To what extent this may have been a product of the relative lack of sophistication regarding spoken English or whether it was a reflection of a broader cultural difference is unclear. Although one group was happy to accept the notion of a "moral" in their play and the other group rejected it, both groups of young people were aware of moral choices inherent in the process of play building.

Bruner states that stories are "viable instruments for social negotiation" and a means of organizing experience through framing them within a narrative:

> Framing provides a means of 'constructing' a world, of characterizing its flow, of segmenting events within that world, and so on. If we were not able to do such framing, we would be lost in the murk of chaotic experience and probably would not have survived as a species. (1990, 55)

Framing experience is what young people do when they create a play, and this framing is given additional socio-cultural significance through performance. It is in the act of performance that the young people's narratives are held up for consideration, and to some extent judgment, by an audience. It is through performance that they have meaning beyond the context of the performing group. In this study, both groups of young people were aware they faced decisions about how they wished themselves to be viewed, by both their peers and others. This involved making moral choices about the content of their play and experimenting with both individual and group identity. Bruner is explicit about the role of narrative within education:

> A system of education must help those growing up in a culture find an identity within that culture. Without it, they stumble in their effort after meaning. It is only in the narrative mode that one can construct an identity and find a place in one's culture. Schools must cultivate it, nurture it and cease taking it for granted. (1996, 42)

Young people's narratives

I want to turn to the young people's narratives and their reflections on the significance of those narratives, both for their peers and themselves. The Anglo-Celtic group created a play called *Without a Trace*, in which a young woman called Tracey returns to her community to look for her sister Stacey, having spent some time away from it. Tracey's search for Stacey also involves her exploring her own difficult and violent life, and the betrayals she has experienced in her life, particularly by men. The play used a crime-thriller genre, explicitly referenced through the use of a "film noir" style private investigator as a narrator. The plot involved a violent, escaped criminal character named "Elmo" who is searching for Tracey because she "dobbed him in to the cops". Audience response data showed that the resultant drama was seen as humane and humorous, as well as violent and confronting.

It is significant that this narrative was based on a film/television genre because this made it accessible to the young people as a vehicle for exploring personal meanings. The resulting story was a combination of this genre and more authentic, deeply personal components. For example, Lisa,[2] one of the older young people involved in this project, strongly identified with the character of Tracey:

> In some ways I am Tracey – my mum kinda left and all this stuff – it's a really meaningful play. Like, to know that we all built it together is really meaningful and [all] that.

When I asked her to talk about the meaning of the play, her answer was complex and very personal:

> Maybe knowledge of, trying to put people into what you think they're going to be, isn't what they necessarily have to be, to be a good person. Like, they've always got morals of: "I've got to look after my sister" or something. People who are in jail still do have feelings: Elmo doesn't like Tracey, he wants to kill her, but he still has feeling in himself where he still loves her.

Lisa is articulating her belief that the play was about people being misjudged through prejudice, and that anyone has the potential to be a moral person. It is interesting that the character she highlighted as having "feelings" and the capacity for love is Elmo, the ironically named, violent

---

[2] All young people's names have been changed.

criminal. Although such a character may easily be seen as a stereotype drawn from popular culture, Lisa's analysis of the character as a real person shows that this figure operates symbolically for her, representing people who have been written off by society.

The dominant narrative of *Without a Trace* concerns a young woman freeing herself from oppressive male characters. This is how some of the young people reflected on this theme:

> Lucy: Tracey, she was strong, tough, she was all that.
> DK: Was it a strength of the show?
> Lucy: Yeah.
> DK: Would it have been different if Tracey was a boy?
> Lucy: Probably it would have been like any other show cos every other show, there's always a tough guy. It was different, building up a tough girl.
> DK: Was it a feminist play?
> Adam: Yes, my mum's a hairy feminist.
> DK: Did she like it?
> Adam: Yeah, my mum thought it was good. And my Nan and my cousin. She said it was good. Feminism, Girl Power! Yeah, it was pretty weird cos I'm not into that.
> DK: How did it feel to be a boy helping girls to make a powerful statement?
> Adam: Felt like George Bush helping Saddam Hussein buy weapons of mass destruction!

Amidst the considerable self-deprecating wit and humor of Adam's "George Bush/Saddam Hussein" remark, there is also self-knowledge and an appreciation of having consciously been part of a play that was perceived by members of his family as being in some ways "feminist". Clearly Adam felt ambiguous about this, but my reading of his comment is that there was an underlying pride in having contributed, as well as a degree of confusion about it. It is also interesting to note the dialogue the play provoked between Adam and his family about this subject.

Certainly for the young woman – Lucy – speaking here, there was a real significance to having a strong female character. This was particularly relevant in the context of the culture of the participant group. An incident that revealed aspects of this culture came from very early on in the process of developing *Without a Trace*. The artistic team set up a scene in which Tracey returns to her old school and reads the graffiti about her, written on a bus shelter. We asked the young people for uncensored suggestions of what might have been written there, and the level of verbal obscenity and misogyny revealed by their comments, from both boys and girls, gave insight into the culture of the group. This is an example of O'Toole's

(1992) concept of subversive meanings, discussed above, because it was used by the young people to make the sort of abusive comments about girls that were normally (and appropriately) prescribed in school. By then asking the young people to call out Tracey's thoughts on reading the graffiti and recording them for the play's script, we started to develop the sort of dialogue about values within the form outlined above.

In the other play *Shana and Ali* by the predominantly Horn of Africa group, two narrative strands stand out as demonstrating young people making moral, artistic statements. The first strand was a narrative about a man who has been damaged by exposure to war and as a consequence, has become dangerously violent. A key scene, created through interaction between the artistic team and the young people, explored this narrative through a dialogue within the drama form. In this scene, the violent character is involved in a fight between two groups of boys over a soccer pitch. Unable to control his violent feelings, he is on the verge of killing one of the boys, when he is "talked down" by his younger cousin. The whole group – both boys and girls – created the scene by working on a fight scene that used basic stage-fighting techniques. It is important to note that the girls found this exercise every bit as engaging as the boys. A basic narrative was then constructed around the fight and Yusef, a Middle-Eastern boy, took the role of the violent man.

Yusef came from a troubled, refugee background, and often seemed particularly aggressive towards his peers. He was in a cultural/ethnic minority of one in this predominantly African group, and his cultural/ethnic isolation may have added to this aggression. In constructing the scene, at the point where the violent character is viciously attacking one of the other boys, I negotiated a switch in roles so that I became the violent character and Yusef became the man's cousin talking him down. In the ensuing dialogue, Yusef was able to offer lines like "It's not a war" and "You're crazy, you'll kill him". This reversal of roles allowed him to oppose violence through the dramatic narrative. Yusef, a Middle-Eastern teenager playing an African boy, was dialoguing with a white English man, who in turn was acting the boy's deranged and war-damaged African cousin. Yusef was controlling and calming the cousin's violent behavior. As an interaction it resonated on many levels: Yusef was talking to a manifestation of his own aggression; he was also talking to a white man who comes from one of the countries that has brought war to his homeland; and he was also talking to the rest of the class about attitudes to violence. One of the teachers in the workshop saw this experience as deeply therapeutic for Yusef and this may well have been the case, although as an artist, I did not consider myself engaged in therapy as such.

In his analysis of such complex interactions in multicultural contexts Winston (2003, 50) states that: "multiple cultural competences cannot only be articulated but also tried out and developed." In an analysis of the same scene, another of the boys in the group said:

> It says: "why do they have to do that, why can't they live in peace?"

There was a general acceptance within the group that this was an important message to have in the play.

Contrasting with this narrative about violence and war was a particular scene of great intimacy that was recognized by the whole of the Horn of Africa group as the most effective and significant moment of their play. This scene was a simple role-play in which a boy is saying goodbye to his best friend because he is migrating. Both of the boys who performed this moment in front of the group had previously resisted engagement in the drama process. They were drawn into engagement through this interaction being modeled by the Greek-Australian teacher of the group and myself, an English-Australian. Both of us had experienced something similar in our own lives and we found the role-play very moving. When the two boys performed the moment, they produced a touchingly simple but extremely honest and heartfelt interaction between a boy and his best friend. The poignancy of this moment was felt by the entire group and was chosen by all of them as the most significant moment of their play. The combination of the two narrative strands discussed – the pain of migration and the rejection of violence – served to make a powerful artistic statement.

Trust and intimacy

At the center of this process of emotional engagement is the development of trust between the participants and the teacher/artist, and trust is a performative act that must be continually renegotiated (Nicholson 2002). Trust is seen as a prerequisite for what Bundy (2003, 5) calls "aesthetic engagement" involving a degree of "personal surrender". Our process intermittently generated moments of insight and intimacy, when the power of the narrative meaning was able to take precedence over the factors working against it. In these moments, the play created a space in which the young people could reveal something of who they were; importantly, it also gave them an opportunity to communicate with an audience of peers. The dialogical play-building process they were engaged in also enabled them to construct moral meanings that represented the "messages" of their play.

In both projects, I set out to develop a process that allowed the young people to create fictional characters and events that related to their own lives, but were not a direct representation of their experiences. There were a number of reasons for doing this. Firstly, it freed us up as a group to produce fight scenes and crime-genre narratives that were fun for the young people to act. Secondly, it enabled us to create a distance between the events being portrayed and the young people's lives. Sometimes this distance was quite wide as in the story of the criminal and the private detective in *Without a Trace* or the fight scene in *Shana and Ali* for example. At other times it was very close, for example, in the portrayal of Tracey's family or the "goodbye" scene in *Shana and Ali*, but on all occasions a fictional distance was maintained. This allowed the *group* to own the story, rather than it being owned by an individual whose story was being directly represented; each young person chose their own relationship to the material they were developing.

Liminality

Recent research into youth theatre in the United Kingdom (Hughes and Wilson 2003) describes theatre workshop contexts as "liminal" spaces, offering the following definition from Schechner:

> A place outside of normal routines where people (temporarily) shed their ascribed roles and take on new ones, a context that is open to all kinds of possibilities and is free from social constraints. (2002, 73)

Liminality is a complex concept developed by Turner (1986) in relation to ritual performance being a space outside the boundaries of society, in which identity and social status are open to renegotiation. In the two projects under discussion, "social constraints" in the form of fear of peer ridicule were present for most of the process. This fear only dissipated temporarily when the young people became intimately engaged in the narrative, as detailed in the examples given above. Yet in both of these projects there were changes in group dynamics and new meanings were made, for example, girls being able to talk to boys in the Horn of Africa group, and boys becoming involved in making dramatic statements that empowered girls in the Anglo-Celtic group. These interactions would not have been possible within the normal constraints of school life. Whether such examples stack up to the workshop spaces of these projects being "liminal" is a matter of interpretation. My interpretation is that a liminal state was achieved fleetingly, but generally not maintained.

Joe Winston in his analysis of drama as moral education sees moral engagement as integral to a successful drama process:

> In other words, for drama to work we have to be morally engaged, to care in either a positive or a negative sense about the people being fictionally represented and what is happening to them. In this sense, consciously or unconsciously, we make choices, deciding where our attachments lie and these choices are value related. (1998, 68)

In both of the projects under discussion this process was manifested. Through complex negotiation, much of it carried out within the art form, the young people in both projects explored their values and made moral choices. In the process there was room for experimentation with identity and morality that allowed young people to explore, in dialogue with artists, their personal values and those of the group with whom they worked.

Performance

When the context was widened to include performance to peers (in the younger African group) or the wider community (in the older Anglo-Celtic group), the stakes was significantly raised. Firstly, there was the very real risk of ridicule if their performance was not perceived as high status within the subculture of the school/community; and secondly there was the belief, common to many of the young people I have worked with, that their dramatic narratives could influence an audience. In an interview conducted a year after the project with members of the predominantly African group, the young people made these statements about how they saw it one year on:

> It [the performance] was important. Connected us, connected to your [our] lives. Explaining our lives to others.

> Most of [the] different cultures come to Australia; they have experience of those things.

> It's important to us and to the audience, not just making things up, but things that happen in this life.

They are describing two related but distinct processes here. Firstly, there is the development of a sense of connection to themselves, both as individuals and as a group, through telling their own story. Secondly, there is the process of "explaining our lives to others". It was important to them that the story they told was based on their reality and that they saw themselves as representatives of a community of people who have migrated to Australia. It was not just their story, but also a story of wider significance.

From the tension generated between the young people's desire to impact positively on their peers/community – "It's important to us and to the audience" – and the more negative feelings that they also needed to express, came a potent dialogic process about values and morality. In the perceptions of the young people, through this process a sense of connection emerged, to themselves, to each other and to their community. For both groups, the relationship between the dramatic narrative they had created and the experience of their own lives was important, because it grounded their stories in their own perception of reality, and thereby added to their significance.

The research data shows that the young people in both projects were constructing a self-narrative of social agency, that is, they believed their stories were important and they had things of significance to say to their peers and to their community. Bruner (1996, 35) sees self-esteem as a complex construct based on an ability to see ourselves as an "agentive self" and on a self-evaluation of our effectiveness as agents. The young people from the Horn of Africa group, who were reflecting one year on from their project, saw themselves as having been agents in the development of awareness in the wider community about not just the issues faced by themselves but by all recent migrants. They felt empowered by this and proud of their achievement. We see something similar in Lisa's analysis of *Without a Trace,* when she spoke about the need to see people's capacity for love. In my experience, the development of self-esteem is frequently cited by people outside the field as one of the principal outcomes of youth arts practice. Self-esteem is often viewed as a simple construct, similar to self-confidence. The understanding that self-esteem is actually an outcome of individual and social agency, plus an evaluation of that sense of agency, seems an important distinction to make.

Conclusion

This study involved two groups of marginalized young people who were "at risk" of social alienation and disconnection. Through the creation of their own enacted stories in dialogue with artists and teachers, they explored some very destructive behaviors, but also *critiqued* these behaviors in ways that impacted positively upon their own community. These drama processes involved resistance and destructive behavior, as well as moments of trust and intimacy. By making the stories fictional and not based directly on the young people's lives, they were liberated to explore narratives that held symbolic importance for them. They saw these stories as having the power to reveal aspects of their society that they wished might be different, and in telling them to an audience they saw themselves, at some level, as agents of social change.

Works Cited

Bruner, Jerome. 1996. *The Culture of Education* Cambridge, Mass.: Harvard University Press.

—. 1990. *Acts of Meaning*. Cambridge, Mass: Harvard University Press.

Bundy, Penny. 2003. "Creating Opportunities for Aesthetic Engagement: Reflections from a Drama Classroom." *Applied Theatre Researcher* 4 (2). Retrieved, http://www.gu.edu.au/centre/atr.

Cunneen, Chris, and Rob White. 1995. *Juvenile Justice – An Australian Perspective*. Melbourne: Oxford University Press.

Freire, Paulo. 1998. "Pedagogy of Hope." In *The Paulo Freire Reader*, edited by A.M. Freire & D. Macedo. New York: Continuum.

Giroux, Henry. 1983. Theory and Resistance in Education: A Pedagogy for the Opposition. South Hadley Mass: Bergin & Garvey.

Hughes, Jenny, and Karen Wilson. 2003. *Playing a Part: A Study of the Impact on the Personal, Social and Political Development of Young People*. UK: Centre for Applied Theatre Research, University of Manchester (Unpublished).

Jermym, Helen. 2001. *The Arts and Social Exclusion. A Review Prepared for the Arts Council of England* 2. Retrieved, www.artscouncil.org.uk

Kelman, Dave, Angela O'Brien, and Kate Donelan. 2005. *My Story Our Stories: Growing and Connecting Through Enacted Stories.* A report for VicHealth. Victoria, Australia: University of Melbourne.

Mackenzie, David, and Chris Chamberlain. 2002. "The Second National Census of Homeless School Students." *Youth Studies Australia* 21 (4): 24-32.

Neelands, Jonathan. 1990. *Structuring Drama Work.* Cambridge: Cambridge University Press.

Nicholson, Helen. 2002. "The Politics of Trust: Drama Education and the Ethic of Care." *Research in Drama Education* 7 (1): 81-92.

O'Toole, John. 1992. *The Process of Drama*. London: Routledge.

Schechner, Richard. 2002. *Performance Studies: An Introduction*. New York: Routledge.

Turner, Victor. 1986. *The Anthropology of Performance*. New York: PAJ.

Winston, Joe. 2006. "Researching Through Case Study." In *Research Methodologies for Drama Education*, edited by J. Ackroyd. Stoke-on-Trent: Trentham.

—. 1998. *Drama Narrative and Moral Education*. London: Falmer Press.

CHAPTER SEVEN

SHAKESPEARE FESTIVALS AND MARGINALIZED YOUTH "AT RISK": SPACE TO RE-IMAGINE OURSELVES AS PART OF A COMPASSIONATE COMMUNITY

JOHN HUGHES & MAT HOWARD

This chapter reports on the role of the Shakespeare Globe Centre Australia Youth Festival, and the effect it has on marginalized participants, in particular, the experiences of a marginalized youth from regional Australia. It was inspired by Angela O'Brien's article (2004) that reports on a marginalized young person, Lucky, and his involvement in an arts program in Victoria. We found the article quite moving and significant in a way that reported research seldom is, giving voice to the subject of the study in a manner that allowed full impact by narrative analysis. Likewise, it honored the work of the participant in the arts project and has the potential to inspire others. Lucky, at the end of the first interview, says "We have a conversation and nobody will listen" (O'Brien, 71). We have heard Lucky's words, and his artistry, and we wish to join and elaborate his journey with Orsino's story.

Findings will be reported from student responses to the Shakespeare Globe Centre Australia's National Youth Festival in the period 1997 to 2005. Longitudinal data and analysis of students' assessments of arts programs are not insignificant. However, Elliot Eisner (1985) reminds us that knowing the outcome of the game tells us little about how the game was played. Therefore we have also chosen to report on the findings of our study of some students involved in the Youth Festival by narrative analysis (O'Brien 2004; Hughes 2003a; Barone 1997; Goodfellow 1997; Clandinin and Connelly 1994) because in narrative case study, the feelings, actions and thoughts of the participant are revealed, and cognitive development is examined with some delicacy. Narrative analysis can therefore reveal what lies behind the numbers.

The case study narrative provided is by Orsino (not his real name), and it is a verbatim autobiographical account of his experiences in the Shakespeare Globe Centre Australia Youth Festival. It was an unsolicited account freely volunteered to both authors. John Hughes (at the time Orsino was participating in the Festival) was Chair of the Festival's Education Committee. Orsino was successful in the Festival and was awarded a scholarship as Young Shakespearean of the Year, which enabled him, once he had completed Year 12, to travel to London to study and work in the Shakespeare's Globe Theatre. John was also visiting the London Globe at that time and we spent some weeks together studying Shakespeare, seeing productions at the Globe and Royal Shakespeare Company, and talking. Mat Howard was a contemporary of Orsino in the Shakespeare Globe Festival, and has worked closely with him on theatre projects since. We will start with part of Orsino's story.

Orsino's background

In so many ways, drama has made me. I was schooled at a series of resolutely Catholic schools in the Southern Highlands of New South Wales, the eldest son in a working class family. At home, I am told, I was always outspoken and playful; the games I roped my brothers and sister into were consistently imaginative and dramatic. At school, I quickly fell into a familiar stereotype: feverishly bookish, awkward looking, but an eternal show-off. I was the drama kid. One of my earliest dramatic memories involves me prancing about the classrooms of a tiny Catholic school, dressed in cricket gear and a green mask I had made out of papier-mâché and a bit of netting, leading a small troupe of girls in a dramatic portrayal of the *Prince and the Pauper*. My Catholic schooling continued at a medium-size Catholic secondary school with a mainly agricultural and sporting focus. In many respects, it was, and is, an extraordinary school. The staff was focused on pastoral care and community, and these are values that continue to inspire and invigorate my theatrical processes.

I was a public speaker for much of my secondary schooling, meaning that I was absorbed in rhetorical and speaking competitions against other classmates and schools. I threw myself into political causes and focused intensively on my schoolwork. I became fiercely competitive and increasingly isolated and frustrated. This was exacerbated by intense bullying I received, which often found expression in physical, as well as verbal and emotional violence. The result, of course, was to turn me further and further inwards.

By 1996, even I could tell that something was not quite right. I became nervous and paranoid, determined that I was alone and the victim of a series of irrational conspiracies. I wrote vicious notes to my classmates and alienated every friend I had, leaving me lonely and often confused. I came first in every class, won every competition and hated myself intensely for it. On a few occasions, the self-loathing found expression in small, precise acts of cruelty against my body that left me feeling angry, but guiltily relieved. I surprised even myself with my own ability to rewrite the nature of my own history. Cuts became cat-related injuries, burns or the outcome of spilt coffee. I fooled myself at the time that much of this behavior could be put down to puberty and a fierce self-obsession, however, it was not until years later that I realized the extent to which I was able to deceive myself about the full scope of these mutilations; one particular incident left me hospitalized. This was bigger than puberty.

In 1997, I was involved in a production of Arthur Miller's *The Crucible*, a production that profoundly revolutionized my life. I forcibly re-entered the world and began, once again, to communicate. It was during the rehearsal process that I first began to realize I was most comfortable around the stage. I adored the process of encountering a text in a scholarly and bodily way, and I also became aware, for the first time, of theatre's ability to effect change and evoke compassion in its audience. Somewhere towards the end of the play, I curled up behind the clapped together flats and peeked through to a soft-lit sea of spellbound faces. It felt natural, and it felt like I was nestled up in the pulse of life somehow. Theatre people, I found, understood me in a way that I did not think anyone else could. There was something about the way everyone made himself or herself so very vulnerable, that encouraged me to lower the gun I was so determined to hold to other people's faces. I played, relaxed and laughed, and most astonishingly, turned my love of literature outwards.

Caught up in the costumes and spinning lights, I also began to tear loose another delicate secret that remained hidden, even to me. And the secret grew and grew until it was obvious to everyone but me, and I again succumbed to the dual processes of self-deception and violence. By this stage, I was able to talk freely to my friends about the troubles that bothered me, but again, dangerous and desperate acts translated as little mishaps, and much of life spiraled into a fiction that has become too hard to remember. Eventually, I suffered a minor breakdown and spent a week in my bedroom terrified that I might be gay. The day that I returned to school, I read a notice calling for submissions for something called the “Shakespeare Globe Centre Australia Festival” and I decided to enter.

Young people and involvement in the Arts

Orsino had entered a youth arts program which, if we review the literature, had the potential to be beneficial to him emotionally, socially and academically. Studies reveal that involvement in the arts has the potential to develop personal and lifeskills, to improve self-esteem, and increase resilience, motivation and retention rates (O’Brien 2004; Catterall 2002a, 2002b; Harland et al. 2002; Heath 2001; Milner 2000a, 2000b; Dalrymple 1998). Further, studies including *Champions of Change* (Fiske 1999), *Critical Links* (Deasy 2002), and the recent *Evaluation of School-based Arts Education Programs in Australian Schools* (ACER 2004) report that important social processes and capabilities are developed in arts though the arts. Heath (2001) notes the pivotal importance of participating in extra-curricular activities and stresses the educational and social benefits of such activities. She notes that whilst schools and families are frequently acknowledged as valuable sources of learning, the activities undertaken by youth organizations are often undervalued and neglected in research (ibid, 10). In addition, there is limited evidence that problems for young people, such as those associated with poverty and marginalization, may be alleviated by opportunities for participation in community, as drama encourages people to work together and express themselves and their cultures (Donelan et al. 2005; Milner 2000a, 2002; Gopalakrishnan 1999).

Educational youth programs, workshops and festivals have been developed all over the world to maximize such social and educational benefits. These occur at different scales from local and school-based programs (Milner 2002, 2000a, 2000b) to national initiatives and funding schemes (Hughes 2003b; Dalrymple 1998). There are also many different types of festivals or programs, each with different aims and methods, and different degrees of youth participation (Woodson 2004). There is some debate and critique of the value of many approaches to youth theatre and its aims, especially when motivated to justify political ends or maximize budgets (ibid). There is criticism that the inner vision of art for art’s sake has been replaced with utilitarian validation of the arts in education (Woodson 2004, 25). Milner (2002, 2000b) similarly claims that political issues and limited budgets have resulted in the justification of arts in terms of measurable and quantitative outcomes. It is problematic when qualitative benefits are overlooked because through such studies young people can "articulate their realities to a world that usually doesn't listen" (Milner 2002, 12). The notion of giving young people freedom and their own voice is widely supported as one of the most important reasons to continue and create such festivals and include young people in performance projects (O'Brien 2004, Woodson 2004; Gopalakrishnan 1999; Dalrymple 1998).

The Shakespeare Globe Centre Australia Youth Festival

The Shakespeare Globe Centre Australia is a charitable organization with the aim of supporting the promotion and development of Shakespearean arts and education in Australia. The Globe Centre conducts a series of festivals that involve high school students (ages 15-18) from New South Wales, Victoria, Queensland, South Australia, Western Australia and the ACT. In 2005 over 230 schools participated: 43% government, 32% independent and 25% Catholic systemic schools. In addition, more than a third of these schools were from rural and regional areas of Australia. The school, regional, state and national festivals involve approximately twenty thousand students. The aim of the festivals is to take Shakespeare off the page and onto the stage. Students are invited to participate in the categories of performance (scenes and duologues), music (composition and performance), movement and dance, and costume and set design. A very important aspect of this festival is that it is student driven, and the guidelines issued to all schools emphasize that the input should primarily be from the students themselves, with teachers acting in an advisory capacity only.

The festival is in four stages. The first is the in-school festival, where each competing school conducts its own competition. The second stage is the Shakespeare Globe Centre Regional Festival. Winners chosen at school level come together and compete against other schools from their region. The third stage is the State Festival. Participation at these first three levels also requires the students to keep a logbook or journal of their thoughts, processes and procedures. These are submitted to the adjudicators at each level, and the students are interviewed to assess their intentions with regard to the piece they are presenting, and the rehearsal process undertaken. The final stage is the National Festival held in Canberra or Sydney, where some thirty to forty students leave the classroom behind and spend ten days immersed in the atmosphere of authentic theatre under the direction and guidance of noted Shakespearean actors and directors, assisted by theatre experts in the fields of dance, music and design. At the end of the week students present a Shakespeare production.

Student responses to the Festival

Current research about youth participation in theatre and drama festivals specifically related to Shakespeare is not extensive. Woodson (2004) comments that such traditional and culturally specific curricula may exclude young people and should not therefore be overused. It is suggested that such classics could be integrated into the production of original works so that young people are "empowered to reflect upon and produce their own knowledge" (ibid, 28). More research into the specific nature of the various programs and festivals is required in order to make helpful comparisons about the differences between them. Research generated by the Shakespeare Globe Centre and its innovative work across Australia, for and by young people, indicates that work in the Shakespearean arts does not need to be alien to student concerns and aspirations (Hughes 2003b).

Between 1997 and 2005 evaluation responses to the Shakespeare Globe Centre National Festival have been received from 242 students. The student responses mirror the findings of several other arts studies (Deasy 2002; Fiske 1999), that is, socio-personal gains are seen by the students as more important than artistic skill/knowledge development. For example, only 33% of the participants said they had achieved a better understanding of Shakespeare. Fifty-one percent of the students indicated they were scared initially whereas, by the end of the project, 83% said they had gained confidence, and learned and developed personal skills. Seventy-eight percent said they had found the experience emotional and life affirming by the end of the project. A high percentage (98%) indicated that a significant issue was that they had made deep and abiding friendships. A high response (86%) indicated they valued working and creating with professional artists, a finding that extends and elaborates the research of Heath and Wolf (2005) which argues that children benefit from working with practising creative artists, albeit their study focuses on four to seven year olds.

Many of the students' unsolicited comments, especially those from regional Australia, revealed they were isolated students with a passion for the arts and as such, they felt marginalized, and in some cases even victimized, by their peers at school. The experience of being in a sustained national arts project, surrounded by like-minded peers and supported by industry professionals had, for these students, been life affirming. Orsino was a member of the Shakespeare Globe Centre Australia's National Student Festival in 1998 and he continued to be involved until 2006. His story continues.

Orsino enters his first Shakespeare Youth Festival

I liked the idea of the acting competition part of the Festival, but decided instead to enter the design section, for reasons I can't quite remember. I decided to design a set and costumes for *Othello*. I asked a friend to enter with me and we both set about drawing sketches and constructing paddle-pop stick models, and I pretty much devoured any book I could find about *Othello*. I was utterly fascinated and began to channel all of my own terror and jealousies into the text and its wealth of characters. I sometimes imagined myself as Othello, brooding and extreme, but quickly fell towards Iago, as most people eventually do, I guess. For one brief moment, I saw myself as Desdemona, and that was too terrifying for words. We progressed through the school and regional levels without difficulty, and quickly found ourselves at the New South Wales State Festival. Accompanied by a wonderful teacher, my friend and I traveled to Sydney's Seymour Centre and were overwhelmed by the sheer number of students competing. We were from a small country town, from a school that had its fair share of drama kids but no real outlet for them, in that we didn't have a drama department or any real opportunity to engage with drama, other than the rare school play. We would discover that Sydney was full of drama kids and we were astonished.

We presented our designs to the judges – three accomplished professional designers – and didn't win the competition. I experienced the usual sense of inertia that follows when an artistic obsession ends. I returned to slightly more dedicated study for the New South Wales Higher School Certificate. Weeks later, I was pulled out of an exam by an ecstatic teacher to be told that my friend and I had been chosen to participate in the Australian National Festival. I was again astonished. My friend wasn't and a month later, I traveled alone to Canberra, where the other national finalists were gathering with a band of professionals to plan, devise, rehearse and perform a pastiche of Shakespearean pieces for a paying audience. This whole process was to happen in just over a week, which is a nightmarish prospect.

I have very distinct memories of arriving at the theatre in Canberra. I was petrified by the prospect of meeting and working with complete strangers. I was very much an internalized loner and the prospect of working so intensively with strangers was anathema. I befriended a girl from Melbourne (who incidentally, at the time of writing, is my flat mate of two years standing) and we got to chatting about the times ahead. Our wildest imaginings could not do justice to the actual experience which followed.

The group was divided up according to its various interests and talents and introduced to a professional theatre practitioner who was to guide us through the process. This was perhaps one of the most significant and memorable aspects of the whole experience; to have a theatre professional support and affirm your contributions gave each of us a sense of confidence and self-worth that allowed us to contest our own artistic and personal limitations. Over the course of the ten-day rehearsal process, I was able to explore and distil a creative ideology that formed the very beginnings of what I now realize to be a formal theatrical career. Each was able to develop our unique contributions in parallel, working towards the one multifaceted yet essentially distinct goal of a production, whilst pursuing our own specific paths. We drew inspiration from our own experiences, honed and developed in a supportive and shared environment and, ultimately, performed them in a very public and confrontational way. This is the perhaps the most phenomenal aspect of theatre making. It is so rare to have the opportunity to work fully through one's private confusions and mishaps in such a safe way.

Drama has always represented the merging of two profound and often conflicted curiosities. On the one hand, drama is about art, the ecstatic exploration of the human condition through literature, music and the body. On the other, and perhaps related to the first, drama is also about personal exploration and subsequently, social and mental instability. When I now try to characterize the nature of my experiences with drama students, both as student and teacher, I am struck by the recurring schizophrenia inherent in the "drama kid". There is the sometimes grotesque, mostly beautiful social-butterfly world of the extroverted drama queen. Playful and imaginative, drama kids are usually the ones who know the answers to the teacher's questions, who sit most attentively in the classroom and who shine most brightly in the playground. Perhaps for this reason, the "drama kid" is also usually the one who bears the brunt of schoolyard jealousies and aggressions, and who is often the most sensitive and fragile of beings.

My own trajectory through the Festival came to an even greater and many-splendored conclusion. Named the Shakespearean Artist of the Year, I was afforded an all-expenses-paid trip to London and Stratford-upon-Avon, where I was to study and work with the Shakespeare Globe Theatre. It was on this trip that I would meet senior members of the International Globe Centre, whose knowing guidance opened up for me a new theatrical world built upon academic investigation and a determined trust in hope and optimism.

Now back to my own little secret. As a participant in the National Youth Production, I was able to find a shape for the blurred and closeted stirrings I had felt for other men. For one, I met other queer men and women. I cannot express just how important that was. Growing up in the country, I did not necessarily have the privilege of knowing many openly identifying gay men. In fact, my first boyfriend, who, incidentally, I met during the two weeks of the National Production, was only the second openly queer man I had ever met. To be able to speak, interact and create with my fellow queers allowed me to find a new, powerful voice for my own faltering identity.

The Arts and marginalized youth

Over the years a number of students in the Shakespeare Festival have self-identified as queer and the acceptance of these students as artists is reported as positive and sustaining. Further, Orsino's experiences at school mirror what is cited in the literature.

Heterosexuality, or the "learning of heterosexuality," is part of the hidden curriculum, or the social norms that students learn without them being part of the formal curriculum (Plummer 1989). As such, heterosexuality becomes part of students' unspoken and assumed identity and becomes a form of cultural and social capital, a valued characteristic within the secondary school setting. The logical counter effect, the subsequent devaluing of same-sex attraction, can be witnessed through both the attitudes and actions of members of the secondary school community (Mikulsky 2005).

Studies have shown that both pre-service teachers and other adults in the school setting, as well as secondary school-aged students, often hold negative attitudes toward homosexuality and homosexuals that can be classified as homophobic (Thurlow 2001; Warwick et al. 2001; Cahill and Adams 1997; Sears 1992). These attitudes, coupled with contextual societal views toward homosexuality, are manifested by teachers' reluctance to address topics related to homosexuality in the classroom, and contribute to an overall silence surrounding homosexuality (Warwick et al. 2001), and students' physical and verbal harassment of same-sex attracted (SSA) students and use of homophobic language in the classroom (Thurlow 2001; Martino 2000; Plummer 1989).

For male students, in particular, homophobia in the classroom is inextricably linked to gender roles and the performance of male sexuality.

Research has consistently shown that gender roles are far more restricted for boys in the school setting than girls, and that boys help to maintain this sense of gender order by "policing" one another to keep each other's behavior on track (Martino 2000). In this sense, the transference of acceptable masculinities to male students is a crucial subscript to the hidden curriculum of heterosexuality (Mac An Ghaill 1994). It is not surprising then that studies have found stricter gender roles are associated with greater victimization of gender-atypical males; male high school students are unfailingly more homophobic in attitudes and behavior than their female counterparts (Rosario et al. 2001), and consequently male SSA students report greater victimization than SSA female students (Bontempo and D'Augelli 2002; D'Augelli et al. 2002).

It is no wonder that SSA male students would make every attempt to seek out a safe haven in the high school setting. Drama class seems to be this safe haven for many SSA young men, as it is seen as a place which first allows, and further encourages multiple expressions of masculinities (Sallis 2004; Perrotti and Westheimer 2001). In the typical high school environment some SSA male students try desperately to go unnoticed to privately come to terms with their sexuality and avoid ridicule and judgment from other students (Town 1996). Drama and theatre can act as a welcome reprieve where they can "try on" different personalities, experiment with their self-expression and be publicly appreciated for doing so. It is not hard to understand the attraction, and it would seem that the Shakespeare Globe Centre Australia's Festival affords similar opportunities.

Cassidy and Watts (2004) reveal there is little literature regarding the arts and rural and regional youth in general, and that therefore this marginalized group's voice is missing. They indicate there are possibilities that rural youth can have their views articulated through involvement in theatre (ibid, 36). Orsino, of course, was experiencing a complexity of problematic issues. Orsino was marginalized as both a SSA student and a rural/regional young person. And there is much in the literature to indicate the severe consequences, including suicide, which this double marginalization can produce (MacManus 2004; Fullagar 2003; Perrotti and Westheimer 2001; Waldo et al. 1998).

Orsino concludes

The Festival allowed me to create more fully, to stretch my own horizons and to fill this new, strange space with confidence and compassion. I felt relaxed, significantly less frustrated and more or less reconnected to the world. And I have seen this in many of the participants, particularly the queer boys, over the years, in my role as participant and director. The results are astonishing. Whilst I have experienced sporadic bouts of depression since that time, I have never felt that things were out of my control, and have not exacted upon my body the cuts or bruises that once brought me calm. With the Shakespeare Festival, I found the very beginnings of my connection to the queer community, and that community has continued to embrace many students since.

So what is a student “at risk”? And I begin to think of the faces of students who I have met during my seven-year involvement with the Globe, as a student, and later tutor and director. I think of myself as well. Our situations might be different, but there is an often unspoken sense of community amongst us that I find truly inspiring. The metaphor of the refugee is an apt one. Many students, like me, in their own worlds, feel isolated or confused, and in the Shakespeare Festival they find community and a sense of self. In my mind, it’s all about space. With its strong focus on collaboration and invention, the Festival allows for a dynamic and safe creative space that privileges those with the courage to be generous with themselves. For us queer kids, particularly those from the country, this space is a rare and beautiful opportunity, not only to find expression for the confusion of sexual difference, but also to re-imagine ourselves as a part of an exciting and compassionate community.

Epilogue

Orsino successfully completed an undergraduate degree in Theatre Studies and now directs a theatre company. Despite his success, we do not wish to imply that theatre experiences are a panacea for all marginalized students, and that the arts can somehow solve every adolescent problem. We agree with Perrotti and Westheimer (2001) that there is a time when the drama club is not enough. However, in some small but not insignificant way, youth theatre festivals, in Orsino’s words, can provide a space to “….re-imagine ourselves as a part of an exciting and compassionate community.”

We have taken the subheading of this chapter from those words from Orsino, and we argue that experiences in the arts can be transformative for some marginalized queer youth, and that the arts can engage students in a dynamic exploration of thoughts and feelings. We do wish to support Heath and Wolf’s argument that creating an environment where students are treated as artists and where their artwork will be used in a genuine and meaningful way is essential in order to help them see the value of the creative arts (2005, 38-9).

The arts can encourage expression in language, movement and aesthetic experiences in community, and enhance the emotional and socio-cultural life of the participants. We also believe that we, as academics and arts practitioners, need to champion students' stories, to learn how to listen to students' voices, hear what they are able to tell us about their involvement in the arts, and thereby honor their work, artistry and life experiences.

Works Cited

Australian Council for Educational Research. 2004. *Evaluation of School-based Arts Education Programmes in Australian Schools*. Victoria: Australian Council for Education Research.

Barone, Tom. *Complementary Methods for Research in Education*. 1997. Washington, D.C.: American Educational Research Association.

Bontempo, David, and Anthony D'Augelli. 2002. "Effects of At-School Victimization and Sexual Orientation on Lesbian, Gay, or Bisexual Youths' Health Risk Behavior." *Journal of Adolescent Health* 30: 364-74.

Cahill, Betsy, and Eve Adams. 1997. "An Exploratory Study of Early Childhood Teachers' Attitudes toward Gender Roles." *Sex Roles* 36 (7/8): 517-29.

Cassidy, Howard, and Vivienne Watts. 2004. "To Leave or Not To Leave: Rural Youth Gain a Voice through Theatre." *NJ (Drama Australia Journal)* 28 (1): 35-45.

Catterall, James. 2002a. "Involvement in the Arts and Success in Secondary School." *Critical Links, the Arts Education Partnership* 11: 1-2. Retrieved June 13 2007, http://www.aep-arts.org.

—. 2002b. "Research on Drama and Theatre in Education." *Critical Links, the Arts Education Partnership* 12: 1-2. Retrieved November 7 2007, http://www.aep-arts.org.

Clandinin, Jean, and Michael Connelly. 1994. "Personal Experience Methods." In *Handbook of Qualitative Research* edited by Norman Denzin & Yvonna Lincoln, 413-27. California: Sage.

Dalrymple, Lynn. 1998. "The Conference of the South African Association of Drama and Youth Theatre (SAADYT)." *Research in Drama Education* 3 (2): 266-8.

D'Augelli, Anthony, Neil Pilkington, and Scott Hershberger. 2002. "Incidence and Mental Health Impact of Sexual Orientation

Victimization of Lesbian, Gay and Bisexual Youths in High School." *School Psychology Quarterly* 17 (2): 148-60.

Deasy, Richard. 2002. "Themes and Variations: Future Directions for Arts Education Research and Practice". *Critical Links, the Arts Education Partnership* 11. Retrieved July 5, 2007, http://www.aep-arts.org.

Donelan, Kate, Angela O'Brien, Kruno Martinac, and Kiersten Coulter. 2005. "Report on the Risky Business Research Project." Paper presented at Backing Our Creativity, National Education and the Arts, Symposium, Australia Council for the Arts, Melbourne, September 12-14.

Eisner, Elliot. 1985. *The Art of Educational Evaluation*. London: Falmer Press.

Fiske, Edward, ed. 1999. *Champions of Change: the Impact of the Arts on Learning*. Washington D.C.: Arts Education Partnerships / Presidents' Committee on the Arts and Humanities. Retrieved October 10 2007, http://www.aep-arts.org.

Fullagar, Simone. 2003. "Wasted Lives: The Social Dynamics of Shame and Youth Suicide." *Journal of Sociology* 39 (3): 291-307.

Goodfellow, Joy. 1997. "Narrative Inquiry: Musings, Methodologies and Merits." In *Qualitative Research: Discourse on Methodologies* edited by Joy Higgs, 61-74. Sydney: Hampden Press.

Gopalakrishnan, Ambika. 1999. "The American Alliance for Theatre and Education (AATE) Conference, 1998." *Research in Drama Education* 4 (2): 265-7.

Harland, John., Kay Kinder, Pippa Lord, Alison Stott, Ian Schagen, Jo Haynes, Linda Cusworth, Richard White, and Riana Paola. 2003. "Arts Education in Secondary Schools: Effects and Effectiveness." *Critical Links, the Arts Education Partnership* 11. Retrieved November 7 2007, http://www.aep-arts.org.

Heath, Shirley Brice. 2001. "Three's Not a Crowd: Plans, Roles and Focus in the Arts." *Educational Researcher* 30 (7): 10-17.

Heath, Shirley Brice, and Shelby Wolfe. 2005. "Focus in Creative Learning: Drawing on Art for Language Development." *Literacy* April: 38-45.

Hughes, John. 2003a. "Performing Shakespeare: A Reconstructed Student Teacher's Tale." *NJ (Drama Australia Journal)* 27 (2): 53-63.

—. 2003b. "Shakespeare Alive: The Shakespeare Globe Centre Australia." *JEDA, the Journal of the Educational Drama Association, NSW* 2: 28-9.

Mac An Ghaill, Mairtin. 1994. *The Making of Men: Masculinities, Sexualities, and Schooling*. Buckingham: Open University Press.

Martino, Wayne. 2000. "Policing Masculinities: Investigating the Role of Homophobia and Heteronormativity in the Lives of Adolescent School Boys." *The Journal of Men's Studies* 8 (2): 213-36.

Mikulsky, Jacqueline. 2005. "Silencing (Homo)Sexualities in School...A Very Bad Idea." *M/C Journal* 8 (1). Retrieved May 26 2005, http://journal.media-culture.org.au/0502/2006-mikulsky.php.

Milner, Jenifer. 2002. "Arts Impact: Arts and Culture in the Community." *Performing Arts and Entertainment in Canada* 24 (1): 11-12.

—. 2000a. "Arts Impact: Improving the Odds for At-Risk Youth." *Performing Arts and Entertainment in Canada* 33 (1): 11.

—. 2000b. "Arts Impact: Research Supports Arts in Education." *Performing Arts and Entertainment in Canada* 33 (2): 11.

O'Brien, Angela. 2004. "Spokesperson from the Margins: 'Lucky' – A Risky Character." *NJ (Drama Australia Journal)* 28 (1): 61-72.

Perrotti, Jeff, and Kim Westheimer. 2002. *When the Drama Club is not enough*. Boston: Beacon Press.

Plummer, Ken. 1989. "Lesbian and Gay Youth in England." In *Gay and Lesbian Youth* edited by Herdt Gilbert, 195-216. New York: Harrington Park Press.

Rosario, Margaret., Joyce Hunter, Shira Maguen, Marya Gwadz, and Raymond Smith. 2001. "The Coming-Out Process and its Adaptational and Health-Related Associations among Gay, Lesbian, and Bisexual Youths: Stipulation and Exploration of a Model." *American Journal of Community Psychology* 29 (1): 133-60.

Sallis, Richard. 2004. "Con and Charlie Do the Splits: Multiple Masculinities and Drama Pedagogy." *NJ (Drama Australia Journal)* 28 (1): 105-17.

Sears, James. 1992. "Educators, Homosexuality and Homosexual Students: Are Personal Feelings Related to Professional Beliefs?" In *Coming Out of the Classroom Closet* edited by Karen Harbeck, 29-81. New York: Harrington Park Press.

Town, Shane. "Is it Safe to Come Out Yet? The Impact of Secondary Schooling on the Positive Identity Development of Ten Young Gay Men." Paper presented at the annual meeting of the American Educational Research Association, New York, April 8-12, 1996.

Thurlow, Crispin. 2001. "Naming the 'Outsider Within': Homophobic Pejoratives and the Verbal Abuse of Lesbian, Gay and Bisexual High-School Pupils." *Journal of Adolescence* 24: 25-38.

Waldo, Craig., Matthew Hesson-McInnis and Anthony D'Augelli. 1998. "Antecedents and Consequences of Victimization of Lesbian, Gay, and Bisexual Young People: A Structural Model Comparing Rural

University and Urban Samples." *American Journal of Community Psychology* 26 (2): 307-34.

Warwick, Ian., Peter Aggleton, and Nicola Douglas. 2001. "Playing It Safe: Addressing the Emotional and Physical Health of Lesbian and Gay Pupils." *The UK Journal of Adolescence* 24: 129-40.

The authors would like to thank Jackie Mikulsky for information on SSA youth and the wonderful students in the Shakespeare Globe Centre Australia Youth Festival.

CHAPTER EIGHT

ARTS PATHWAYS: BUILDING BRIDGES

SHARON HOGAN

Many "at risk" young people are blocked from following education or employment pathways by a range of environmental, social and personal factors. Futures can be limited due to young people's lack of resources, restricted opportunity and networks, negative experiences of past schooling or work, personal trauma and emotional or social barriers. Participation in arts-based programs has been suggested as an effective intervention strategy to re-engage the marginalized. However, it could be argued that "at risk" young people require more scaffolding to bridge these barriers. This chapter expands upon the key research findings of the *Arts Pathways Initiative* to propose how arts-based programs for "at risk" young people might be organized, to provide a more effective bridging experience to a wider range of employment and education pathways by addressing the creative, physical, social and emotional essentials.

The Queensland context

In February 2003 the then Queensland Minister for Employment, Training and Youth and the Arts delivered an address in the Queensland Parliament reporting that "10,000 young Queenslanders aged fifteen to seventeen years are out of school, out of work and out of training." These alarming statistics represented a growing number of young people who had opted to leave school and effectively disengage from employment or further formal learning.

Several government departments combined forces and funds to initiate a pilot program that could explore how "innovative and practical strategies and partnerships create better options for young people through involvement with the arts" (Hogan et al. 2005, 2). The *Arts Pathways*

Initiative was developed as a partnership between Arts Queensland, part of the Department of Education and the Arts, and the Department of Employment and Training. This initiative was linked to state policy directions such as *Education and Training Reforms for the Future 2002* and the *Creative Queensland* cultural policy (ibid).

The Arts Pathways Initiative 2004/5 aimed to re-connect "at risk" young people with learning and potential pathways to employment using different art forms as an engagement tool or bridging strategy. Seven arts-based programs were conducted across four locations in South East Queensland: Sunshine Coast, Gympie, Ipswich and Brisbane in venues such as TAFE campuses, alternate school settings, and other spaces familiar to young people, including parks and youth centers. The *Arts Pathways Resource Guide,* launched in May of 2005, describes artistic outcomes of the seven programs:

> Over 120 young people participated in a range of arts experiences and workshops including photography, image creation and manipulation using multimedia software and cameras, painting and drawing, traditional crafts and arts, screen printing, circus workshops, writing and recording music and lyrics. They produced textiles, artworks, music, films, posters and clothing, which were showcased in their local community. (Hogan et al. 2005, 2)

Programs involving young people and the arts with creative outcomes similar to those mentioned above are not new, yet there has been little research in Australia into the efficacy of arts-based programs or the benefits for the "at risk". Despite this lack of Australian studies or evidence, many claims have been made about the potential positive benefits of participation in the arts for this target group.

Arts and the "at risk"

Findings from several US studies have prompted government bodies in Australia to recognize the potential of arts-based programs to engage "at risk" young people, and offer intrinsic and extrinsic benefits for this target group, such as improved "pro-social" attitudes, stronger community involvement, increased personal agency and higher academic achievement. These studies include *Coming up Taller* (Weitz 1996), *The Arts and Pro-social Impact Study* (Stone et al. 1998) and *Champions of Change* (Fiske 1999).

The seven *Arts Pathways* pilot programs targeted young people aged fifteen to eighteen years experiencing a range of risk factors. Participants were young mothers, homeless youth, youth offenders who had recently spent time in detention and were under court orders, and some who were dealing with emotional or other health issues. Many of the participants had been expelled from school without completing Year 10, and some participants were already enrolled in alternate schooling. As a result of this demographic, there were varying degrees of "risk", interest and readiness to engage in any form of short-term program amongst the participants.

The labeling of young people as "at risk" can be a problematic notion (Sullivan 2001), as "risk" can be constructed along a continuum of life factors for all young people and adults; some are minimally at risk, while others are further advanced in terms of risk and vulnerability (Batten and Russell 1995). The period of adolescence in youth development models is often marked as a transitional time of risk taking and vulnerability. However Wyn and White (1997, 70) argue:

> ...behaviors that are described as risky from the youth development perspective may be understood as the result of young people's negotiation of the complexities of gender, class, race and age relations.

The Department of Education, Science and Training (2001, 2) links the term "at risk" to young people's "successful transition to adult life", explaining that the concept of risk can also be viewed within an individual's physical, emotional, cognitive and social developmental trajectories, and can be cumulative and circular. In the process of identity development, the need to provide security and accept risk is a complicated affair. The way adolescents differentiate themselves and discover their capacity for solitude and responsibility is by taking risks (Hogan et al. 2004, 9).

Many young people (and adults) struggle with issues of identity, independence, competency and social role. Research conducted in the United States as part of the *Coming up Taller* initiative claims that the arts help to mediate this confusion:

> Creative art activity allows the adolescent to gain mastery over internal and external landscapes by discovering mechanisms for structure and containment that arise from within, rather than being imposed from outside. The artistic experience entails repetition of actions, thoughts or emotions, over which the adolescent gains increased tolerance or mastery. While providing a means to express pain and unfulfilled longings during a distinct maturational phase, the arts simultaneously engage the competent, hopeful and healthy aspects of the adolescent's being. (Milkman 1995)

Bonnie Benard (2004) summarizes the last ten years of research into the development of personal resiliency and identifies the key indicators of supportive communities and schools. Benard defines the four personal capacities for resiliency: social competence, problem solving, autonomy and sense of purpose/future. Benard identifies the arts and the arts teacher as vital in assisting young people to build these capacities. She particularly looks at the role of imagination and creativity in the development of personal resiliency, stating that: "resiliency research documents the critical role that creativity and imagination play in surviving and transcending adversity, trauma and risk" (ibid, 29). Deeper involvement, engagement and participation are developed by "flow" experiences described by psychologist and researcher Csikszentmihalyi (cited in Benard 2004, 1). Benard links the positive effects of the arts to the "flow" experiences they offer. In a "flow" moment, concentration and immersion are so intense that all self-consciousness or problems are forgotten.

Drawing upon the literature surrounding "at risk" youth and the arts, the *Arts Pathways Initiative* explored how arts-based programs could assist young people develop capacities for resilience, provide a safe environment to explore their own identity, define their social role and provide a transitional space to new pathways.

The research

Independent researchers were employed to evaluate the seven pilot programs. I joined the *Arts Pathways Initiative* research team in the early stages, and recall my initial reaction to the request to evaluate such diverse programs was one of wary trepidation, due to the negative notions of judgment that can be attached to an evaluation process. However, there was potential for this study to document successful strategies and approaches identified by the participants and stakeholders. Consequently, the study focused on documenting the learning and action research already taking place at each program site, rather than imposing external measures or criteria for success.

The key research question was:

- How do/can *Arts Pathways* programs provide participants with a greater understanding of the options available to young people who are currently not in education, training and/or employment to enter or re-enter learning or earning, and gain the self-confidence to continue along a recognized pathway?

The research focused on monitoring and evaluating:

- Program structure: partnerships, recruitment of participants, staffing, resources
- Program curriculum: skills and knowledge, processes, participant evaluation
- Participant engagement: achievement, attitude, attendance, outcomes

The research and evaluation involved visiting the program sites, observing workshops and interviewing key people involved in the *Arts Pathways* initiative. There were many stakeholders working across the complex layers of each program, which brought the welfare/service, arts and education/training sectors together to form new partnerships. Over seventy semi-structured interviews were conducted with a cross section of stakeholders "including TAFE tutors, program coordinators, youth workers, arts workers, service providers and the young people who participated in *Arts Pathways*" (Hogan et al. 2004, 5). Data was systematically collected from each program site, ensuring the range of stakeholder perspectives were collected at the beginning, middle and conclusion of each program. Successful strategies were identified from each case study considering, the unique context, interests of participants, stated program aims and the demands of the selected art form. The final research phase involved a thematic analysis of the transcripts from each stakeholder group, including young people, tutors, program managers and youth workers to identify common findings from the seven case studies.

The limitations

According to the major study *Champions of Change* (Fiske 1999) positive outcomes for young people often occur in arts-based programs that have regular contact with participants over a long period of time. *Arts Pathways* programs were short-term and one-off, therefore this evaluation could not assess their long-term impact or the efficacy of the specific arts experiences. Instead, this study focused on the potential of the arts-based programs to engage and retain the target group of "at risk" youth, and stimulate their interest in other pathways.

> Attraction, recruitment and retention of participants emerged as major challenges at several program sites. Developing arts-based frameworks and programs that encourage sustained and frequent contact proved difficult in a post school environment involving isolated and often transient youth, who are not connected to a learning organization or a community group (Hogan et al. 2004, 14).

Numbers and attendance fluctuated with a core group of around six to eight participants emerging at each program site around the third or fourth week of the program. This made it difficult to assess the before and after impact of *Arts Pathways*. However, young people who became core participants and experienced more frequent contact and sustained attendance spoke positively about the impact of the program. For the core group, *Arts Pathways* programs "re-ignited their interest in re-engaging with learning, training or work. Several participants returned to school, enrolled in alternate education programs or approached organizations for further funding for training" (ibid, 14).

The findings

Arts-based programs alone offer little benefit to "at risk" young people unless support structures are in place. While the *Arts Pathways* initiative aimed to assist young people to find some future direction, this trial program became more about developing an understanding of bridge building. This pilot initiative helped organizations to identify essential support needs and scaffold arts-based programs that assist "at risk" young people to walk into new territory. Most importantly the young people participating in the *Arts Pathways* initiative were involved in the evaluation process and, as key stakeholders, had the opportunity to articulate what they needed, describe what worked for them and the changes required in program design and content.

The research identified five critical success factors in the development and delivery of arts-based programs that successfully re-engaged young people, including the importance of the following:

1. Building partnerships
2. Rebuilding relationships and trust
3. Designing curriculum for learning through the arts
4. Scaffolding for successful outcomes
5. Flexible frameworks for learning

1. Building partnerships

Collaboration with partners contributed to the success of *Arts Pathways* programs. The sharing of expertise and merging of resources from youth service organizations and educational institutions enriched the learning experiences and support mechanisms available to "at risk" young people. Many of these partners approached the program with different values and objectives. It took time for partners to develop a common platform of understanding and shared aims; however, this negotiation and agreement on values, objectives and program design had a direct impact on outcomes and the experiences of young people.

This finding is clearly described in the *Arts Pathways Resource Guide* as:

> organizations that negotiate a clear memorandum of understanding with partners at the senior level including shared program philosophy, values and objectives, prior to the commencement of the implementation phase, delivered more effective programs. (Hogan et al. 2005, 5)

Some young people involved with the *Arts Pathways* were eager to continue with further arts activity or pursue other educational programs after the program had finished. This raises the issue of how programs can support participants and offer pathways or mentoring beyond the finish date. In these case studies partnerships allowed for the continued support and the building of relationships beyond the boundaries of the program. For example, links to TAFE meant that further opportunities could be offered after the initial *Arts Pathways* experience. One participant went on to enrol in photography at TAFE and other young people were interested in pursuing more multimedia training. Partnerships with service organizations and local artists opened up other potential pathways for young people to develop mentoring relationships after program completion.

Without partnerships with service organizations, the identification, recruitment and retention of participants proved difficult. Youth workers were vital to the effectiveness of several programs. It was the youth worker, for example, who promoted programs, secured participants and played a significant communication role between all stakeholders.

2. Rebuilding relationships and trust

Participation and retention rates in *Arts Pathways* programs were directly affected by the attributes of teaching staff, their experience in working with "at risk" youth, the manner in which they interacted with participants, and their demonstrated level of respect and empathy for young people. One of the program designers described the need for both intellectual and emotional support. He commented that:

> At the end of the day, all the best structure and all the best strategies in the world won't replace the heart stuff. It's heart and head stuff. For me it is

> respect that is fundamental, and unless you respect young people I don't believe you can actually work with them. (Mark, *Arts Pathways* program designer and coordinator; Hogan 2003a, 6)

In the seven *Arts Pathways Initiative* programs it was often necessary to address the social and emotional needs of the participants while simultaneously pursuing the artistic objectives of the program. In over thirty interview transcripts, young people participating in *Arts Pathways* stated that relationships, particularly the rebuilding and establishment of trust, influenced their level of engagement and dominated their concerns. They were anxious about being accepted, how they would be spoken to and allowed choice within the program. They wanted to feel welcome and be treated with respect, and this was something that many of the "at risk" young people interviewed felt was missing in their previous school experience. One participant spoke about her fear of entering a new institutional setting,

> …that's why I originally left school because I didn't get on with the teachers. They're really nice people [*Arts Pathways*] to get along with because they're out there to help us kids…they were hell, nice, they would laugh with you and they didn't make you feel bad about yourself or anything, so it was really good. (Jessica, young person; Hogan 2003c, 1)

For many "at risk" young people attending *Arts Pathways* was a challenging experience. They needed support on many levels, physically, emotionally, socially and artistically. Artists, program managers and youth workers were needed to provide these complex layers of assistance, each with clearly defined roles and boundaries of responsibility. In many cases, the youth worker supported the emotional journey, as well as providing practical assistance with physical needs such as transport, clothing, accommodation and links to other support services. Counseling and emergency assistance were required to maintain the engagement of some young people. Partnerships with youth workers or the presence of someone the young people could attach to as a "significant" person, who would cater for their personal needs, impacted on the success of *Arts Pathways* programs (Hogan et al. 2004, 15).

This finding presents several implications for the rebuilding of relationships and trust in the planning and development of future arts-based programs for "at risk" young people. There is a need to source and engage technicians, artists, tutors and educators who have the proven ability to build positive relationships with young people. A team of staff are required that have empathy for and experience with the target group, including professional attributes such as clear boundaries, conflict resolution skills, positive values and respect, inclusiveness, non-judgmental attitudes, awareness of self and others and flexibility. Adequate briefing and training must be provided for all workers/tutors to manage complex learning issues associated with "at risk" young people (ibid, 178).

3. Designing curriculum for learning though the Arts

Arts Pathways programs that catered for diverse abilities and included learning strategies that were inclusive of a range of learning styles were most effective in retaining attendance and participant engagement. Curriculum design that combined the opportunity for play, individualized learning plans, and a variety of learning experiences appropriate to visual, kinesthetic, aural and oral learners were more effective.

The quality of the arts experience influenced the young people's engagement. In some cases the arts were a tool used for other means, therefore the quality of the arts experience and resources varied from site to site. For example, some programs saw the artistic process as secondary to concentrating on developing literacy, computer skills or social competencies that would enable young people to engage with adults within their community or the workplace. This influenced the choice of resources and mode of arts instruction or program design. Access to resources varied with some young people using commercial grade screen printing and graphic design software, while others used domestic equipment. Some participants experienced an apprenticeship model of arts education. They observed demonstrations by a tutor or artist to develop new skills in a particular art form and then applied these to their own design. Others participated in a collaborative community arts model, where they developed their own vision and made a short film with timely support from local artists.

Tension between the requirements for facilitating technical training and artistic process was evident in how programs were staffed and learning experiences sequenced. One TAFE tutor commented that while he had the technical skills, he did not have the process skills or ability to assist the participants in developing their design or artistic vision. He welcomed the support of the professional artist to lead this process, allowing him to concentrate on the use of technology.

A carefully sequenced curriculum that supported the artistic process and included technical skill development fostered inspiration and engaged young people at a deeper level. This idea was reflected in a comment by a program coordinator:

> We spent a lot of time encouraging the creative process … we need to have them inspired, to be able to see the outcome in their eyes, before they actually did any work. It certainly didn't work unless they felt inspired to do so. (Alex, *Arts Pathways* program designer and coordinator; Hogan 2003d, 2)

The word "fun" featured in many interviews with young people participating in *Arts Pathways* (Hogan et al. 2004, 168). They spoke about how they wanted to have fun as opposed to being bored, to be immersed in a program and to forget their problems for a while. They were looking for a "flow" experience. Young people were excited about the opportunity to make a film, a CD, to screen print their own clothes or produce a poster. The opportunity to make a tangible artistic product was engaging, providing an outlet for creativity, the development of personal agency and the opportunity to build positive relationships. The young people interviewed were proud of their creative achievements. They were excited by access to resources and the opportunity to establish new relationships with members of their community, including artists and technicians:

> I wanted to get out of the house. I wanted to actually do something rather then sitting down all day and just reading and writing and whatnot, and I felt doing this would have been a good release, finding out new artistic practices and everything, that was fun. (Phillipa, young person; Hogan 2003b, 4)

Many of the "at risk" young people participating in the *Arts Pathways* programs preferred a mediated arts experience where they were not the direct means of expression. They wanted to use technology or other tools or materials to make products external to themselves. Moments when they were required to be on "show", such as recording their singing voice or appearing in film, often caused the most tension in the group and anxiety for the individual. Individually based programs using art forms such as visual art, craft or graphic design, where participants could move forward at their own pace, worked effectively and were easier to manage for program coordinators. However, young people at one site developed communication and conflict resolution skills when required to collaborate on a group film project, indicating that group processes needed to be managed effectively for the overall group to leave the program with a positive experience.

The findings from this study indicate how future programs may be structured to engage participants, such as the need to involve young people from the target group and relevant staff, including tutors, art workers and youth workers in the planning and design of the program framework, content and objectives. It is necessary to design a learning program that is inclusive of the diverse capabilities and literacy levels by incorporating a variety of learning experiences in each module or session. Participant feedback indicates the need to include learning experiences that make learning fun, incorporate play and encourage creativity. Programs must be designed to provide scaffolding for arts-based learning experiences that facilitate and support young people's creative ideas and self-expression. This requires staff with expertise in arts education and creative practice to play a key role in program design/development. Young people must be inspired, and this could occur through the inclusion of strong aesthetic material in the inception/orientation phase of the program to engage young people in creativity and learning, rather than beginning with an emphasis on training (Hogan et al. 2004, 179).

4. Scaffolding for successful learning

Creating a "safe" space became vital to the achievement of the outcomes for each program, and this required a carefully planned induction or orientation phase, often with a series of activities in spaces that were already familiar to the participants. Participants could not relax and engage in activities unless they felt accepted and comfortable with the group or with staff. Who will be working with each group, staffing structures and participant numbers are key considerations in scaffolding effective arts-based programs. *Arts Pathways* participants felt safer in smaller groups and with a high tutor to participant ratio.

Issues of safety and respect were also linked to logistical considerations such as food. The provision of food became a key social component of each program. Participants were very positive about access to free lunch, with some participants mentioning that this initially was one of their key motivations to join the program. For one case study group, the opportunity to sit in the dining room each day and eat a meal with staff and their peers was mentioned by all of the participants as a highlight of the program. They mixed and conversed with youth workers, TAFE tutors and artists in a relaxed and pleasant environment. This interaction had a positive impact on the social health of the group.

The opportunity to debrief with a youth worker was often needed after each day in order for some participants to maintain their attendance or interest. Many of the participants struggled with conflict resolution skills and were emotionally fragile. They lacked the emotional and social competencies described by Benard (2004) as central to resilience. Therefore emotional and relational factors are central to any scaffolding and planning considerations. This was highlighted in the interviews. Participants and program officers commented that:

> The first part is the hardest part because you're getting to know everyone and what they think of you. At the start we all fought on the first week, but we all got along in the end. (Jessica, young person; Hogan 2003c, 3)

> …working with "at risk" populations, there's this sort of assumption made that they get along, and that they like each other, and that they have a common culture. In reality, what you find is that you have a very diverse set of people. Some are "at risk" because they have mental health issues or a disability, and so those set of young people will not necessarily feel comfortable working with a group of young people who may actually have a drug issue and continue some of the drug culture things that impact on their lives, and bringing that into the group. They may not feel very comfortable, and with good reason, to work with this group. So those things can impact. (Brad, *Arts Pathways* program officer; Hogan 2003e, 2)

This finding indicates that careful consideration needs to be given to the length and sequencing of each phase of arts-based programs. Timelines affect every aspect of a program from the establishment of partnerships, the acquisition of resources, outcomes for participants and effectiveness of the arts experience. Longer and realistic timelines are needed for the development of arts-based programs, so that appropriate and effective scaffolding can be in place prior to the implementation phase. Most importantly, the inclusion of an effective orientation phase can significantly impact on the social health of the group, the commitment of participants, retention, completion rates and learning.

5. Flexible frameworks for learning

Program frameworks that were flexible and responsive to the needs and capabilities of young people were more successful in re-engaging them in learning and encouraging participation. Content and structure played a strong role in determining the outcomes of each program, directly influencing the recruitment and retention of young people. They wanted the program to be flexible, to be responsive to their feedback and allow them to pursue their own personal creative goals. Young people were also at different stages in terms of their readiness to engage in each program. Those in stable accommodation wanted certificates and qualifications that would assist them in finding employment, while others were looking for "something to do".

What emerged as a key planning principle in program design was the need to provide multiple exits and entry points (Hogan et al. 2005, 8). Some young people elected to come to one-off workshops until a core group emerged who wanted to take their creative pursuits further. Other participants wanted the opportunity to reconnect at a later phase. Similar to the snowball effect of gaining momentum, building in size and impact, programs gained broader interest and uptake in the community as they reached their conclusion. Word spread among young people and celebratory events that involved friends and family helped promote programs. More young people were interested in joining programs in the later stages. Ideally programs need to recycle or loop several times allowing greater access for more young people. This finding is illustrated in a comment from one program coordinator:

> Really we want every young person here to be able to build on and maximize their own learning to the level that they're comfortable with at that particular point in time, and then be able to exit with a sense of achievement and a pat on the back. "You made it", that's our preferred option in terms of program design… providing multiple exit and entry points. (Alex, program designer and coordinator; Hogan 2003d, 4)

Another finding that emerged from the research data was the need for the "dignified" exit (ibid, 5). This celebration of all achievement, no matter how long their time commitment, enables "at risk" youth to avoid replicating past feelings of failure, or to feel like a "drop out" when circumstances beyond their control do not allow them to continue. Young people could attend a two-hour workshop for a day, perhaps a week, but they are empowered to self-select and come and go until they choose to engage in a more intensive program.

Conclusion

The experiences of the stakeholders during these pilot *Arts Pathways* programs raised issues regarding program structure, and the importance of timelines and frequency of attendance in participant engagement and outcomes for young people. This short-term program exposed young people to a range of options and possible future pathways in arts-related fields. Eight-week programs were not long enough to build skills, competencies or the confidence to enable participants to move into arts-related work. To develop pathways into arts-related industries stronger industry links would need to be made during the program implementation. Programs would need to be longer, possibly repeat or cycle, link to work-related competencies and include supported work, mentoring or work experience (Hogan et al. 2004, 14).

It is clear that finding employment in the arts was not the main objective of the initiative, as many "at risk" young people participating in *Arts Pathways* were not ready for work, or in a position to commit to longer-term training. Instead, this initiative focused on using the arts as a reconnection tool that could encourage the participants to consider a range of pathways. *Arts Pathways* programs worked, but only if sufficient scaffolding was in place. Programs that catered for the emotional, social and physical needs of the young people "provided a valuable first entry point or first step towards re-engaging with the community, learning and building their personal confidence and awareness of other pathways" (ibid).

The key overall finding to emerge from research of the *Arts Pathways* initiative is that access to an artist, arts equipment and even a space in which to be creative are not enough for "at risk" young people to fully engage in any program. The arts can engage young people and assist them to re-imagine a future, but only if the program structure and other conditions are appropriate. Before "at risk" youth can access potential pathways they need a bridging experience with appropriate scaffolding to breach real or perceived barriers. Program design impacts on participation with key issues such as the need to rebuild relationships and establish a safe environment and trust, overshadowing any attempt to use art making to attract and retain the interest of "at risk" young people.

The *Arts Pathways* initiative proved, yet again, that the arts do work. They provide an effective engagement tool, but more importantly, they offer "at risk" young people opportunities for creativity, fun and the development of personal agency. When questioned about what they had gained one young woman commented: "A lot of achievement, and a certificate and it proved that I could do a lot more than what I thought I could" (Hogan 2003c, 5). These trial arts-based programs highlighted the capacity for arts programs to embed a range of literacies including technology. However, program structure and design plays a key role in determining the outcomes for young people. Specific bridge building strategies are needed to address the barriers to participation experienced by "at risk" youth. These strategies include key considerations concerning timelines, partnerships, resources, scaffolding, sequencing of arts experiences, flexibility and appropriate staffing, if arts-based programs are to offer young people an effective experience. "At risk" young people need programs with ongoing funding, flexible program design and delivery, programs that offer activities and rich arts experience that loop and loop again, offering multiple exit and entry points, each with acknowledged and celebrated achievement.

Works Cited

Batten, M., and J. Russell. 1995. *Students at Risk: A Review of Australian Literature 1980–1994*. Melbourne: Australian Council for Educational Research.

Benard, B. 2004. *Resiliency: What We Have Learnt*. San Francisco: West Ed.

Department of Education, Science and Training. 2001. *Innovation and Best Practices in Schools: Review of Literature and Practice*. Commonwealth Publication Department of Education, Training and Youth Affairs. Retrieved August 7 2003, http://www.detya.gov.au/schools/publications/2001/fss/index. htm.

Fiske, E.B. 1999. *Champions of Change: The Impact of Arts on Learning*. Washington, D.C.: Arts Education Partnership and the President's Committee on the Arts and Humanities.

Hogan, S. 2005. "Respectful Pathways," *Artwork Community Arts Network*: 34-6.

—. 2003a. "Mark" Interview Two Transcription: *Arts Pathways* program coordinator/designer, 16 December.

—. 2003b. "Phillipa" Interview One Transcription: *Arts Pathways* young person participant, 15 September.

—. 2003c. "Jessica" Interview One Transcription: *Arts Pathways* young person participant, 15 September.

—. 2003d. "Alex" Interview Two Transcription: *Arts Pathways* program coordinator/designer, 16 December.

—. 2003e. "Brad" Interview Two Transcription: *Arts Pathways* program coordinator/designer, 10 November.

Hogan, S., L. Munro, and J. McLean. 2005. *Arts Pathways: A Road Map to Engaging with Young People. Arts Pathways Resource Guide.* Arts Queensland and Department of Employment and Training. Retrieved February 16 2007, http://www.trainandemploy.qld.gov.au/client/about_us/research_publications/strategic_policies/arts_pathways/index.html

—. 2004. *Internal Report: Arts Pathways.* Brisbane: QUT CIRAC Arts Queensland and Department of Employment and Training.

Milkman, H., K. Wanberg, and C. Robinson. 1995. *Project Self-Discovery: Artistic Alternatives for High Risk Youth.* Retrieved December 4 2003, http://www.cominguptaller.org/report/chapter2-1.

Stone, A., T. Bikson, J. Moini, and D. McArthur. 1998. *The Arts and Pro-Social Impact Study: Program Characteristics and Pro-Social Effects.* Santa Monica: Rand Corp CA. Inst. of Education and Training. ERIC Document Reproduction Service no. D444898.

Sullivan, R. 2001. "Identifying and Meeting the Needs of 'At Risk' Young People." ACER Research Conference, *Understanding Youth Pathways: What Does the Research Tell Us?* Retrieved June 4 2004, www.acer.edu.au/workshops/documents/confpro2001JC.

Weitz, J. H. 1996. *Coming Up Taller. Arts and Humanities Programs for Children and Youth at Risk.* President's Committee on the Arts and Humanities, Washington. Retrieved December 4 2003, http://www.cominguptaller.org/report/chapter2-1.

Wyn, J., and R. White. 1997. *Rethinking Youth.* St Leonards: Allen & Unwin.

Youth Arts Queensland. 2004. *Arts Pathways*. Retrieved October 11 2005, http://www.yaq.org.au/arts_pathways.

CHAPTER NINE

ACTING AGAINST BULLYING IN SCHOOLS

BRUCE BURTON

Acting Against Bullying (AAB) is the result of ten years of action research into conflict and bullying in schools. The project began in Queensland in collaboration with the international DRACON research program into conflict within schools, with partners in Sweden, Malaysia and Australia. The program, using a unique combination of drama and peer teaching, was constructed, tested and trialed by Bruce Burton and John O'Toole, first through Education Queensland, then through the New South Wales Department of Education and Training. The project (known in NSW as "Cooling Conflicts") has been implemented in more than eighty schools in NSW and it continues to expand each year.

The DRACON program was a trailblazer in the emerging discipline of Applied Theatre and actually helped to define the field. Since the DRACON project commenced more than a decade ago, a number of texts have been published attempting to identify and describe Applied Theatre as a separate discipline (Nicholson 2005; Taylor 2003; Thompson 2003). The DRACON project has significantly contributed to the definition of these parameters and it provides an effective model for the emerging field. First of all, DRACON draws on the paradigms and techniques of two separate disciplines, drama and conflict management. Secondly, it involves the cooperation of a range of practitioners in these fields, in this case from international locations. Thirdly, it is a clearly defined and delineated project in its own right that combines research and practice to achieve its objectives. Finally, its stated purpose is both individual and social change. It can be argued that these four characteristics are all fundamental to Applied Theatre as a discipline.

The final phase of the DRACON project, AAB, was funded by an Australian Research Council Linkage Project in association with Education Queensland, and focused specifically on addressing bullying in schools. The project began in four Brisbane high schools in 2003, and it was progressively implemented in more than twenty primary and secondary schools, urban and regional. Although the research component of the project finished in 2006, a number of Queensland schools continue to run the program on an annual basis, and some schools have taken the initiative and implemented the program themselves.

Summative data is now available from the four high schools initially involved in the project for three years. In each school, Year 10 or Year 11 classes were taught on concepts relating to the nature and management of bullying, and Enhanced Forum Theatre was used to explore and deal with a range of bullying situations. These schools then taught Year 8 and Year 9 classes in exactly the same way. In turn, these junior secondary classes taught peer students at their neighborhood primary schools, who in turn, taught younger students.

Extensive data was collected during the three-year duration of the program in both the high schools and associated primary schools. The data included hundreds of pre and post questionnaires administered to all students who took part in the project in each school, and to the administrators and teachers also involved. Focus group interviews were held during and after the operation of the project each year with students from each class who participated. Individual interviews were also conducted summatively with students from each class, and with administrators and teachers involved in the project for each of the three years. The data was collected by the chief investigators, Bruce Burton and John O'Toole, a PhD researcher and a number of research assistants. A number of classroom teachers also took an active part in administering questionnaires and conducting interviewers. The statistics and quotations that follow are all drawn from this questionnaire and interview data.

This chapter describes the structure and implementation of the project and reveals how it provided a positive and valuable experience for most of the students and teachers involved. Constraints and problems encountered during the project are also identified:

> Before I did AAB, I didn't know how to deal with a situation when I got into it, so I got like, I didn't think about what I was doing, and about the consequences of what I was doing, and about how it would make other people feel. Since doing AAB people have said that whenever I get into fights and stuff, which sometimes I do, that I've dealt with it in a more mature way and it hasn't got me into so much trouble as before. (Year 9 student)

> It really worked for kids who were "at risk" or who were bullies. It really helped them to look at who they were and their relationships with others and you can notice that when the program was on, they were treating others differently. Their tolerance and acceptance of others improved. Their behavior had improved. (Year 9 teacher)

The structure of the AAB project

Bullying

Bullying in Australian schools is an issue of increasing concern and research over some years (O'Toole et al. 2005; Rigby 2002; Bagshaw 1998; Australian Government 1994) indicates that both teachers and students lack the skills and strategies to deal with the problem. Surveys conducted in the United Kingdom, Europe, Canada, Australia and New Zealand indicate that in excess of 20% of all students have been involved in bullying, either as bully or victim (McCarthy et al. 1996), whilst Rigby's (2002) meta evaluation of bullying indicates that one child in six is bullied on a weekly basis. Other estimates suggest that two-thirds of all schoolchildren are affected by bullying at some time in their lives (O'Toole et al. 2005).

Furthermore, a wide-ranging review of conflict management and peer mentoring programs in a number of American secondary schools across several states revealed that all the programs surveyed were ineffective, and in at least one case, counter-productive (Powell et al. 1994). This research is in line with the international quantitative data on bullying over the past two decades that reveals there has been almost no change in the incidence of bullying despite numerous intervention programs (O'Toole, Burton and Plunkett 2005).

Addressing bullying in schools

Rigby (1996) and McCarthy et al. (1996) argue that any attempt to deal with bullying must involve a whole of school approach and must empower the students. Rigby (2002) asserts that bullying is a problem that the students themselves must deal with, and they must do so through pro-social means, not punishment. His research reveals that students believe this to be true, and also believe that students and teachers need to work together to achieve this aim. Rigby (1996) also points out that the majority of students have an empathetic regard for the victims of bullying, and argues that this needs to be increased and somehow extended to the bullies themselves.

A consistent thread through the AAB data has been the realization by participants of the impact of their bullying on other students – and a determination to stop bullying:

> The interesting thing that we come across is the students who tend to be bullies – when they are acting out the scenarios – have taken sometimes the role of the bullied, and it's very interesting to then speak to them about that role afterwards, and they say "yeah I think I know now, miss, how they feel, and I know that it probably isn't a real cool thing to do." (Year 10 teacher)

> Well, I thought it was a really good thing for me to do. I think it's changed me. I used to be a bully myself, being a mean person, but I actually changed and I've actually stopped doing that. I really don't like it. (Year 9 student)

McCarthy et al. (1996) state that the curriculum itself should be a potent plank in anti-bullying policy in schools, because it is a vehicle for influencing the way young people think, changing and developing attitudes and behavior. The AAB research clearly indicates that the most successful way to implement a program is to integrate it into existing curriculum rather than simply an add on.

> They [the schools] have to make a commitment that is seen to be valued, seen to work, seen to be accessible to students and not something that is going to make a lot of extra work for somebody, but it can be done through the curriculum. (School Administrator)

Integrating the AAB program into the curriculum can create serious organizational and timetabling problems for schools, particularly secondary schools. In one of four schools, the program was not fully implemented initially because of these logistical problems and the departure of a key teacher. However, the school did reintroduce the entire program into the school in 2005 and completed a full cycle, including the peer teaching in the local primary schools.

In fact, the demands on the teachers and lack of support from colleagues in administration have proven to be the most significant factors in reducing the impact of the program on a school.

> We were thrown into this, and then I came back and I was like not getting support from partners and the principal. I kind of feel like it's expected of me to do it all and it's a bit hard for me. (Drama teacher)

Drama and change

Most subjects in the secondary school curriculum deal in knowledge outside the personal and subjective domains. The very content of drama is human relationships, conflict and power. It operates through invoking both cognitive understanding and empathy, to generate what Carroll (1989, 20) describes as "real learning". Through drama students imitate and refract life through constructed, hypothetical (i.e. fictional) contexts and situations. They make realistic events and characters that can be manipulated and reflected upon, and issues of relationships are dealt with in a safe, fictional context (O'Toole et al. 2005; Burton 1991). In this way, the participants are both actors and audience, able to experience fictional roles and situations, whilst perceiving and reflecting on the meaning of these experiences at the same time (Boal 1995; Carroll 1989; Bolton 1984). Erikson (1975, 173) identifies this form of knowledge as insight: "...the act of seeing into a situation and into myself at the same time."

This imitation of actual events and the creation of realistic characters are crucial to the AAB project. Students are able to explore a variety of bullying situations, taking on a range of roles that are as authentic as possible, but deliberately distanced from individual encounters with bullying and enacted within the safe, fictional world of the drama classroom. The students are able to choose the nature and extent of their involvement, and participate in ways that give them the greatest insight into the specific bullying situation being enacted, and the nature of bullying itself. The teacher's role is therefore not primarily as a transmitter of received knowledge, but a facilitator of shared transformation into potentially useable learning. The freedom and autonomy to create roles and situations and explore their possibilities through drama has been fundamental to the success of the project:

> I think they enjoyed exploring bullying and solving it under an alias, especially as I know some of them had been bullied as younger students. Also solving it – how can you do that?....Instead of writing about it, they are actually doing it, which is real life; which is an empowering thing. (Year 9 teacher)

> It's definitely made my relationships stronger. With the people in my class doing the project with me. Like, this one girl, I felt very intimidated by her, and we actually had to do a play together and she would bully me, and then we had to swap the role around so we both know where each other stood then, and now we're actually friends. (Year 9 student)

> I found a lot of people growing through the program…At the beginning they actually thought they weren't bullies at all and after the project some of the girls realized that they actually were. You don't always realize when you're bullying someone all the time or just ignoring someone, you don't realize it's the same thing. You just don't realize that. (Year 11 student)

Peer teaching

In conjunction with the use of drama as an agent of change within the school, the AAB project uses peer teaching as an innovative form of instruction that empowers students to confront the issues associated with bullying. As peer teachers, students also provide exemplary models for the younger students they teach.

Extensive research has identified peer teaching as a particularly potent approach to stimulating learning in schools (Rubin and Herbert 1998; Simmons et al. 1995; Bilson and Tiberius 1991; Forsyth and MacMillan 1991). These studies have found clear and convincing proof that peer teaching can be an extremely effective tool for improving learning in the classroom. Goodlad and Hirst (1989) identify the positive impact that peer tutoring has on student self-esteem. The specific benefits of peer teaching for those doing the teaching are described by Rubin and Herbert (1998) as an increase in both social and intellectual awareness; significant gains in empathy; the clear recognition that they could change habitual patterns of behavior; and finally, that peer teaching empowered the students, increasing their sense of mastery and self-esteem. They conclude that it would be hard to think of another method that would enable so much intellectual, social and personal growth.

Other research has focused on the effects of peer teaching on the students being taught. Rubin and Herbert (ibid, 2) claim that this form of learning is superior in "…application of concepts, problem solving, attitude, motivation, group membership and leadership skills." Overall, the research has produced clear evidence that teenagers often learn more effectively from their peers than from traditional, teacher-centered instruction.

Furthermore, recent research on the use of peer teaching to re-engage negative leaders in secondary schools (Morrison et al. 2006) has clearly demonstrated that it has the power to transform the behaviors and attitudes of students with serious behavioral problems who have a high status amongst their peers. Not only do these students re-engage in the schooling process, but also their peer teaching experiences appear to reorient them towards positive leadership roles.

Despite clear evidence that peer teaching is extremely effective in both enhancing learning and empowering students, it has been a neglected resource in the field of bullying. In particular, there is no evidence in the current literature on bullying, nationally or internationally, that peer teaching has been empirically tested as a mechanism to address bullying. Instead, peer mediation has been the preferred approach. Nevertheless, the DRACON project produced consistent confirmatory evidence that peer teaching generates genuine understanding in learners and then as peer teachers, empowers them to deal with cultural and other conflicts. In fact, both the DRACON research and the AAB project suggest that students, especially secondary school students, are far more likely to become competent at dealing with bullying in their own lives if they are empowered to do so by confronting it through drama, and then teaching what they have learned to their peers:

> The peer teaching, I think, was a great aspect of it. I mean, I think a lot of the kids related a lot more towards students teaching classes other than the teachers. It wasn't just teachers rattling off facts again. (Year 10 student)

> I can think of one particular student who actually has really benefited from this and he was a student who interacted a lot with the school behavior management focus – the program. He was often on suspension, things like that. And I noticed especially when we went to the primary school that he was a bit of a role model…I think something happened to him because of his involvement in this [program]. The fact that he had younger kids looking up to him – I noticed him being quite different in that context than he had ever been at school. (Year 9 teacher)

> It [AAB] opens up channels of communication, establishes relationships with Grades 11 and 8 or 9, and provides a supportive environment for victims of bullying. (Year 11 teacher)

Forum Theatre

Over the ten years of the DRACON project, a number of drama and theatre forms were used experimentally to address conflict and bullying. The key form that evolved, and was applied in the AAB project, was Enhanced Forum Theatre. Because Forum Theatre is interactive, allowing the audience to intervene and take on roles in the play, it has proved particularly useful for addressing a range of issues in the developing world. Theatre for Development practitioners, particularly in Africa, use Forum Theatre to empower rural villagers and the urban poor to understand and address the problems which confront them, including poverty, lack of essential services such as water, the scourge of AIDS and social and political injustice in all its forms.

However, during the course of the DRACON project aimed at constructing an effective model for using drama to address conflict and bullying in schools, the research demonstrated that it was necessary to make five major adaptations to Forum Theatre, for both educational and aesthetic reasons. In each case, the impact of the enhancement was recorded and once evaluated as effective, was incorporated into the next action research cycle, and the final model was applied consistently throughout the AAB project.

Bullying actually involves complex behaviors that escalate through a number of identifiable stages (Glasl 1999), and often need a complex process of identifying appropriate ways of dealing with the situation (O'Toole et al. 2005; Rigby 2002). "Classic" Forum Theatre's single scene cannot incorporate all the relevant contextual factors, nor depict the escalation process of bullying. The first enhancement therefore re-structures the initial performance into three scenes, depicting in turn one of the three stages of bullying escalation. The second enhancement involves audience members being invited and encouraged to intervene during any one of these phases. Furthermore, the third enhancement allows audience members to intervene as any one of the characters in the play, not just the protagonist. The fourth enhancement allows the possibility of a fourth scene to be incorporated into the structure, giving both the actors and audience the opportunity to further explore ways of dealing with a bullying situation which has proved impossible to manage within the three-scene structure.

As well as these alterations to the structure of Forum Theatre, the final enhancement involved the insertion of a number of participatory techniques, from process drama into theatrical performance. These permitted the audience to stop the action and find out what the character was actually thinking at any point – and even invited the audience to interview characters placed in a "hot seat" (O'Neill 1995). This fleshes out for the audience their contextual understanding, so that their interventions can be better informed and more aware of pitfalls. Boal too has moved to this kind of added improvisation, in some of his allied therapeutic theatre work, including the idea of putting the protagonist and the antagonist in the hot seat (1995, 123).

The nature and impact of the enhancements

Enhancement one: three scenes, not one

Enhanced Forum Theatre involves the creation of a realistic play in three scenes, rather than the single scene structure of Boal's version. The action of the play occurs over a period of time, and the bullying escalates during this time, as it does in reality. Three identifiable stages of escalation in bullying are taught to the students both conceptually and through the drama work. These stages are defined as latent, emerging and manifest, and in the planning and structuring of their Enhanced Forum Theatre performances, students are encouraged to develop each scene to represent a specific stage in the escalation of the conflict they are exploring. They are also encouraged to make sure that days or weeks elapse between each scene, so there is a genuine development of the plot, the characters and the issue being explored, and a genuine understanding of how bullying develops:

> It's changed because I now know and understand a lot more about bullying. I am now aware of the three stages...All the different forms of bullying, where it may come from and what can come from it. (Year 9 student)

> I don't participate in latent bullying any more. (Year 8 student)

Having three scenes means that the audience can intervene early in scene one or scene two in a bullying situation, before it becomes critical. Boal's traditional structure of a single scene is appropriate for his purposes in focusing very tightly on an instance of oppression, and on what means are directly at hand to deal with the oppression. However, it means that even the most complex forms of oppression are portrayed only very briefly, without any exploration of the history or context of the issue. Furthermore, in the initial phase of the research, when conventional Forum Theatre was being used, students were reluctant to intervene in the single scene of the play, most often because they did not feel they understood enough about the causes and nature of the issue, and the interventions that occurred were frequently ill conceived and inappropriate. With the introduction of the three-scene enhancement, there was a significant increase in effective interventions, particularly during the latent and emerging scenes of the forum.

Students as young as Year 3 have found no difficulty in remembering the terminology of latent, emerging and manifest, and in being able to describe the nature of each stage and discuss its representation in specific scenes. Questionnaires over the past two years have recorded a rate of 99% in students' ability to remember and define the three stages of bullying, and identify these stages in their own drama work. A clear outcome of the research has been that almost all students recognize the need to intervene in a conflict before it becomes manifest and students are able to articulate a clear understanding of the nature and implications of bullying:

> Bullying is a transition of power between people. It is a method people use to make themselves feel superior to others. (Year 9 student)
>
> The result of an imbalance of power. (Year 8 student)
>
> Bullying can cause major physical and psychological damage. The victims in a bullying situation can suffer more than people realize. These people have the power to stop the bullying if they don't let themselves be bullied, or give the bully power, it may stop. (Year 11 student)

Enhancement two: multiple interventions

In Boal's original model (1979), the actors normally perform a single scene that dramatizes a particular instance of oppression, with the protagonist as the oppressed. The scene is then replayed, with audience members invited to intervene in the scene only in the role of the oppressed person, seeking to alleviate or counter the oppression.

However, the purpose of the AAB program is to encourage the participants to explore bullying situations coolly and discover that all parties – bully, bullied and bystander – have some agency and potentially some power to resolve or alleviate the situation. This meant widening the possibilities of intervention to permit the audience to take on a role as any of the characters depicted in the dramatic scene and intervene as often as they wished. This is particularly important when exploring bullying situations because very often, it is the bystander or an outsider who can most effectively modify what is happening, and a range of interventions are then needed to address the problem. It also allows the participants to use their interventions to explore the concept of mediation, a core concept in conflict and bullying management, and to experiment with the use of mediation in practice within the drama.

The questionnaire and interview data have consistently revealed that students feel that they are able to empathize, with both the bullied and the bully, when they have the opportunity to experiment with these roles and intervene as both parties. Furthermore, the majority of students involved in the AAB project over the past three years have identified the role of bystander as crucial in a bullying situation, and students intervene more often as bystanders in Enhanced Forum performances than as bullies or the bullied. The following Year 8 and 9 students from different secondary schools all identified the crucial role of the bystander in bullying situations:

> Bystanders are the most powerful person in a bullying situation. They have the capacity to make or break the bully. If bullying continues, it is as much the bystander's fault as it is the bully's.
>
> I have stopped becoming a silent bystander and have intervened more.
>
> Before I was a bystander but now, I'm going to help the people who were been [sic] bullied.
>
> I don't sit by the bullying, I do something about it.
>
> I know you can actually make a difference by stepping in, like a bystander can actually stop the people fighting, understand what the people are doing. They can solve it.

Enhancement three: the fourth scene

Boal's classic model seeks to raise consciousness in his audience by highlighting an instance of oppression, and giving them a brief opportunity to directly counter it in the safety of fiction, thereby stimulating the audience to further action in the real world.

However, when working with young people in conflict management, the needs are different. For one thing, basic conflict resolution and counseling practice, and its handbooks (Glasl 1999) and position papers (Jones 2004), caution that simplistic intervention in bullying, especially intervening in the heat of angry confrontations, can do more harm than good. It is basic police procedure when called to a "domestic" or a neighborhood brawl, to firstly identify and separate the key protagonists, and then get them to cool down apart, before trying to mediate in their quarrel. Inviting a student audience to intervene in scenes of direct confrontation, far from helping them to manage bullying effectively, might be actively giving the students poor models of mediation practice to follow.

Therefore, the AAB program employs a new enhancement of Forum Theatre, a "Scene Four". After the initial three scenes of a bullying scenario have been performed and a number of interventions have been tried and have failed, or have had limited success, the audience is invited to construct a fourth scene. This takes place in another time and/or place, and includes other characters whose involvement in the conflict or bullying might mean that it is handled better. They could be outside mediators brought in to address the problem, or one of the characters who can intervene in the situation and is least emotionally involved, but has authority, for example, a teacher. The audience groups can then perform this fourth scene themselves, taking on the characters from the original play, or they can brief the actors who performed the first three scenes, and ask them to perform the fourth scene. This invariably brings out new material for discussion and debate, and the articulation of new understandings gained through the theatre work.

Over ten years of the DRACON research in more than 100 schools, students have very seldom been able to "solve" serious conflict and bullying situations within the three scenes. This is hardly surprising when bullying, in particular, is one of the most persistent and intractable behavioral problems faced in schools (Rigby 2002).

In the majority of instances where the fourth scene has been incorporated, the situation has not been fully resolved either. However, in a significant number of cases recorded by the researchers, the actors and the audience have constructed authentic and realistic scenarios which offered effective, and sometimes very sophisticated, possible strategies for addressing the particular issue. In essence, the fourth scene allows the participants to demonstrate their developing confidence and competence in dealing with bullying, and this sense of empowerment has been the major outcome of the research at every year level and in every school.

Enhancement four: process drama additions

Finally, Enhanced Forum Theatre also uses some of the specific process drama techniques in common use in drama classrooms (O'Neill 1995) to make the performance and the situation more realistic, authentic and complex. In the early stages of the work, when the students are improvising bullying scenarios, they are encouraged to use a Role Circle, where each student can add a fictitious but authentic detail to the construction of the characters and the scenario. This also allows the students to distance the bullying from its source in the group, if they are using someone's direct experience of bullying. Using a Role Circle means that the original story is fictionalized and the whole group takes on ownership. This protects the original storyteller and also allows the group creating the play to make it their own. Only one student has ever indicated in a questionnaire that the use of his bullying story had negative repercussions and led to him being teased by the other students. The overwhelming majority of students whose stories have been used have felt that this benefited them, either by helping them to see the experience in perspective or making them feel more confident to deal with similar issues in future.

In the structure of Enhanced Forum Theatre performance itself, other process drama techniques are also integrated. These include Thought Tracking, where any member of the audience can stop the action and ask any of the actors to speak aloud what is in the mind of their character at that moment, a kind of stream of consciousness for the character. At the end of a scene a hot seat is conducted, where a chair is placed in front of the audience, and they are invited to question one of more of the characters in the play. The characters take it in turns to sit in the hot seat and the audience cross-examines them to find out more about the motivations, attitudes and emotions behind their behavior. Hot seating can be a very effective technique for exploring conflict and bullying, and students will often ask perceptive and profound questions of the characters in the hot seat (Bolton 1992). Students performing these roles are equally capable of thoughtful and sophisticated responses, including elaborate justifications for their behavior, and sometimes the Host or MC (Boal's Joker) who controls the Forum, will have to demand that the absolute truth is spoken. One of the features of this form of hot seat is that it generates intense debate amongst the audience, often involving the actor as well, about the issue being explored.

Hot seating has been identified by the students as the most effective and engaging drama technique used in the research. Sustained observation of Enhanced Forum Theatre performances consistently record significant improvement in the students' ability to understand the causes of behavior being enacted in the performance when hot seating is used. There are also significant increases in the ability of audience members who intervene after thought tracking, to make valid and authentic changes to the behavior of those involved in the conflict being represented, and to empathize more fully with people involved in bullying situations:

> If my friends are bullying I tell them to stop being so mean or I just don't participate. (Year 9 student)

> Danny was the student who I observed the most change in during the program... Interestingly, he was one of the students who admitted to being a bully when we started the program. His enthusiasm for the AAB program appeared to flow into Drama generally. During the beginning of the year

he didn't submit all of his assessment and he was failing, then during Semester 2, he submitted all this assessment and began passing Drama. (Year 10 teacher)

Conclusion

The summative evidence from three years' operation of the AAB program in four urban high schools clearly indicates that the combination of peer teaching and enhanced Forum Theatre can assist students to deal more effectively with bullying in their own lives. On a whole school basis, considerable reductions have been reported in the incidence of bullying, based on teacher and administration responses. Only one school has kept reliable recorded data over the period. This school was confronted with serious bullying problems five years ago, serious enough for the school to be identified as a center for harmful bullying activity. The school has made a sustained effort to construct a behavior management program, with Acting Against Bullying at its center. In the past two years, school records indicate a significant decline in reported bullying throughout the school, and the disappearance of serious bullying incidents as a discipline problem.

The lack of reliable statistical information on bullying within individual schools has been a problem throughout the DRACON project in measuring the impact of the use of drama and peer teaching. However, data currently being collected in Sydney, as part of a longitudinal study of the outcomes of the DRACON project there, indicate major changes in the whole culture of a number of schools that have been running the Cooling Conflict program for five years.

The questionnaire data collected over three years of the AAB project in the four Brisbane high schools involved does demonstrate extensive and significant changes in students' understanding of bullying, their attitudes to it and their behavior related to bullying. Almost all the students surveyed (99%) were able to identify the three stages of bullying (latent, emerging and manifest) and every student correctly described the three types of participants (bully, bullied and bystander).

Furthermore, 87.2% of all students involved in the project stated that they were more able to recognize when bullying was taking place, and 87.1% believed that bullying could be de-escalated or stopped. In response to the question "have you learned to manage bullying situations better?" 63.8% of all students responded positively. Most significantly, when asked how they would respond as a bystander to a bullying situation, 61%

replied that they would intervene. A further 38% replied that they would report the incident, and only 1% said they would watch, but do nothing.

The final word should go to a drama teacher who has been involved in the project for the entire three years with a range of classes, both senior and junior secondary, in a school identified by Education Queensland as having serious bullying issues:

> A lot of the students who have been involved in this project have generally been those who have not participated in this sort of thing before and have absolutely delighted me – to see how some of them have grown. They appeared to have grown in self-esteem and confidence. Their ability to communicate to a group and to feel personally proud of what they achieved at the end of the program, sometimes in fairly challenging situations, had increased. I think that the whole process has been a big benefit for those students…my observation was that a number of them certainly got a personal "high" from being involved in that program.

Works Cited

Australian Government. 1994. *Sticks and Stones: Report on Violence in Australian Schools*. Canberra: Australian Government Printing Services.

Bagshaw, Dale. 1998. "What Adolescents Say About Conflict in Schools." *Children Australia* 23 (3): 17-22.

Bilson, Janet M., and Richard G. Tiberius. 1991. "Effective Social Arrangements for Teaching and Learning." *New Directions for Teaching and Learning* 45: 21-4.

Boal, Augusto. 1996. "Politics, Education and Change". In *Drama Culture and Empowerment: the IDEA Dialogues* edited by John O'Toole & Kate Donelan. Brisbane: IDEA Publications.

—. 1995. *The Rainbow of Desire*. London: Routledge.

—. 1979. *The Theatre of the Oppressed*. London: Pluto.

Bolton, Gavin. 1992. *New Perspectives on Classroom Drama*. London: Simon & Schuster.

—. 1984. *Drama as Education*. London: Longman.

Burton, Bruce. 1991. *The Act of Learning: The Drama-Theatre Continuum in the Classroom*. Melbourne: Longman Cheshire.

Carroll, John. 1989. "Terra Incognita: Mapping Drama Talk." *NADIE,* vol. 12 (2): 13-21.

Erikson, Erik. 1975. *Life, History and the Historical Moment*. New York: Norton.

Forsyth, Donelson, and James McMillan. 1991. "Practical Proposals for Motivating Students." In *College Teaching from Theory to Practice*, edited by Marilla Svinicki. San Francisco: Jossey-Bass Inc.

Friere, Paolo. 1973. *The Pedagogy of the Oppressed*. London: Penguin.

Glasl, Friedrich. 1999. *Confronting Conflict: A First Aid Kit for Handling Conflict.* UK: Stroud.

Goodlad, Sinclair and B. Hirst. 1989. *Peer Tutoring: A Guide to Learning by Teaching*. London: Kogan Page.

Healy, Sue (ed). 1998. *Bullying and Peer Pressure*. NSW: The Spinney Press.

Johnson David, and R. Johnson. 1996. "Conflict Resolution and Peer Mediation Programs in Elementary and Secondary Schools: A Review of the Research." *Review of Educational Research* 66 (4): 459-506.

Jones, Tricia S. (ed). 2004. "Conflict Resolution in the Field: Assessing the Past, Charting the Future." *Conflict Resolution Quarterly* 1-2 (22).

Lofgren, Horst and Briget Malm. 2005. "Bridging the Fields of Drama and Conflict Management: Empowering Students to Handle Conflicts through School-based Programmes." *Studia Psychologica et Paedagogica Series Altera CLXX.* Sweden: School of Teacher Education, Malmo University.

Morrison, Morag, B. Burton, and J. O'Toole. 2006. "Re-engagement through Peer Teaching Drama – Insights into Reflective Practice." In P. Burnard and S. Hennessy, *Reflective Practices in Arts Education.* Netherlands: Springer.

Nicholson, Helen. 2005. *Applied Drama: The Gift of Theatre*. UK: Palgrave Macmillan.

O'Neill, Cecily. 1995. *Drama World: A Framework for Process Drama.* Portsmouth NH: Heinemann.

O'Toole, John, B. Burton, and A. Plunkett. 2005. *Cooling Conflicts: A New Approach to Conflict and Bullying in Schools*. Sydney: Pearson Education.

Powell, Kenneth E., et al. 1995. "A Review of Selected School-based Conflict Resolution and Peer Mediation Projects." *Journal of Social Health* 65 (10): 427-31.

Rigby, Ken. 2002. *New Perspectives on Bullying.* London: Jessica Kingsley.

—. 1996. Bullying in Schools – and What to Do About It. Melbourne: ACER Publishing.

Rubin, Lewis, and C. Herbert. 1998. "Model for Active Learning: Collaborative Peer Teaching." *College Teaching Winter* 4 (1): 26-31.

Simmons, Deborah et al. 1995. "Effects of Explicit Teaching and Peer Tutoring on the Reading Achievement of Learning-disabled and Low-performing Students in Regular Classrooms." *The Elementary School Journal* 5: 26-31.

Svinicki, Marilla. 1991. "Practical Implications of Cognitive Theories." *New Directions for Teaching and Learning* 45: 30.

Tatum, D., and E. Tatum. 1996. In Paul McCarthy, Michael Sheehan & William Wilkie, *Bullying: from Backyard to Boardroom*. Alexandria, NSW: Millennium Books.

Taylor, Philip. 2003. *Applied Theatre: Creating Transformative Encounters in the Community*. Portsmouth NH: Heinemann.

Thompson, James. 2003. *Applied Theatre: Bewilderment and Beyond*. Oxford: Peter Lang.

Van Ments, Morry. 1983. *The Effective Use of Role-play*. London: Kogan Page.

CHAPTER TEN

RECONFIGURING INTELLECTUAL DISABILITY THROUGH INTEGRATED DANCE THEATRE

ANNA HICKEY-MOODY

Discourses of risk (Lupton 1999; Beck 1995, 1992; Douglas 1992) are the predominant theoretical paradigm used to research youth who are statistically likely to fail mainstream educational systems. Frameworks of risk often link young peoples' intellectual ability, their socio-economic status, race and gender to low educational success (Rasmussen and Harwood 2004; Angwin, Shacklock and Blackmore 2001; Wynn 2000). With regard to the areas of disability, youth disengagement and youth "at risk", a particular point of critique advanced by scholars in the field is, within risk discourses, educational disadvantage is arbitrarily linked to poor wellbeing (Leahy and Harrison 2004; Wright 2000). Such connections are statistically supported, yet research needs to construct positive systems of engagement and new ways of thinking about success and wellbeing for disadvantaged students, particularly for those with intellectual disability (Barton 1986). Research conducted within the paradigm of risk tends to create "assemblages of disadvantage" in which limited future trajectories are constructed for the student statistically "at risk" of educational failure (Hickey-Moody 2007). This creation of limited opportunities is the product of assembling[1] readings of particular aspects

[1] I employ the word "assemblage" as an articulation of Deleuze and Guattari's desiring-machine (1983, 1987). Desiring-machines are empirical assemblages that articulate social bodies and meanings through connecting materialities. For example: the desiring-machines that articulate "intellectual disability" connect IQ tests as signifiers of failure and/or success with particular behavioral characteristics and physical attributes in order to "assemble", or produce, the intellectually disabled subject.

of students' lives as signs of disadvantage, aspects such as IQ, class, race, gender and low socio-economic status. There can be readings of the same signifiers that are not negative (Skeggs 2000). What is of interest is that "risk" as a paradigm tends to read signs such as "intellectual disability" and "low socio-economic status" as indicators of "lack" and "disadvantage", which, when connected together, produce a deficiency of possibility. Rather than reinforcing assemblages of disadvantage currently produced within risk discourses, and linking educational disadvantage to poor health and wellbeing, research needs to focus upon articulating new affective images through which young people with intellectual disability can be regarded in terms of their productive capacities. Dance theatre offers one medium through which research can source positive images, or affects, of young people with intellectual disability. In advancing this polemic, I examine the process of constructing and performing Restless Dance Company's (RDC) major new work for 2001, *Proximal*. The RDC is critically regarded as Australia's leading youth dance company inspired by cultures of disability. It remains one of a select number of companies operating in the field of integrated dance in Australia. I employ the phrase "integrated dance theatre" to discuss dance theatre devised and performed by people who identify as being with and without intellectual disability. In contexts other than this, the term "integrated dance theatre" is also employed to discuss dance theatre performed by people who identify (more broadly) as being with and without disabilities.

I take up Deleuzian concepts of affect and sensation[2] in order to explicate integrated dance theatre as a politically affective realm that changes the ways that bodies with intellectual disability are thought. In *What is Philosophy?* Deleuze and Guattari argue that:

> A thinker may…modify what thinking means, draw up a new image of thought, and institute a new plane of immanence. But instead of creating new concepts that occupy it, they populate it with other instances, with other poetic, novelistic, or even pictorial or musical entities… These thinkers are "half" philosophers but also much more than philosophers…They are hybrid geniuses who neither erase nor cover over

[2] The texts I mainly draw on are: Deleuze, G. 2003. *Francis Bacon: The Logic of Sensation,* translated by Daniel Smith. London and New York: Continuum Press; Deleuze, G. 1988. *Spinoza: Practical Philosophy.* San Francisco: City Books; Deleuze, G. 1990. *Expressionism in Philosophy: Spinoza,* translated by Martin Joughin. New York: Zone Books; Deleuze, G. 1990. *The Logic of Sense,* translated by M. Lester and C. Stivale. New York: Columbia University Press; Deleuze, G., and F. Guattari. 1996. *What is Philosophy?* London: Verso Publishers.

> differences in kind but, on the contrary, use all the resources of their "athleticism" to install themselves within this very difference, like acrobats torn apart in a perpetual show of strength. (Deleuze and Guattari 1996, 66-7)

The "very difference" (ibid, 67), to which Deleuze and Guattari refer in the above quote, is *sensation*. A *being of sensation* is the unique and characteristic affective capacity of a work of art. In dance theatre, dancers themselves are installed within the entity of sensation, an entity that both articulates new differences in kind and speaks to emergent images of thought. An affective, creative entity, such as a *being of sensation* in dance theatre, is a method for expressing the unique nature of the multiplicities that constitute our world. Creating a *being of sensation* is a way of conceptualizing difference in a material sense. Integrated dance theatre is expressive of change within social imaginaries. It shifts understandings in bodies through staging relationships between dancers and audience members. The aesthetic, embodied labour of restless dancers affectively disrupts medically based discourses of intellectual disability, such as those that were established by the work of Édouard Seguin (1856) and Thomas Merton (1968). These medically based discourses are also clearly reflected in the later model for disability service provision developed by Wolf Wolfensberger (2001, 1991, 1989, 1975). Contemporary scholars such as Edgar Miller (1996) and Mark Rapley (2004) have critically reflected on the ways in which early projects have led to circumstances in which bodies with intellectual disability are popularly understood in negative or patronizing ways. This chapter extends such critical arguments by explicating a physiology of audience–performer relations, associated emotional connections and possibilities for constructing images in thought, which are articulated by integrated dance theatre.

Configuring intellectual disability

The intrinsic paradox created by Descartes' (1986a, 1986b) claim that the positioning of corporeality outside thought, that is constitutive of thought itself, haunts academic discussions of intellectual disability. One of the negative consequences of Cartesian dualism for thinking about people with intellectual disability, is that models of thought developed to theorize "intellectual disability" have constructed and maintained deficit ways of thinking about bodies with intellectual disability. These inadequate methods of thought construct people with intellectual disability as lacking a relationship with "pure" epistemology. The idea of a "pure" epistemology was, for the most part, popularized in Western philosophical thought by Descartes. As the construct "intellectual disability" suggests, it is a way of thinking about bodies in terms of what they *cannot* do.

The primary "regimes of signs" (Deleuze and Guattari 1996, 137) that I am concerned with are generated within medical and sociological discourses of intellectual disability. The "abstract machines" (Deleuze and Guattari 1987, 4) of such discourses are, respectively, an "apparatus of capture" (ibid, 424-73), and territorializing machines that map bodies as being "intellectually disabled". In so doing, these discourses frame bodies in terms of what they are *not* capable of, and confine the potential for theorizing their corporeal capacity within a discursive "set of limits" (Deleuze and Guattari 1996, 141). These limits are constructed in relation to majoritarian (Deleuze and Guattari 1987, 140) "norms" and are informed by a Cartesian understanding of the territorialized, intellectually disabled body. I critique aspects of medical discourses of intellectual disability on the premise that Cartesian methods for thinking about the body are recreated within such discourses (Hickey-Moody 2006, 2005, 2003, 2001a, 2001b). Further, I contend that Cartesian ways of conceiving corporeality can be traced through select studies of the social construction of intellectual disability.

In opposition to Cartesian methods of thought, I argue for an understanding of corporeality that medical and sociological discourses of intellectual disability are not able to realize. Translating this aesthetic labor into thought, it is my contention that performers re-territorialize their bodies through affectively disrupting medical and sociological territorializations of bodies with intellectual disability.

In stark contrast to medical and sociological discourses of intellectual disability, within Restless Dance, *beings of sensation* (Deleuze and Guattari 1996, 165, 177) are created. These *beings* (ibid) that inhabit integrated dance theatre texts are specific to the bodies of the dancers and thus are a performance of the dancers' personal and cultural histories. Furthermore, it is through the production of *beings of sensation* (ibid) that performers with intellectual disability deterritorialize medical and sociological discourses of intellectual disability, and create space for the disruption of dominant discourses of intellectual disability. As a place of collective imagining in-between thought and flesh, *sensation* is what Deleuze (1988, 49) has read as the space:

> ...between the body's affection and idea, which involves the nature of the external body, and the affect, which involves an increase or decrease of the power of acting, for the body and the mind alike.

Between emotional, embodied affect and images in thought, there are *beings of sensation* and there is cognitive labor. Imaginings of the intellectually disabled body – that can be connected in a range of different ways – are born of sensation. These sensory imaginings are then translated into thought through cognitive labor. Such thought is the political and scholarly work of studies such as this chapter. A glacial zone, in which dominant cultural assumptions surrounding bodies with intellectual disabilities are frozen and reconstructed; the sensory being that inhabits the Restless Dance Company production *Proximal* can be translated into thought as an affective disruption of intellectual disability.

Integrated dance theatre: Restless Dance Company's *Proximal*

This chapter draws on ethnographic research journals[3], in which I documented the process of devising and performing *Proximal.* The production was primarily funded by the Australia Council Dance Fund and the South Australian Youth Arts Board. Ingrid Voorendt was commissioned to devise and direct the work, in collaboration with the Youth Performance Ensemble. Sally Chance, the (then) Artistic Director, also worked on later stages of the project. South Australian composer and musician, Heather Frahn, was commissioned to develop and perform a score for the work. The company's resident designer, Gaelle Mellis, conceived the costumes and set for the production. The lighting designer was David Gadsden, and the production sound technician was Nick O'Connor. It was the company's first substantial foray into video technologies. The company collaborated with Tamsin Sharp, an Adelaide-based film and video maker, in devising video text that spoke to the choreography, and which constituted a core component of the performance. *Proximal* was devised in the (then) Restless Dance Studio in Franklin Street, Adelaide and the North Adelaide Community Centre in Tynte Street, North Adelaide. The work was performed at the South Australian State Opera Studios from October 23 to 26. The Ensemble's work began in July 2001 and, as such, the production was a four-month project for the dancers and a longer, more extensive process for the company's Manager, Artistic Director, Director and Stage Manager.

---

[3] These journals draw on six years of ethnographic fieldwork with Restless Dance Company in South Australia. The journals were written in 2001. See references for further information.

The directorial concept that underpinned *Proximal* was concerned with interrogating, mapping and re-imagining the dancers' lived bodies. The performance director, Ingrid Voorendt, modelled the choreographic techniques employed to devise the work around the idea of the body as a map of life histories, and bodily actions as (re)positionings of these embodied histories. The title of the work *Proximal* was chosen to highlight the importance of in-between bodily spaces, those spaces which we simultaneously inhabit and move away from unwittingly in the pedestrian experience of living as a body. It is in and through proximal spaces that embodied histories are carried, performed and re-framed.

The stage space was shockingly white and shot through with a thousand tiny cracks. Upon this stage, the dancers' bodies were framed by clumps of young willow, which reached with twisted spindles towards the sky. This foliage articulated notions of youth, possibilities and immanent futures. The world to which this space belongs was timeless and somehow unnervingly dense; speaking at once of the infinite, fresh possibilities of youth and also of generations of pain. This is a universe perched perilously close to the edge of a "Body without Organs" (Deleuze and Guattari 1987, 1983) produced by bodies with intellectual disability, a social/psychological mass of majoritarian cultural denial, anger, fear and prospective genetic annihilation. A "Body without Organs" is the virtual power of a collection of singularities. The virtual power of Restless Dance, its "Body without Organs," is constantly feeding back into the dancers' art, as bodies on stage perform generations of embodied and institutionalized majoritarian social disavowal.

A screen fixed upon the splintered white surface that marks the back of the stage shows up minutiae of physical details. Here the body is objectified; scrutinized, and seemingly unrelated corporeal parts are perversely connected. The viewer is a voyeur of sites of corporeal rupture, and their potential for subverting ways of thinking about bodies. The screen becomes a technology of the dancers' corporeality as it performs the interconnectedness of singularities inscribed in flesh. It traces life histories through corporeal inscriptions, connecting the audience and the performer in uncertain understanding. The viewer connects to the eye of the camera, as it connects to a dancer's extensive head scar, which connects us to the surgeon's scalpel, and an operating theatre. Body technologies and the embodied histories (durations) that constitute them are coupled through the eye of the camera and the eye of the viewer, as the film screen becomes a bodily extension. Movement excerpts that are included in the film see the images morph film into dance, in a becoming-dance of the usually stable screen.

The dancers' bodies echo, or reverberate, the sensations that inhabit the film screening on the wall behind them. Youthful, bright, "innocent" 1950's style dresses or pastel pants and shirts garb the scarred bodies that move through this thickened atmosphere, which literally pulses with the sounds of amplified heartbeats and rushing blood. Here, bodies step into a gallery of corporeal inscriptions in order to etch themselves again through movement. Chance (2001) suggests that:

> *Proximal* does what dancers do best – it creates abstract, multi-layered images resonant with sensation. Further layers are provided by Tamsin Sharp's bold, magnifying glass screen, the controlled intensity of Heather Frahn's magical music.

Through movement, dancers explore the stories that their bodies tell, and the ways their histories are constantly imprinted upon the spaces surrounding them. Here, re-territorializing the body becomes an art form, in which corporeal boundaries blur into a performance space. The overall "affect" (Spinoza 2001; Deleuze and Guattari 1996, 1987) of the work, the *being of sensation* (Deleuze and Guattari 1996, 165) that is produced, is that of a "liminal zone" (Turner 1967). In this liminal zone, "worldly" conceptual boundaries are pushed away and bodies are reconstituted in sensation upon their own terms.

Reconfiguring bodies

In choreographic terms, proximal space is the area closest to a dancer's body; a virtual extension of corporeal surface area. Taking this notion as a starting point for devising performance material, Ingrid Voorendt encouraged the Youth Performance Ensemble members to extend their proximal space in order to encompass an entire performance venue. As such, not only concepts of corporeality, but also those of spatiality were re-territorialized through the dancers' work in *Proximal.*

The space that bodies performed in became more than a given condition of performance, akin to what Deleuze and Guattari (1987, 488) define as a "smooth space", an environment in which ratios between matter and energy are reworked. They state:

> What defines smooth space, then is that…space and that which occupies space tend to become identified, to have the same power…a smooth, amorphous space of this kind is constituted by an accumulation of proximities, and each accumulation defines a *zone of indiscernibility* proper to "becoming" (more than a line and less than a surface).

In Voorendt's (2001) words, this sensory atmosphere evolves from an exploration of "the space we occupy and the spaces in between". The atmosphere we move through in life is an inextricable part of what we "are", what we can and cannot do.

Dancers created answers through movement to questions such as: how can you write yourself into space; become void? As such, the devising process for *Proximal* began in a collection of in-between spaces, sites of corporeal rupture which performers were asked to identify, speak and dance on. Dancers responded to this task by categorizing parts of their body that open out and connect with other assemblages: Simone's armpit is scarred with a razor cut, which connects her to socialized ideas of gender, "femininity" and consumerism.

Ellie's childhood knee injury – the product of an unfortunately placed stick when falling – has left traces of white scar tissue running across her leg. These silvery lines tie Ellie into childhood memories, her brother, and her engagement with sympathy as a powerful social tool. A purple welt on Aislinn's thigh marks a cut from a surfboard, connecting her to "surfie" youth subcultures and her idea of being a young person in Australia. The burn on Tom's thigh from a match links his body with practices of sadomasochism, dissent, subversion and addiction.

The number of sites of corporeal rupture upon the company members' corporealities as a whole, and the multiple significances of these sites for company members, is potentially infinite. These lines of connection are moments of tenuous union between the corporeal form of the dancer and the Body without Organs which produces the energy and intensity that offers these performers the force they give form to through creating sensation. Here I use "Body without Organs" to mean virtual possibility. "Body without Organs" can be read as the *virtual possibility of matter* – unstructured potential.

The connections forged by making dances about sites of corporeal rupture are immanent. For example, Nicola's grown-out piercing scar in the webbing between her thumb and index finger embodies subcultural practices of body modification, a friendship bonding ritual between two girls, and the years that it has taken for the jewelry to be rejected by her flesh. This scar is inseparable from these processes. These bodily marks are a performance of the ways in which we are always already part of a range of different machines at any given moment in time. Nicola's scar is but one cog in a subcultural machine of body modifications; a small component of her own friendship machine and a marker of the passing of time.

As well as inspiring choreographic material, the dancers' assortments of corporeal brandings formed material for filming. These bodily marks are personal intensities, erogenous zones that are coded through duration (embodied time) rather than processes of psychoanalytic sexualization. The often hetero-normative libidinal economies of the body, economies that are invested and coded through psychoanalytic sexualization, are reworked here. Individually specific personal intensities of the body are shot close-up and cut together in an unlikely series of connections. To reappropriate a popular Afro-American folksong, in the video text "the backbone's connected to the eyeball, the eyeball's connected to the fingertip…the fingertip's connected to the nipple…". This ever increasing "body machine" (body parts compiled on to video) was screened during the performance of *Proximal*, serving as a poignant reminder of the constructed nature of libidinal economies of anatomy. The point here is that becoming in art, the sensory becoming one undertakes in crafting a *being or bloc of sensations*, will always push a body past its purported limits.

Compounds of percepts and affects – *beings or blocs of sensation* – are distinctly different in nature to the raw materials from which sensation is crafted, or the methodological tools employed in the process of construction:

> Sensation is not the same thing as the material. What is preserved by right is not the material, which constitutes only the defacto condition… Sensation is not realized in the material without the material passing completely into the sensation, into the percept of affect. All the material becomes expressive. (Deleuze and Guattari 1996, 166)

As this quote suggests, a *bloc or being of sensation* is a synergy, a whole that is equal to more than the sum of its parts. The trajectories of *blocs of sensation* cut across the territories of those who produce them; dancers, directors, technicians, musicians, designers, and also those who behold the sensation, audience members.

In *Proximal*, embodied percepts, the product of ensemble process and company politics, collect along with other synthetic media in order to create a *being of sensation* that is generated by bodies with intellectual disability, yet does not frame these bodies in terms of discourses of intellectual disability. Junction points of choreography, design, music, lighting and film are movements of "deterritorialization" and "destratification", or "becomings", which change the capacity of the bodies who intercept these radical trajectories, or "lines of flight"[4] (Deleuze and Guattari 1987, 1996). These junction points are movements of destratification, corporeal transformations undertaken through group process. Their limit, which is never reached, is chaos (Deleuze and Guattari 1987, 503).

Somewhere in between the "territory" and the point of disarticulation, a radical production occurs – the production of *blocs of sensation*. As a kinaesthetic force, the affect of *Proximal* cuts across closed ways of reading bodies with intellectual disability, positing a liminal reality, in which assumed conceptual boundaries and ways of knowing are reworked. This liminal reality has the capacity to alter the ways in which audience members think about intellectual disability. When experienced by an observer, sensation produced by integrated dance theatre is a site of multiple processes of becoming-other. These processes are corporeal affects, which involve renegotiations of viewers' subjective limits.

Reconfiguring thought

In making the argument outlined above in written form, this chapter translates the collective, creative and embodied work of the Restless Youth Performance Ensemble into thought. This process of translation from art to thought, and the contextualization of Restless Dance Company's work amongst bodies of scholarship, produces space for what Deleuze and Guattari (1996) term "conceptual personae", figures of thought that act within and upon thought. Creative thought is affected by conceptual personae, as personae are a *technique of invention* within thought:

> The role of conceptual personae is to show thought's territories, its absolute deterritorialisations and reterritorialisations. Conceptual personae are thinkers, solely thinkers, and their personalised features are closely linked to the diagrammatic features of thought and the intensive features of concepts. (ibid, 69 [original emphasis])

Personae are non-intentional, in the sense that one does not "set out" to imagine a persona that produces certain kinds of concepts (77). The persona (rather than the "author") is the means through which thought is actualized.

---

[4] Movements of deterritorialization cut across the territories of other species, or intercept each other (Deleuze and Guattari 1996, 185). They occur largely through lines of flight. Carried to its end, a line of flight will effect complete disarticulation of form.

A *being of sensation*, in its affective capacity, creates movements within thought, journeys conducted by "aesthetic figures"[5] (177) who exist in meta-contextual relationship with other works of art. In so doing, aesthetic figures dialogue, or resonate, with other aesthetic figures and conceptual personae. It is through these exchanges between aesthetic figures and conceptual personae, through a dialogue between art and thought, that art can instigate becomings of thought (ibid). By inviting us to think outside the boundaries of "majoritarian" Cartesian thought, aesthetic figures push sensory becomings into the realm of the conceptual, by creating experiences in which one is challenged to partake in "the action by which the common event itself eludes what it is" (ibid). Audiences are forced to rethink how they conceive the bodies they are viewing on stage. Here, the event of a body on stage is no longer the performance of accepted or predictable cultural norms. Rather, within the work of Restless Dance, bodies pose questions that the audience must endeavor to answer, such as: What is intelligence? What can a body with intellectual disability do? Which bodies can hold power? How are bodies with intellectual disability transformed through their relations with others?

The work of Restless Dance questions the nature of Cartesian assumptions in thought and draws upon what Deleuze and Guattari (ibid) have called "the possible as an aesthetic category". Through producing *beings of sensation* (Deleuze and Guattari 1996, 165), or sensible inhabitants of a work of art, performers with intellectual disability de-territorialize medical and sociological discourses of intellectual disability. Seemingly unified and continuous surfaces of medical and sociological discourses of intellectual disability are shattered by the many "becomings" (Deleuze and Guattari 1996, 1987) of performers with intellectual disability. Corporeal becoming is "the action by which something or someone continues to become other (while still continuing to be what it is)" (Deleuze and Guattari 1994, 177). These becomings map as yet uncharted aesthetic and sensory terrains. They also push thought, or structures of thought through which the intellectually disabled body can be thought, beyond the limits of medical and sociological discourses. Bodies become multiplicities, as an ensemble becomes a *being of sensation*, part of a synergy of movement, music, design, staging and conceptual

[5] Deleuze and Guattari (1996, 177) contend that Aesthetic Figures, and the style that creates them, have nothing to do with rhetoric: "they are sensations, precepts and affects, landscapes and faces, visions and becomings…Aesthetic figures are not the same as conceptual personae. It may be that they pass into one another, in either direction…insofar as there are sensations of concepts and concepts of sensations."

development, which produces a whole that is more than the sum of its parts.

Conclusion

Integrated dance theatre critically reconfigures the ways in which spectators perceive performers with intellectual disability. It also reconfigures the ways in which performers with intellectual disability perceive themselves. This chapter has theorized the means by which integrated dance theatre affects the viewer, by discussing the process of devising and performing *Proximal*. There were a number of components that fed into the dance theatre text that became *Proximal*. The particular critical power or force of *Proximal*, as an integrated dance theatre text, has been theorized here in terms of affect and sensation. The practical, choreographic and material nature of constructing such an affective entity, alongside the embodied conceptual work that accompanied these choreographic techniques, is inseparable from the aesthetic nature of *Proximal* as a dance theatre text. The *being of sensation* produced by this text literally constitutes a place upon which new conceptions of bodies with intellectual disabilities can be produced. It is in, or through, the translation of *beings of sensation* and aesthetic figures into thought that this chapter also reterritorializes, or affectively disrupts, dominant conceptual paradigms through which we can think the intellectually disabled body.

Works Cited

Angwin, J., G. Shacklock, and J. Blackmore. 2001. "Once You Get into the Box You Can't Get Out: Schools Managing At Risk Students & their Post-school Options." *Crossing Borders: New Frontiers in Educational Research. Australian Association for Research in Education, International Education Research Conference*. Fremantle: AARE.

Barton, L. 1986. "The Politics of Special Educational Needs." *Disability, Handicap & Society* 1: 273-90.

Beck, U. 1995. *Ecological Politics in an Age of Risk*. Cambridge: Polity Press.

—. 1992. *Risk Society: Towards a New Modernity*. London: Sage.

Chance, S. 2001. *Proximal Program Notes.* Directed by I. Voorendt, State Opera Studio, Netley, SA, October 23-26.

Deleuze, G. 2003. *Francis Bacon: The Logic of Sensation,* translated by Daniel Smith. London & New York: Continuum Press.

—. 1990. *Expressionism in Philosophy: Spinoza,* translated by Martin Joughin. New York: Zone Books.

—. 1990. *The Logic of Sense,* translated by M. Lester, and C. Stivale. New York: Columbia University Press.

—. 1988. *Spinoza: Practical Philosophy.* San Francisco: City Light Books.

Deleuze, G., and F. Guattari. 1996. *What is Philosophy?* London: Verso Publishers.

—. 1987. *A Thousand Plateaus: Capitalism & Schizophrenia.* Minneapolis: University of Minnesota Press.

—. 1983. *Anti-Oedipus, Capitalism & Schizophrenia.* Minneapolis: University of Minnesota Press.

Descartes, R. 1968a. In *Discourse on Method,* edited by F.E. Sutcliffe, 27-94. London: Penguin Books.

—. 1968b. In *The Meditation,* edited by F.E. Sutcliffe, 95-169. London: Penguin Books.

—. 1999. *The Principles of Philosophy.* Retrieved September 22 2003, http://www.philosophy.leeds.ac.uk/GMR/hmp/texts/modern/descartes/principles/dcprince.html.

Douglas, M. 1992. *Risk & Blame: Essay in Cultural Theory*. London: Routledge.

Hickey-Moody, A. C. 2006. "Folding the Flesh into Thought: Vitalism and Reading Theory through Movement." *Angelaki: Journal of the Theoretical Humanities* 11 (1): 189-97.

—. 2005. "Unimaginable Bodies: Intellectual Disability, Performance and Becomings." PhD diss., Adelaide: SA, University of South Australia.

—. 2003. "Turning Away from Intellectual Disability: Methods of Practice, Methods of Thought." *Melbourne Studies in Education* 44 (1): 1-22.

—. 2001a. *Proximal.* Reflective ethnographic research journal. World Dance Centre, Adelaide & North Adelaide Community Centre, North Adelaide & The Opera Studio, Netley.

—. 2001b. *Proximal.* Documentary ethnographic research journal. World Dance Centre, Adelaide & North Adelaide Community Centre, North Adelaide & The Opera Studio, Netley.

Leahy, D., and L. Harrison. 2004. "Health & Physical Education & the Production of the 'At Risk Self'." In *Body Knowledge & Control: Studies in the Sociology of Physical Education & Health,* edited by J. Evans, B. Davies and J. Wright. 130-9. London: Routledge.

Lupton, D. 1999. *Risk.* London: Routledge.

Merton, T. 1968. *Mankind in the Unmaking: The Anthropology of Mongolism*. Sydney: Bloxham & Chambers.

Miller, E. 1996. "Idiocy in the Nineteenth Century." *History of Psychiatry* 7 (3): 361-73.

Rapley, M. 2004. *The Social Construction of Intellectual Disability*. Cambridge: Cambridge University Press.

Rasmussen, M.L., and V. Harwood. "Using Ethnography to Enhance Contemporary Understandings of Australian Youth Underachievement." Melbourne: AARE Conference, December 2004.

Restless Dance Company. 2001. *Proximal* Program Notes, directed by I. Voorendt. State Opera Studio, Netley, SA, October 23-26.

Seguin, E. 1986. "Origin of the Treatment & Training of Idiots." *American Journal of Education* 2: 145-52. Retrieved February 29 2008, http://www.disabilitymuseum.org/lib/docs/1437.htm.

Skeggs, B. 2000. "Cultures of Class." In *New Developments in Sociology,* edited by M. Haralambos, 1-25. Ormskirk: Causeway Press.

Spinoza, B. 2001. *Ethics.* England: Wadsworth.

Turner, V. 1967. "Betwixt & Between: The Liminal Period in Rites de Passage." In *Forest of Symbols: Aspects of Ndembu Ritual.* Ithaca: Cornell University Press.

Voorendt, I. 2001. *Proximal* Program Notes, directed by I. Voorendt. State Opera Studio, Netley, SA, October 23-26.

Wolfensberger, W. 2001. "The Story of the 'Cruickshank Chairs' at Syracuse University: A Contribution to the History of the Brain Injury Construct." *Mental Retardation* 39 (6): 472-81.

—. 1991. *A Brief Introduction to Social Role Valorization as a High-Order Concept for Structuring Human Services*. Syracuse, NY: Training Institute for Human Service Planning, Leadership & Change Agency.

—. 1989. "Human Service Policies: The Rhetoric Versus the Reality." In *Disability & Dependency,* edited by L. Barton, 23-41. London: Falmer Press.

—. 1975. *The Origin & Nature of our Institutional Models*. Syracuse: Human Policy Press.

Wright, J. 2000. "Disciplining the Body: Power, Knowledge & Subjectivity in a Physical Education Lesson." In *Culture & Text*, edited by A. Lee and C. Poynton. Sydney: Allen & Unwin.

Wyn, J. 2000. "Youth, Education & Risk: Facing the New Millennium in Social Changes and Youth Development Policies in the New

Millenium." In *Promoting Youth Rights & Adolescents' Social Participation*. Seoul: Korea Institute for Youth Development.

CHAPTER ELEVEN

"DOING GOOD": THE ETHICS OF ARTS INTERVENTIONS WITH "AT RISK" YOUTH

ANGELA O'BRIEN & KATE DONELAN

The *Risky Business* project

This chapter critically examines the *Risky Business* research project, a four-year study of the efficacy of arts interventions for young people "at risk" in urban and rural Australia. *Risky Business* was the first longitudinal, interdisciplinary analysis of the creative arts as intervention activities for highly marginalized youth in Australia. The *Risky Business* research team included researchers from the fields of the creative arts, arts education and criminology[1]. We attempted to address two broad interrelated problems: the qualities of effective diversionary programs for "at risk" young people and the social impact of the creative arts. Within the context of a burgeoning literature on the social benefits of arts participation, we designed the *Risky Business* study to investigate the involvement of highly marginalized young people in arts making, creative expression and performance. Our aim was to examine whether and how the creative arts might increase self-esteem and wellbeing, improve lifeskills and build social inclusion for young people "at risk".

The *Risky Business* research project was conducted in three distinct geographical areas in Victoria, Australia, all of which were identified as having a high proportion of young people who could be described as "at risk". Using an ethnographic, multi-site design, we investigated the participation of young people in ten arts programs in custodial and community settings. Within each program we documented the working

[1] The criminologists involved were Associate Professor Christine Alder and PhD candidate Kiersten Coulter.

processes and arts products, generated field notes, and conducted interviews with young people, artists and support workers; these data sets were analysed as a "collective case study" (Stake, 1995) across the research project. The programs covered a range of art forms: drawing and painting, photography, drama and theatre, dance, rap and hip-hop music, stand-up comedy, creative writing and puppetry.

In our monograph, *Risky Business: Creative Interventions for Marginalised Youth* (Donelan and O'Brien 2008), we discuss the findings of this cross-disciplinary study, and analyze some of the challenges the research team encountered in implementing and researching arts-based interventions with diverse groups of highly marginalized young people. The data indicates that the young people who engaged with particular arts programs gained significant personal, social and artistic benefits. However, many of the young people were difficult to engage and this impacted negatively on the frequency of their attendance and sustained participation in arts making. We argue that engagement is facilitated by the provision of a "safe" working space, appropriate programs and artists with a commitment to working with highly marginalized young people, and the achievement of a publicly disseminated arts product as a culmination of each program.

Whilst acknowledging the positive outcomes of this complex and difficult project, as researchers we are left with some unresolved questions. This chapter interrogates the *Risky Business* study in relation to the ethics and efficacy of applied arts practice in the contemporary world. We consider, from a more critical and detached stance, the motivations of researchers and community artists who choose to work with highly marginalized young people, the social and artistic expectations of creative arts interventions, and community responses to the personal and artistic products of "at risk" young people. On the basis of our experiences within the *Risky Business* project, we examine some underlying assumptions about ethical research practices with "at risk" young people, and the potential of the creative arts to facilitate transformative social and individual change given the needs and aspirations of highly marginalized young people.

The concept of "risk"

The concept of "risk" was central to the *Risky Business* study, including the problem of how we understand and manage risk. A preoccupation with risk is a feature of the modern age (Bernstein 1998). Risk perversity or an attraction towards risk is seen as destabilizing to our safe society and so we often choose to marginalize and label those who take risks, particularly adolescents (Giroux 2000; Bessant and Watts 1998; Wyn and White 1997). There has been a tendency to problematize youth and to perpetuate negative stereotypes of young people as "victims, potential criminals or agents of social disorder" (Cahill 2002, 20). The more they are categorized as rebels or risk takers, the more likely adolescents are to engage in risk taking behavior, and the more socially marginalized and "at risk" they become.

The young people in the ten *Risky Business* case studies presented with a multitude of complex risk factors including disconnection from family, poverty, exposure to violence, homelessness, academic failure, illiteracy and school exclusion, histories of offence and drug use, teenage single parenting, mental health issues, marginalization through refugee status and Indigenous cultural background. Most young participants had incomplete schooling and limited experiences of the arts within their formal education. However, the *Risky Business* research was concerned not only with risk factors but also with the kinds of risks young people are prepared to take. We recognized that the concept of "at risk" is complex, contested and open to interpretation (Oakley 2007, 28). As arts researchers, we operated from two broad assumptions: that there is latent or unrecognized potential in marginalized young people, and that making art is about taking risks. We were interested in whether "at risk" youth, often with a background in harmful risk-taking behavior, are more likely to respond to intervention programs that focus on creative expression and involve excitement and risk, but within a safe framework. We hoped the research would establish a relationship between positive arts interventions and a decline in self-destructive behaviors as a corollary to an improvement in young people's wellbeing, self-esteem and social integration.

In many ways the outcomes of the *Risky Business* research supports attempts to involve young offenders and other troubled youth in creative diversionary programs. The study demonstrates that young people can assert their identity in new ways through the arts, beyond the prescriptive labeling of being "at risk" or "delinquent".

Claims made for the arts and social change

The *Risky Business* study took place at a time of prolific research into the social, cognitive and community-wide impact of the arts, with implications for policy and practice. Building on groundbreaking studies such as *Champions of Change* (Fiske 1999) and *Critical Links* (Deasy 2002) in the US, and the UK publication *All our Futures* (National

Advisory Committee on Creative and Cultural Education 2000), research has burgeoned, both intensifying and diversifying public interest in this area (Oakley 2007; Bamford 2006; Hughes and Wilson 2003). A significant amount has been written about the instrumental benefits of arts programs for young people (McCarthy, Ondaatje and Brooks 2004; Jones 2000; Marsden and Thiele 2000; Brice Heath and Roach 1999; Dreeszen et al. 1999; Stone et al. 1998, 1997; McArthur and Law 1996). In the Australia Council's 2004 study *Art and Wellbeing*, special attention is given to the use of arts practice as a way of connecting people to support networks and community to achieve better health outcomes (Mills and Brown 2004; Thiele and Marsden 2003). Young people "at risk" and marginalized social groups are the focus of a number of case studies included in this report; it argues that engagement in arts practice can promote individual efficacy including confidence, communication and resilience.

The value of the arts is receiving increasing recognition in Australia from people working with offenders and other disadvantaged populations. Health and welfare organizations are using a range of arts practices including visual arts, sculpture, music, theatre, dance and multi-media to engage with and stabilize the lives of "at risk" young people (*ANAH Newsletter* 2000; Jones 2000; Marsden and Thiele 2000; Murray et al. 1999; Nunn and Bull 1995). Many of these programs are aimed at young people experiencing a range of risk factors including homelessness, criminal histories, and significant drug dependence. A number of organizations are using the arts to engage with young people who fall through a service gap. Diagnosed with dual disorders, drug dependency and mental illness, this growing population of young people are often not accepted into drug treatment or psychiatric services (Marsden 2000; Jones 2000; Murray et al. 1999). The arts are regarded by these organizations as the key to positive shifts and outcomes. They claim it is often through their engagement with the artists and their arts practices, rather than through formal counseling, that problems and needs are identified and addressed. Young people are attracted to and access arts programs, thereby introducing them positively to community services and other resources (Redshaw 2000). Thiele and Marsden have developed a theoretical model of practice in which the artistic framework of the arts studio is balanced with "social and developmental outcomes" that drive their work within a health, welfare and community development context. They identify five key principles within their practice: "artistic function and outcome; building connectedness; exchange of knowledge; respect; and possibility" (2003, 83–97).

A number of other recent studies have focused on the positive social impact of engagement with the arts for young people considered to be "at risk" (Roberts 2006; Brice Heath and Wolf 2005, 2004; Hunter 2005). Participation by young offenders in theatre and visual arts programs have been shown to stabilize their lives in unexpected ways, leading to compliance with orders, employment and establishing themselves in stable housing and community networks (Marsden and Thiele 2000; Walters 1997). Both the health and welfare sectors make substantial claims about the kinds of outcomes that emerge from arts projects: the reduction of illicit drug use and offending, assistance with psychological and emotional issues in a young person's life, and a range of educational, social and lifeskills that are transferable to further education and employment situations.

Questioning these claims

It is pertinent to consider the ethical and political motivations driving this burgeoning interest in arts interventions with marginalized communities both locally and globally. The movement has generated vigorous debate. Nicholson critiques what she sees as a contemporary "culture of altruism" (2005). She argues that many academics, arts practitioners and policy makers adopted the term "applied drama" during the 1990s to describe arts practices that primarily exist outside conventional mainstream institutions and which are "specifically intended to benefit individuals, communities and societies" (ibid, 2). She suggests that these community practitioners are motivated by a belief in the arts to effect individual and social change. They draw on the libertarian practices of twentieth century arts education and alternative or political arts practices to claim that the social impact of these interventions is socially radical and instrumental, simultaneously justifying the artistic efficacy and social good of arts interventions.

Essentially, the applied arts movement picks up on the idealism associated with modern romanticism. Ackroyd, for example, argues that academics and artists who are engaged in applied arts work believe in the power of the arts to address something beyond the form itself (cited in Nicholson 2005, 168). Somers suggests that "drama performances of all kinds have as their roots a belief that by making drama we are doing good" (cited in Balfour and Somers 2006, viii). The applied arts movement is underpinned by a shared conviction that creative engagement facilitates redemptive change for both the individual and the community. Thiele and Marsden (2003) use the term "community cultural development" to define a process in which an artist practitioner works with a community to develop artistic outcomes, while at the same time acknowledging "the unique knowledge, skills beliefs and values of the participants". They claim their work offers "a model of arts practice that...delivers broad social change outcomes for marginalized young people" (ibid, 22). For these practitioners, the arts are seen as transformative, facilitating a transition from the margin to the social norm.

Kershaw argues that western mainstream theatre culture is "a social engine that helps to drive an unfair system of privilege" involving class and cultural exclusion and undermining broad community participation (1999, 31). His argument might also be applied to other art forms, particularly modern and post-modern art which assume a level of intertextuality available only to the culturally initiated. What assumptions then do practitioners, imbued with romantic and elitist notions of artistic form and social purpose, bring to those who have been traditionally excluded? What assumptions underpin the creation of art-works by marginalized young people and the claims made for the role and status of participants as emerging artists? Is it possible in the contemporary global community to reclaim the arts as a vehicle for individual, social and political change?

Ethical research with marginalized youth

Claims about the positive impact of arts interventions with "at risk" young people have generated questions about the nature and ethical challenges of arts-focused youth research (Oakley 2007; Bamford 2006; Hughes and Wilson 2003). While the field of educational research is currently dominated by calls for "evidence-based" research and experimental trials, there is an increasing interest in alternative, socially engaged, arts-based approaches to conducting and writing research texts (Cahnmann-Taylor and Siegesmund 2008). Barone argues that arts-informed narrative research texts can "artfully change the conversation", opening up critiques of social structures that powerfully inform public policy (2008, 47). Contemporary qualitative research methodologies are seen to provide more collaborative, ethical and reflexive modes of inquiry than traditional forms of empirical and experimental research. The emergence of participatory and critical ethnographic and action research has informed the approach of many of those studying arts-based interventions with vulnerable populations (Gallagher 2007; Madison 2005). Finley champions "radical, ethical and revolutionary arts-based inquiry" as a form of socially responsible political activism that gives agency to disenfranchized, marginalized and oppressed communities (2005, 689).

The *Risky Business* project was underpinned by many of the principles of contemporary ethnographic and arts-based social research (Denzin and Lincoln 2000; Janesick 2000; Tedlock 2000; Stake 1995; Wolcott 1995, 1994). The research design emphasized collaboration, social engagement, contextualized field-based data, and grounded and emergent theory. We conceived of the young people, artists and other community members as research participants rather than "subjects", and we attempted to build and sustain relationships of trust as the study evolved. The field-based researchers in each arts program attempted to access the multiple perspectives of the participants and stakeholders: the young people, the artists and the administrative and professional staff associated with the community organizations and host institutions. Although the *Risky Business* researchers focused on building a deep understanding of each arts program as a complex socio-cultural event, we were mindful of the need to generate a strong "evidence base" to underpin a set of findings that were meaningful to our partners and other stakeholders. We acknowledge that our research report reflects the tensions we encountered in working across these two divergent research paradigms (O'Brien and Donelan 2008, 2007).

The research team encountered ethical and logistical challenges in conducting this multi-site study with a team of researchers and diverse groups of highly marginalized young people. Wherever possible we chose field researchers who were culturally and age appropriate for interacting with the young participants and documenting their art making. In each program the fieldworkers undertook their participant observation role differently; some participated in the arts workshops, building at least temporary relationships of trust with the young people and fostering dialogue with the artists. Some took an active role as a "privileged observer" fulfilling the tasks associated with a project manager, while others remained as a "passive observer" (Wolcott 1995). The positioning of the researcher, their fieldwork experience and skills, and their capacity to build rapport with the young "at risk" participants impacted significantly on the nature and quality of the data collected within each program.

We tried to ensure that the research was conducted in an ethical manner that extended beyond the mandatory ethics clearances and protocols required by the University and the government departments involved. Given the nature of the demographic, informed consent and longitudinal data collection proved problematic. We were concerned that many of the young people were prepared to agree to participate in the project without looking at the plain language statement, and that some could not read or did not understand the consent forms. The mobility of the young people and their unstable life circumstances made continuity of data collection difficult, and privacy regulations meant that it was often impossible to maintain contact with young people after they left custodial settings.

In the researchers' briefing sessions with the young people we explained the research as a collaborative endeavor designed to improve the provision and quality of arts programs for young people. In their interviews with researchers, many of the young participants revealed that a key motivating factor in their involvement with the project was their desire to assist others in similar circumstances. They asked for their views, as communicated through their artwork or in their discussions with us, to be recorded and disseminated. This created an ethical dilemma for the research team as we had undertaken an agreement to protect the identity of the young people, particularly those in custodial institutions where it is a criminal offence to identify a young person residing in a custodial facility. As chief investigators we observed a tension between the young people's need for public communication and recognition and the constraints of the research agreement and the provisions of the Privacy Act and other aspects of the law.

We were surprised by the extent to which involvement in the research component of the *Risky Business* project seemed to give some young people agency. The participants said they enjoyed the opportunity to offer their views and to be heard by an adult who might be able to affect change. For example, a young man in the hip-hop music program was clear in his commitment to support the research: "Obviously I want to help youse out and get all this stuff down" (O'Brien 2004a). The young people's interviews with researchers provided a forum for expressing their opinions on the social world and reflections on the process of art making. In retrospect, however, we wonder about the young people's experiences of these encounters with adult researchers. What were their motives for contributing to a dialogue with researchers about the benefits of the arts program? And what were their expectations of the rewards and consequences of speaking about their views of the world to adults with life experiences so different from their own?

Reporting the benefits of the *Risky Business* programs

The *Risky Business* study provides compelling evidence that the "at risk" young people who engaged in the arts programs achieved positive outcomes and personal, social and artistic skills (Donelan and O'Brien 2008). Drawing on data from the young people, the artists and support workers within the custodial and community settings, and the observations of field researchers across the ten programs, we identified a range of instrumental and affective outcomes. The young participants indicated that they had increased self-esteem and confidence; improved communication and presentational skills; developed their artistic skills; and gained a sense of artistic achievement through the experience of art making and contributing actively to a public arts event. The data indicated that for many of the young people their experiences within the arts programs transformed their sense of identity, enabling them to make new and positive relationships with people and, in the words of one young man: "to be the person I just want to be".

A key finding is that the young people perceived themselves "as artists" working within a larger community of artists, and flourished in arts programs in which their ideas, artistic development and problem solving were recognized and respected, especially if they were overtly recognized as having "expertise". A public presentation of the artistic work developed during an arts program provided a highly valued culmination and affirmation of the young people's engagement in the process.

In writing our *Risky Business* research report we wanted to include and privilege the voices of young participants, including those in custody who are largely absent from the research literature. Interwoven through the report their words provide "evidence" of a range of instrumental benefits and positive social outcomes of these arts interventions. We constructed individual case studies of young people and wrote vignettes drawn from the data. Apart from providing support for our interpretative account of the impact of the arts interventions, the inclusion of young people's voices and the participant vignettes are intended to give readers a sense of the diverse life histories, subjectivities and experiences of those within the arts programs (Donelan and O'Brien 2008).

However, it is important to interrogate the choice of data we included in the report and to analyze the gaps, for example, the limited interview material gathered from young people in transition, those who came to a session once and did not reappear, those who were silent and withdrawn, or, after the initial interview, were not available for follow-up discussions. Across all programs the numbers of young participants dropped after the initial sessions, attendance in both community and custodial settings was unpredictable, motivation and interest levels were often low, and behavior was volatile and challenging for the artists and community workers. We regret now that we were unable to access and include the voices of those young people for whom the arts programs were not meaningful, or for whom the immediate life circumstances were more compelling than continuing to participate. It is the words of those who remained within the programs, who engaged with aspects of arts making, and who participated in public performances and exhibitions that we use to illustrate and support our claims about the efficacy of arts interventions (ibid). Because data was generated before, during or soon after the culminating public event and we were unable to stay in contact with most of the young people, we were unable to ascertain the extent to which the positive impact of participation and engagement in the *Risky Business* arts programs had a lasting impact on their lives.

Artists and working methods

The *Risky Business* study argues that the selection of artists with the capacity to engage marginalized young people is a key factor in the effectiveness of arts interventions (Donelan and O'Brien 2008, 55–63). We found that artists require complex pedagogical and interpersonal skills in order to manage difficult groups of young people with diverse personal, logistical and social needs. On reflecting on this finding we realize that there is an inherent assumption. One of our industry partners was clear on what he saw as essential for arts interventions: "the greatest programs that are run with kids often stem out of the worker's own passions" (ibid, 55). In this romanticized view of the arts and community artists, efficacy is driven by passion. Arts participation is seen as transformative for marginalized young people as long as the facilitator has commitment and the capacity to engage young people. Inherent in this vision is an assumption that the arts training methods and aesthetic outcomes are of secondary concern. In this section we identify the qualities that community artists bring to their work with young people and question whether workers with these qualities can both bring about social change in their interactions with young people and create effective arts learning outcomes.

The *Risky Business* study identified that the young people had strong views about essential qualities for those artists who worked with them: they needed to develop and sustain one-to-one relationships; build a positive group dynamic and emotionally supportive environment; and demonstrate a grounded aesthetic and a sense of youth culture, as well as being seen as a "real artist" (ibid, 61). Many of the artists in the *Risky Business* case studies expressed their commitment to creating a working environment that was emotionally supportive, productive and responsive to the needs of all participants, and which in some way rescued participants from their position on the margin. The role of the artist working with young people "at risk" is not just to involve participants in art making, but also to use the arts for positive instrumental change and to make "the world a better place" (ibid, 58).

When we asked the artists about their background and training, many privileged their professional training in human sciences such as psychology or teaching rather than their artistic training; they saw these skills as "missing with pure arts people". Some of the artists identified a capacity to empathize with the participants through their parallel life experiences as important. One artist commented: "well I guess I was once a young girl 'at risk'" (ibid).

The role of a community artist working with young people in difficult contexts is generally unsupported by training, professional networks or arts bodies and poorly paid. The artists with whom we worked juggled the challenges of community arts building with the necessary pastoral care of needy young people. It seemed to us that it was often difficult for artists to mediate the complementary but different roles of arts therapist, arts educator and community artist. The artists did not have the time or power to negotiate with the institutions in which they worked or to influence policy makers about the importance of this work. Although their backgrounds, arts practices and working methods varied, all artists in the *Risky Business* project were deeply committed to the wellbeing of the young people, and the idea that involvement in arts programs offered the participants a chance to express themselves and make meaning of their lives. In their discussions with us, most of the artists were explicit in their desire to "do good".

We became interested in the motivations of the artists who worked in the *Risky Business* programs because it was evident to us that the desire to "empower" young people was more important than financial remuneration or artistic outcomes. We observed that most of the artists remained committed to the arts programs even when the young participants were negative or disengaged and there seemed to be little evidence of positive outcomes. Nicholson interrogates the "good intentions" of applied arts practitioners. She suggests that self-interest and altruism are "interrelated rather than oppositional", that altruistic acts may be "socially and psychologically beneficial to the giver because altruism is a significant part of his or her identity".

> Miller's and Badhwar's research confirms that there is still an uneven balance of power between altruist and recipient, with the uncomfortable implication that, however well intentioned, some acts of altruism may have the effect of keeping "other" people in their place. Because practitioners often work in contexts in which they are outsiders, for all kinds of reasons, their good intentions about "helping" others in "need" may be construed as patronizing or authoritarian, contributing to keeping "others" on the margins rather than taking centre stage. (2005, 30)

One of the artists rejected the "empowering" potential of arts engagement, and found himself frustrated by a mismatch between his aims and those of the other artists with whom he worked:

> My role is as a professional artist and a young man. To be uncompromising in the sense that it is potentially unlimited and I want to illustrate for them that this hippy therapy thing is a crock of shit as far as I am concerned. I'd be more interested in them holding the possibility that they could be a professional artist. That's what I'm interested in. (Donelan and O'Brien 2008, 64)

For one of the *Risky Business* programs, we engaged a professional theatre company to work with a highly marginalized group of Indigenous students in a rural secondary school (Donelan and O'Brien 2006). The professional artists who worked on this project articulated the frustrations they experienced in working within this challenging school-community setting. We observed that they were motivated by their artistic goal of creating a product; when the young people became bored with the tedious work of creating puppets for the final performance, the artists simply finished the job. In reflecting on the puppetry making and performance program, and the artistic growth for these young people, the artists' assessment was comparatively negative. However, as the difficulties they encountered led them to reassess their working methods, they believed their own learning as arts facilitators had been profound. They recognized that they needed to be "more prepared to accept things might be different from what they had expected" and let go of "expectations of what the (artistic) outcome might be" (Donelan and O'Brien 2008, 60).

Some of the artists in the *Risky Business* programs had developed formulaic processes for their work with the young people; positive outcomes were predictable and assured and artistic expectations had been modified by experience. In the painting program, the particular skills-based approach, which involved the reproduction of images and a high level of artistic guidance, ensured instant "success" for the majority of participants. The artist worked with each participant in identifying an image to work from, and his teaching style included transferring the image to the canvas and then modeling the technique on the participant's canvas, which the participant, in turn, painted over (O'Brien 2004b).

For this artist, as for most of those with whom we worked, enabling methods, positive outcomes and positive feedback were part of the essential pedagogical discourse of arts interventions with marginalized youth. Concomitantly, these artists worked within a social development culture. We noticed that for many of the artists their pre-existing beliefs in the efficacy and benefits of the arts for troubled young people circumscribed their responses as reflective practitioners. It seemed to us that belief in the transformative power of the arts locked artists and community workers into an unwavering position of advocacy that prevented them reflecting critically on the young people's responses to the arts programs and the difficulties they encountered.

A safe space

For most of the young participants whose lives and learning experiences had been inconsistent, chaotic and fragile, consistent adult support, structured programs and familiar physical environments offered security and safety. Our analysis of the *Risky Business* data shows the importance of establishing a safe working space for all participants (Donelan and O'Brien 2008, 51–5). In the context of these arts programs, a "safe" space is defined both broadly and specifically, providing for physical, emotional and aesthetic safety. A safe physical space is not only one where physical harm is avoided, but where the participants feel a sense of privacy and comfort. Ritualization of the space is important, so that participants can associate positive and predictable social or artistic activities within the space. For the artists and young people "a safe space" was a liminal space that fostered a sense of community and social connectedness, "a family sort of environment" where transitions and transformations were possible.

The significance of space is highly contested and our identification of a "safe" space as an essential prerequisite for effective arts engagement became a matter for considerable debate between members of the research team. The ten *Risky Business* arts programs were conducted in different spaces including juvenile custodial centers, a school, a university drama workshop room and theatre, a former YMCA building and community arts centers. None of these spaces was "empty" in terms of cultural associations and values (Lefebvre 1991). Physically and symbolically they were part of larger institutional contexts and had been inscribed and re-inscribed with various social meanings.

Nicholson makes the point that a symbol of the modernist Utopia is the "empty space designed to liberate the soul and the imagination by insulating actors and audiences from the restrictions of history, the regulations of place and the materiality of everyday life" (2005, 125). It is a place of potential transformation aesthetically and socially. One can extend Nicholson's point to the metaphor of the blank canvas or page on which one might recreate oneself and one's image or rewrite one's history and future. Nicholson suggests that the idealization of the empty space and the assumption that temporary isolation from other social practices leads to social transformation rests on a belief that a space is "ideologically neutral and without cultural inscription". She argues that the notion that participants can emerge from the empty space "transformed as individuals and ready to transform society" is a modernist re-working of a romantic view of the arts and the artist, dependent on "idealist constructions of the creative imagination" (ibid,126).

In institutional settings, spaces are conceived because of power and the regulations governing their movement and behavior. The arts themselves impose forms, languages and social constructions on the blank artistic space before the writer picks up her pen or the actor physically inscribes the space. Transforming spaces within highly regulated institutions into enabling artistic spaces is challenging. Balfour (2004) discusses the challenges for arts practitioners working in prisons where surveillance is the institutional norm, as characterized by Foucault when he invokes Bentham's metaphor of the panopticon (Rabinow 1984, 216-19). Balfour argues that practitioners must ensure that there is an imaginative escape from the physical and symbolic corrective structures within prisons for there to be successful artistic practice. Artists need to understand how the discourses of power and authority are reproduced in physical spaces and symbolically on the blank canvas in order to assist participants to rewrite or overwrite these restrictive and codified spaces.

Cultural anthropologist Victor Turner's notion of liminality emerges out of his understanding of ritual processes. The liminal space is the space "betwixt and between" for the initiate, a borderland between childhood and adulthood where the participants are expected to subvert and challenge cultural norms (Turner 1986). Liminal spaces allow for play, but following playful subversion the initiates are re-integrated into the adult world. For Turner, in post-industrial societies, artistic creativity takes place within a "liminoid" space – a place that is voluntary and not so contained, with the potential to challenge societal norms and generate "the seedbeds of cultural creativity" (1982, 28).

The spaces in which the *Risky Business* arts programs were conducted were certainly not neutral. The extent to which the artists and participants were able to re-inscribe these as "safe" artistic spaces depended on multiple factors, including not just the physical and symbolic spaces in which the workshops were held, but also the skills of the artists, their working methods and the relationships between the participants. Coulter believes it was not possible to create a "safe" space within a juvenile justice center:

> The facility is locked: once you are in, you are locked in. One whole side is glass with no curtains so that it is possible to look out and for others to look in. The nature of the space, the proximity of the boys' unit and the gym room, made it difficult to create an emotionally and aesthetically "safe" unencumbered quiet space that was private, comfortable, warm and uninterrupted. It would never be an intimate space. (2006, 51)

While we argue that a safe space is an essential factor for engagement, we believe instances of a "safe" space, where participants were able to take risks and where personal and artistic transformation occurred, were relative and rare but occurred across all *Risky Business* programs.

The following two examples of performance events illustrate when the artistic space became liminal. The public performance for a giant puppet-making project at a residential school for Indigenous youth took place outdoors where the young people felt comfortable. The artists believed that it was unlikely that the young Indigenous participants would or could have performed in a traditional theatre space. The use of huge puppets supported their engagement in the dramatic storytelling and preparedness to perform. The young actors manipulated the huge puppets by getting inside them and being fully enclosed so they were "protected" from public exposure. Young people involved in the custodial programs were motivated by their plays being performed in a theatre at The University of Melbourne, which they perceived as an environment in which they could meet the "outside" community on equal terms. Over the one-week rehearsal period these young people were able to develop a level of comfort in a space to which they might not otherwise have had access. It became a safe space, geographically and socially removed from the youth custodial centers.

For all the young people, but particularly those in custody, the presence of family members at performance events contributed significantly to the young people's sense of self and connectedness. In the boys' program, organizers went to some lengths to ensure that the mother of one of the young men was given time off work and brought to the theatre by taxi. Because she did not speak English, her son translated his scene into his native language, and performed in two languages, speaking each line twice. His performance was a moment of intense connection between performer and audience member, mother and son, and enhanced the social and theatre dynamic for the audience as a whole. Similarly, the experience of huge puppets interacting within the outdoor setting of the Indigenous school took on a spiritual dimension for performers and audience alike, connecting the community in a liminal time and place, allowing for transition and transformation (Donelan and O'Brien 2006).

Artistic product

An important finding of the *Risky Business* study was the importance of an artistic product in a public space as a culmination of each arts program. This was essential for young people's engagement in programs and a significant factor in participants achieving many of the personal and social outcomes that we discuss earlier in this chapter. These public arts events also provided a tangible demonstration of the social networks that the young people formed within the arts programs and their desire to communicate with a broader community. In this sense, each performance or exhibition was evidence of increased social connectedness and community engagement. Even the most highly marginalized young people were motivated by an expectation of high standards in public output and an approach that assumes they were working as "emerging artists" (Donelan and O'Brien 2008, 79). Artists working in the custodial programs noted a significant increase in commitment and focus by the young people during the production week. A tangible goal of producing a digitalized music track or completing an artwork ensured that most participants remained motivated. The strong positive response by artists, family, support workers and the general community to the public outcomes encouraged the participants to feel both proud and confident about what they had achieved.

In interrogating the significance of these findings a number of questions arose for us. Was it important to ensure that the public outcomes were of a threshold standard in aesthetic and production terms? As researchers, how should we interpret the positive audience feedback? What messages were the young people receiving about their work and their potential as artists?

Very few of the young participants had previous experience with the arts; most of them had never attended a performance or exhibition, and had little idea what a public outcome might involve. Almost all of the artists, on the other hand, were concerned to ensure a successful arts product, and most expressed high satisfaction with the level of achievement by the participants. As arts educators and critics, we believe that the arts have the capacity to communicate metonymically by using symbol, metaphor and representation. At times we were uncomfortable with some of the public exposure associated with the *Risky Business* arts programs. In creating their artwork, the young people drew on their lived experiences, including traumatic events involving refugee experiences, family violence, drug overdose and extreme loss and grief; often the starting point for the work was personal story. The drama, theatre and performance based programs allowed participants to engage with personal issues and social skills, primarily because the form demands social interactivity and embodied meaning making.

Fundamental to our research approach was that the arts interventions were not therapeutic but about creating artworks that transcended the personal and everyday. We believed that art making could be transformative as it allowed the participants to actively engage in constructing and reconstructing meaning about self, their communities and the broader world. When the arts products allowed the public to witness disadvantage and lived trauma, we were concerned this might reinforce the marginalized position of the participants. The model of confessional art, which reinforces the maker as victim, engages the audience as voyeurs to the victimhood, placing them in the dominant position as judge or protector, rather than as members of a shared community. Audiences responded very positively to the work of the young participants but we were concerned that the praise was qualified – that the young people were brave to reveal themselves and that they had achieved personally and artistically in spite of their status. One might argue that the experience of attending "outsider" art is transformative and redemptive, allowing members of the audience to assuage their collective social guilt and experience a kind of spiritual and moral catharsis. The witness performance has its roots in the public confession where the public hear and forgive, reinforcing a social and moral hierarchy. We wondered whether it was ever ethically appropriate for vulnerable young people to mark themselves by publicly revealing their social disadvantage and legal transgressions. We felt more comfortable as audience members when the art product processed and transformed personal stories, allowing for alterity[2] and the creation of metaphoric representation and metanarrative.

Maxine Greene emphasizes the importance of young people developing self worth and agency, but highlights the unspoken and inherent controls and expectations society imposes on youth:

> Young people are seldom looked upon as capable of imagining or choosing…Instead they are subjected to outside pressures, manipulations and predictions. The supporting structures are not used to sustain a sense of agency among those they shelter; instead they legitimate treatment, remediation, control – anything but difference and release. (1995)

There was evidence in the *Risky Business* study that some members of the wider community had expectations about the kind of work that young people "at risk" should exhibit. Nick, a young homosexual man in the painting program, was deeply disappointed when his painting "Preaching to the Perverted" was censored out of the final exhibition:

> Only two (of my paintings) went into the exhibition because the third one was a bit risqué because it had penises on crosses and apparently we're not allowed to have that in this gallery. Which I think is absolutely ridiculous. You shouldn't censor art but they do anyway. Well the idea was that I wanted to talk about homosexuality and Catholicism. I didn't aim to shock people. That's not my idea. I have a point that I wanted to make.

As researchers, we believe this work, while confronting, was appropriate in the context of a contemporary exhibition; had the young man been a recognized artist, we suspect that the work would not have been censored. In the stand-up comedy program, by contrast, participants and artists recognized that subversive and often inflammatory commentary was supported and sanctioned by the conventions of the form "because comedy is very democratic" (Donelan and O'Brien 2008, 75).

We also had some concerns that the young people with whom we worked might be easily seduced by the immediacy and ease of achieving success and public attention through their art. The artists who worked on the programs were highly committed and prepared to assume personal as well as educational responsibility for the arts outcomes by building puppets, writing songs and scripts, choosing images to paint and performing alongside the participants. A number of the participants indicated that they enjoyed the arts experience and believed they might

---

[2] "For outness is but the feeling of otherness rendered intuitive, or alterity visually represented" (Coleridge).

become successful artists. These were clearly inflated expectations given that most of the young people had very little idea of the commitment necessary for artistic training, and the fact that only a small proportion of arts workers ever achieve significant public recognition or remuneration. A young man for whom we organized an audition in an elite arts training school felt out of his depth; we were concerned this negative experience may have counteracted the positive benefits of his *Risky Business* experience.

We have stressed the importance of young people having the opportunity to show their artwork in a supported public environment and experiencing the excitement and "professional" demands of preparing for an exhibition or performance. While we have emphasized the necessity for the young people to see themselves as part of an artistic endeavor, we believe it is unrealistic to judge the products on a solely aesthetic basis, or to expect marginalized young people to attain a high level of skills development through their brief exposure to an art form. Public responses to the artwork in the *Risky Business* programs were complex, often involving pleasure and surprise at the young people's artistic and social development and an emotional involvement in the evident joy, pride and growth demonstrated by them at these public events. We wonder now if some of these responses reflected the sense of unease felt by privileged spectators exposed to social disadvantage.

Conclusion

In this chapter, we have interrogated the ethical challenges associated with arts interventions with this cohort, and, particularly whether the desire to "do good" obscures both the most efficacious approach to arts interventions with youth "at risk" and our understanding of the artistic and instrumental benefits or disadvantages of this work. It has not been our intention to dismiss our own commitment to the social applications of the arts nor the contribution of the many committed and skilled artists and researchers who are working in this field. Rather, we have tried to interrogate the assumptions researchers and artists may bring to work with young people "at risk", the way in which we construct interventions and the selection and interpretation of data.

The *Risky Business* study, in line with other international research, found that young people who engaged in the arts programs experienced a broad range of personal and social benefits, including enjoyment, increased self-esteem, artistic and communication skills development, the experience of achievement, an improved sense of wellbeing, community connectedness and social inclusion.

The arts give young people agency and a voice. The arts are risky, inherently subversive and challenge expectations. Through the opportunities the arts offer to test out ideas and for arts makers and performers to be heard and seen, they attract young people and particularly those on the margins who lack access to supportive adults. The arts offer opportunities for facilitating a dialogue. Working with marginalized young people, however, presents a range of challenges for researchers and artists, not the least of which is the burden of ethical and moral responsibility to do more than just "good".

Works Cited

ANAH. *ANAH Newsletter*, no. 7, October 2000. "News and Views of the Australian Network for Arts in Health, New Farm, Queensland". Retrieved February 1 2008, http://www.powerup.com.au/~anah.

Australia Council for the Arts. 2006. *Community Partnerships Scoping Study: Creative Communities.* Sydney: Australia Council.

Balfour, Michael, ed. 2004. *Theatre in Prison*. Bristol: Intellect Books.

Balfour, Michael and John Somers, eds. 2006. *Drama as Social Intervention*. UK: Captus University Publications.

Bamford, Anne. 2006. *The Wow Factor: Global Research Compendium on the Impacts of Arts in Education*. New York: Waxman Munster.

Barone, Tom. 2008. "How Arts-based Research Can Change Minds". In *Arts-Based Research in Education*, edited by Melisa Cahnmann-Taylor & Richard Siegesmund. New York: Routledge.

Bernstein, Peter L. 1998. *Against the Gods: The Remarkable Story of Risk.* New York: John Wiley and Sons.

Bessant, Judith, and R. Watts. 1998. "History, Myth-making and Young People in Time of Change". *Family Matters* 49, Autumn: 5-10.

Brice Heath, Shirley and Shelby Wolf. 2005. *Dramatic Learning in the Primary School*. London: Creative Partnerships.

—. 2004. *Visual Learning in the Community School*. London: Creative Partnerships.

Brice Heath, Shirley and A. Roach. 1999. "Imaginative Actuality, Learning in the Arts during the Non-school Hours". In *Champions of Change: The Impact of the Arts on Learning* edited by E. Fiske. Washington D.C.: Arts Education Partnerships /Presidents' Committee on the Arts and Humanities. Retrieved February 1 2008, http://www.aep-arts.org.

Cahill, Helen. 2002. "Teaching for Community: Empowerment through Drama". *Melbourne Studies in Education*, 43:2, 12-25.

Cahnmann-Taylor, Melisa, and Richard Siegesmund, eds. 2008. *Arts-Based Research in Education*. New York: Routledge.

Coulter, K. 2006. "The Arts: A Program Model in the "Rehabilitation" of Young Offenders in Custody." Risky Business Working Papers (unpublished). Risky Business Project Custodial Case Studies 1 and 2. University of Melbourne, School of Political Science, Criminology and Sociology, Australia.

Deasy, Richard J, ed. 2002. *Critical Links: Learning in the Arts and Student Academic and Social Development. Washington*. D.C.: Arts Education Partnership.

Denzin, Norman K., and Yvonna S. Lincoln, eds. 2000. *Handbook of Qualitative Research*, Second Edition. California: Sage Publications.

Donelan, Kate, and Angela O'Brien. 2008. *Creative Interventions for Marginalised Youth: The Risky Business Project*. Brisbane: Drama Australia.

—. 2006. "Walking in Both Worlds: Snuff Puppets at Barak Indigenous School". *The Applied Theatre Researcher/IDEA Journal*, 7, 1-14. Retrieved February 1, http://www.griffith.edu.au/centre/cpci/atr/content_journal.html.

Dreeszen, Craig, Arnie April and Richard Deasy. 1999. *Learning Partnerships: Improving Learning in the Schools with Arts Partners in the Community*. Washington D.C.: Arts Education Partnership.

Fiske, Edward, ed. 1999. *Champions of Change: the Impact of the Arts on Learning*. Washington D.C.: Arts Education Partnerships/Presidents' Committee on the Arts and Humanities. Retrieved, February 1 2008, http://www.aep-arts.org.

Gallagher, Kathleen. 2007. *The Theatre of Urban: Youth and Schooling in Dangerous Times*. Toronto: University of Toronto Press.

Giroux, Henry A. 2000. *Stealing Innocence: Youth, Corporate Power and the Politics of Culture.* New Sussex: Harvester Press.

Greene, Maxine. 1995. *Releasing The Imagination: Essays On Education The Arts And Social Change.* San Francisco: Jossey-Bass Publishers.

Hughes, Jenny and Karen Wilson. 2003. "Playing a Part: A study of the Impact of Youth Theatre on Young People's Personal and Social Development". *Research in Drama Education*, 9 (1): 57-73.

Hunter, Mary Anne. 2005. *Education and the Arts: Research Overview, A Summary Report Prepared for The Australia Council for the Arts*. Sydney: Australia Council.

Janesick, Valerie. 2000. "The Choreography of Qualitative Research Design: Minuets, Improvisations and Crystallisation". In *Handbook of Qualitative Research*, second edition, edited by Norman Denzin & Yvonna Lincoln. Thousand Oaks: Sage Publications, 379-400.

Jones, A. 2000. *Visionary Images: A Model Of Practice For Delivering Multiple Media Art Programs To Marginalized Young People*. Moonee Ponds: The Salvation Army Crossroads Network.

Kershaw, Baz. 1999. *The Radical in Performance: Between Brecht and Baudrillard.* London: Routledge.

Lefebvre, Henri. 1991. *The Production of Space*, trans. D. Nicholson-Smith. Oxford: Basil Blackwell.

McArthur, D., and S. Law. 1996. *The Arts and Prosocial Impact Study: A Review of Current Programs and Literature*. Santa Monica, California: The RAND Corporation.

McCarthy, K., E. Ondaatje, and A. Brooks. 2004. *Gifts of the Muse: Reframing the Debate about the Benefits of the Arts.* Santa Monica, California: The RAND Corporation.

Madison, Soyini D. 2005. *Critical Ethnography: Methods, Ethics and Performance*. Thousand Oaks: Sage Publications.

Marsden, Sally, and Martin Thiele. 2000. *Risking Art – Arts for Survival: Outlining the Role of the Arts in Services to Marginalised Young People*. Richmond, Melbourne: Jesuit Social Services.

Mills, D., and P. Brown. 2004. *Art and Wellbeing: A guide to the connections between Community Cultural Development and Health, Ecologically Sustainable Development, Public Housing and Place, Rural Revitalisation, Community Strengthening, Active Citizenship, Social Inclusion and Cultural Diversity*. Sydney: Australia Council. Retrieved February 1 2008, http://www.ozco.gov.au.

Murray, D., R. Ellis, J. Enter, and C. Richards. 1999. "Connexions – A Program of Jesuit Social Services, an Integrated Service For Marginalised Young People". *Youth Studies Australia*, 18 (1), March.

National Advisory Committee on Creative and Cultural Education. 2000. *All Our Futures: Creativity, Culture and Education*. London, UK: DfEE Publications.

Nicholson, Helen. 2005. *Applied Drama: The Gift of Theatre*. Hampshire: Palgrave Macmillan.

Nunn, P., and S. Bull. 1995. *Sounds of the Street. Music/Education Course Training Manual*. Sydney, Australia: Sydney City Mission.

Oakley, K. 2007. *Educating for the Creative Workforce; Rethinking Arts and Education*. Sydney: Australian Research Council Centre of Excellence for Creative Industries and Innovation, QUT and Australia

Council for the Arts. Retrieved February 1 2008, http://www.ozco.gov.au.

O'Brien, Angela. 2004a. "Spokesperson from the Margin: Lucky, A Risky Character". *NJ (Drama Australia Journal)*, 28:1, 61-72.

—. 2004b. "Teacher, mentor or role model? The role of the artist in community arts work with marginalised young people", *Change: Transformations in Education*, 7 (2), November: 74-88. Sydney: Division of Professional Learning, University of Sydney.

O'Brien, Angela, and Kate Donelan. 2007. "*Risky Business*: Engaging Marginalised Young People in the Creative Arts", *the International Journal of the Arts in Society*, 1 (6): 15-23. Retrieved, February 1 2008, http://www.arts-journal.com or http://ija.cgpublisher.com.

Rabinow, P. 1984. *The Foucault Reader*. London: Penguin Books.

Redshaw, A. 2000. "Cellblock Arts Program – Cellblock Youth Health Service". In. *Risking Art – Arts For Survival, Outlining the Role of the Arts in Services to Marginalised Young People,* edited by Sally Marsden & Martin Thiele. Richmond. Melbourne: Jesuit Social Services, 16-17.

Roberts, P. 2006. *Nurturing Creativity in Young People: A report to Government to Inform Future Policy*. Canberra: Commissioned and published by Departments of Education and Skills, Creative Industries and Tourism, Culture, Media and Sport.

Stake, Robert. 1995. *The Art of Case Study Research*. Thousand Oaks: Sage Publications.

Stone, A., T. Bikson, J. Moini, and D. McArthur. 1998. *The Arts and Prosocial Impact Study: Program Characteristics and Prosocial Effects*. Santa Monica, California: The RAND Corporation.

Stone, A., D. McArthur, S. Law, and J. Moini. 1997. *The Arts and Prosocial Impact Study: An Examination of Best Practices*. Santa Monica, California: The RAND Corporation.

Tedlock, Barbara. 2000. "Ethnography and Ethnographic Representation". In *Handbook of Qualitative Research*, second edition, edited by Norman Denzin & Yvonna Lincoln. California: Sage Publications, 455-86.

Thiele, Martin, and Sally Marsden. 2003. *Engaging Art: The Artful Dodgers Studio: A Theoretical Model of Practice*. Richmond, Melbourne: Jesuit Social Services.

Turner, Victor. 1986. *The Anthropology of Performance*. New York: PAJ Publications.

—. 1982. *From Ritual to Theatre: The Human Seriousness of Play*. New York: PAJ Publications.

Walters, R. 1997. "Big hArt: The Theatrical Side of Youth Crime Prevention". *Youth Studies Australia*, 16 (4): 22-6.

Wolcott, Harry F. 1994. *Transforming Qualitative Data: Description, Analysis and Interpretation*. California: Sage Publications.

—. 1995. *The Art of Fieldwork*. California: AltaMira Press.

Wyn, Johanna, and Rob White. 1997. *Rethinking Youth*. St. Leonards, Sydney: Allen & Unwin.

CHAPTER TWELVE (EPILOGUE)

MINIMIZING RISK: NEITHER MESSENGER NOR MISSIONARY

PETER O'CONNOR

"Go on, take a risk, just take a risk. What have you got to lose?" Just last week I was in a classroom of Year 7 and 8 students in one of the poorest areas in the Far North of New Zealand. Over 80 percent of the school students are Maori. Gangs are prevalent in the area and our classroom has a number of gang prospects. It was the first day of the most recent Everyday Theatre tour and I was being hot seated as Bernie, a twelve-year-old, who the students had seen in a piece of theatre earlier as both a victim and perpetrator of violence in his family. I was being encouraged to tell my story to Enid, my father's girlfriend in our drama. I was resisting with every bone of my role.

"Go on, take a risk, take a risk, what have you got to lose?" persisted the bright thirteen-year-old, determined that I find a way out of the mess Bernie was in. What young people and adults see as risky might be two very different things. In the hot seat as Bernie, I learnt risky business when you are twelve is trusting an adult with a secret; risky business when you are twelve is how to get away from your mum who is beating you, whilst at the same time, not telling on her to the police. I was reminded that what are "at risk" are often not young people, but our faith that they are not the problem.

> If youth once symbolized the moral necessity to address a range of social and economic ills, they are now largely portrayed as being the source of most of society's problems. Hence, youth now constitute a crisis that has less to do with improving the future than with denying it. No longer viewed as a privileged sign and embodiment of the future, youth are now demonized by the popular media and derided by politicians looking for quick-fix solutions to crime, joblessness, and poverty. In a society deeply

> troubled by their presence, youth prompt a public rhetoric of fear, control, and surveillance. (Giroux 2003)

Youth “at risk” can become another label to justify a range of programs to contain the threat and risk they pose without needing to address the underlying causes of global instability, particularly the growing disparity between rich and poor.

Charitable visits

When I was eight my father had a stroke that left him paralyzed for the last years of his life. For our family of seven children it was a devastating time. Financially, it meant real and genuine hardship, and inevitably, because of poor nutrition and other factors, we were identified by a range of social agencies as requiring their help. Our file at the local social welfare agency was no doubt quite large. We were visited by, it seemed, armies of social workers, and we also became recipients of food parcels from our local church. I don’t know if “at risk” was a term used to describe families like mine in the 1970s. I think our family label was “dysfunctional” and a number of my siblings at school were identified as “low achievers.” Of the seven children, I was the only one to finish high school and go on to university.

I remember, in particular, the good church ladies who brought around the food parcel on a Friday morning. They always seemed immaculately dressed, spoke a variant of English I was aware of from BBC period dramas, and they never came inside the house. They delivered the parcel with what my mother described as “the smug look of self-satisfaction, knowing they would get to heaven”. I have no doubt the parcel was genuinely given, but as a family we hated the food parcel, and we hated those who delivered it. As my mum said as she looked at the wholesome and boring food: “Why isn’t there a packet of cigarettes in there, or a bar of chocolate? I guess because we are poor we aren’t allowed to ask for things we want.” It was clearly up to the good ladies to decide what it was we needed, and we were never in a position to ask for anything or even worse, complain about being helped. In the end, my mother ended up in hospital with malnutrition just after my fourteenth birthday, and she said: “I’d rather that than have to be grateful for their help.”

I’ve spent the last twenty years using applied theatre as a way of working with those who are marginalized within society. It has meant I have worked in secure units for young adolescents labeled too dangerous to remain in society. I’ve worked in forensic psychiatric institutions, and in hospitals and units for those whose needs are described as special. In the back of my mind throughout that time, I have always remembered our kind ladies with the food parcels. Do I give only what is needed but never what is wanted? Do I ask if I am doing more harm than good? Do I gain more from the work than the group I work with? I know I am really grateful that it was only food parcels they came to the house with. If they'd come to empower us with the arts or drama, I'd have run a hundred miles.

It has meant I have a very healthy suspicion of why anyone, including myself, wants to use the arts with people "at risk". It is why I'm nervous about people who do things for people rather than with them. New Zealand as a nation has had more than its fair share of missionaries who have gained far more from their salvation narratives than the recipients who, as in all colonized societies of course, end up, in fact, the givers.

Everyday Theatre

So when I was asked in July 2003 by the New Zealand Department of Child, Youth and Family to create a show on child abuse for schools, I was wary and cautious about the notion. Thankfully, so was the Department. As the government agency responsible for the care of children and young people, Child, Youth and Family had become the victims themselves of very negative press and constant posturing by opposition members of parliament over failures in their service delivery. Several high profile deaths in care had created almost a siege-like mentality within the department, and although keen to engage in their educational role, they were wary of the risks the department faced in engaging in something as risky as theatre in education. It meant that nearly a year was spent in negotiation before Everyday Theatre made its first appearance in schools. By then, we were able to position our work to be neither missionaries nor messengers.

The basis for the work was summed up in the final contract letter between Applied Theatre and the Department in 2003:

> The purpose of the theatre in education programme is not to provide or teach simple solutions to the issues but to provide safe and structured environments for teachers and students to discuss these issues and find the answers relevant and suitable in their own contexts. The programme will allow students to think about, reflect on and talk about their own stories by investigating the story of someone else. This distancing process provides

> the necessary protection for students to both think and feel deeply about the issues but to do so in a protected manner.[1]

In our negotiations we worked with the notion that we had to find ways for young people to feel safe enough to take the risk of talking about abuse, and to support those for whom the work might reactivate past traumas so they too were safe at the end of the work.

Two structures were used to provide the necessary safety. One was the use of a double frame in the fiction we worked with. The second was the wrap around services provided by Child, Youth and Family to support the school in the use of the program.

Playing the most important game in the arcade

On the day of Everyday Theatre's visit to a school, three classes totaling on average ninety students gather in the school hall to view a twenty-minute performance which tells the story of a family in the local area. It is a complex family and the students meet its various members through the eyes of teenager, Ramesh Patel, a video gamesmaster who sees life as a video game. At times, the action of the play is performed both naturalistically, and at other times as a video game. Ramesh enrolls the students as trainee gamesmasters, whose first job is to help fix the broken family game. At different times, the game requires the students to consider the perspectives of witnesses to abuse or confidantes, the victims of abuse and the perpetrators of abuse.

We based our workshops on the process we had developed for the New Zealand Mental Health Foundation as part of a youth suicide prevention program (O'Connor 2005). Students work with the teacher/actors through four levels of the game, each level lasting an hour and with a different teacher actor from the performance, using dramatic conventions to explore the story and to work out answers to what might help the family. For example, at level one, students explore the narratives of the video game by hot seating different characters, while at level two students create still images from the family's life to explore the issues which sit underneath the violence. In level three the students play the decision game, where they decide what will happen to the children in the family. In the final and most difficult level, the students recreate what they have learnt in video game format. Like any video game, at each level, students gain a password that

---

[1] Personal communication between Applied Theatre Consultants and Child, Youth and Family.

allows them entry into the next level. At the end of the day they have the full password "Every Child has Hopes and Dreams" which entitles them to become gamesmasters.

Double framing

The students therefore work on their own family issues through a double-framed distancing device. Framing refers to the position of the students in relation to the family. The most straightforward dramatic approach would be to have the students simply act out the family's story. This first level of framing would not have provided the distance from the events of the family for the students to feel free to explore it. We could have distanced the students by enrolling the students to be social workers, working with our fictional family. However we decided that double framing, that is, putting one perspective to the events within another, would provide the greatest safety and paradoxically, the greatest investment for the students to engage with the story. They do work with a fictional family and their issues, but not directly, playing instead with a broken video game, helping Ramesh put it back together. The fun and excitement of playing a live video game provides the distancing and protection for the students to engage effectively with the serious and difficult issues that sit underneath the game structure. Students become so engrossed in making it to the next video portal to get the next word or phrase, they actively engage in challenging and difficult work inside the game structure to help the family.

The risk of opening things up in school for the young people in a way that is difficult to manage is avoided by the double framing. But it allows, as Gavin Bolton (1999) famously suggested, "for students to be protected into emotion," not from it. The double frame provides a double protection, but paradoxically, a double opening for young people to feel the issues of the video game family.

On that first day of our latest Everyday Theatre tour last week, a group of young girls struggled with the decision of where the two children, April and Bernie, were to go. However, for two young girls the answer was not so difficult. In their group they argued passionately for the children to go to the grandparents. They told the group how they themselves had been sent to live with their grandparents. They wanted to tell Bernie that this was okay; it was not something to be ashamed of, that he would be all right. When, as Bernie, I asked them in role whether he might be hit again at his grandparents', they remained true and honest and said: "You might get hit but it won't be as bad." Their honesty provided reassurance to me as Bernie, from their own lived experience, but within the safety of the game structure. They were also able to risk looking at their own lives and feel a sense of whether the decision they had made was right.

I had forgotten that as a boy I had spent many times at my grandparents, sometimes through whole school terms, as one crisis or another rocked my family. I'd never really thought about it, what it might have meant for my grandparents to take me and one or two of my brothers or sisters in. I realized it had taken me till I was forty-six to even be grateful for what they had done. Maybe the "at risk" child I had been gained something from the drama I did last week.

The effectiveness of using the game as a framing device was evident when, after a break for morning tea, we came back for the final session of the day. I said that as this was the final level of the game it would be much more difficult than the previous levels. The tasks set for the students in this level of the game are aesthetically more demanding and also require considerable emotional engagement with the story. One of the students, the same one who, we were told by the principal when we arrived, was unlikely to last the morning said: "Oh great, if it gets harder we take the cheats off." In video games, cheats are instructions that allow you to make mistakes or tell you short cuts. The students told us they wanted to play the game with the cheats off. They decided this meant that there would be no second chances in improvized work, no help from us as gamesmasters.

The level was played at a pace and focused beyond the imagination of the principal and teacher who watched, as the students worked through the level and gained their badges as gamesmasters. Playing level four with the cheats off is now a standard part of our day in schools.

As part of our work with the school we ran a session for parents, staff and the Board of Trustees that evening. We invited the students to come along and bring their parents. Five young men arrived with their mums, dads and some of their brothers and sisters, and some chose to come alone. We welcomed the group and acknowledged we had new gamesmasters who could help the parents sort out the problems in our fictional family. We worked solidly for two hours. Our young gamesmasters took the roles of the characters in the story, at different parts of the hall for the hot seat session. Parents and teachers asked questions and listened to our new gamesmasters tell them about their fictional family. They led the discussions with groups about the decision for the children. The discussions were intense and focused. One young man who was leading a group of adults who were seeking an easy answer told them: "there's no cheats in this level. You got to work hard to sort this out." The groups had to give their decisions to the new gamesmasters now back in role. They knew this game and made the parents sweat over each decision. They challenged their parents and teachers for clarity around the decisions and pressed them on whether it was the right one.

The usual dynamic of adults empowering youth "at risk" was turned on its head. The young people risked talking to and teaching their parents and teachers. If there was any empowering going on it was two-way. I too had always thought my own family had a few things we could have given those women who came around with the food parcels, if they had just been willing to accept what our family had to offer.

Ako (to teach and to learn)

In the Maori language the word for "to teach" and "to learn" is the same: *ako*. Metaphorically, *ako* emphasizes reciprocal learning. In a traditional house of learning pre-colonization it was said it was impossible to distinguish the learner from the teacher. Russell Bishop, Chair of Maori Education at Waikato University, suggests *ako* implies that "teachers and students can take turns in storying and restorying their realities, either as individual learners or within a group context" (1999, 6). *Ako* implies a narrative pedagogy where students can investigate those things "which arise from the conversation heard about the story and a relationship can then emerge in which both stories are heard or where a new story is created by all the participants" (ibid, 8). Where Everyday Theatre might be successful then, is in simply providing the space where new stories, new narratives about family abuse and violence, may be established.

A few days after the evening, I spoke to the *kaumatua* (tribal elder) who had joined us for the evening with his grandchild. I asked him how he had found the evening. He said: "it's a spiritual thing we had connected with; we connected with something that was deep inside who we were as people." He told me that there were no English words to describe what happened, as what had happened was too deep for words.

Nearly five years ago I had worked in the Far North with a largely Maori group as part of the work I was doing on the national campaign to counter stigma and discrimination associated with mental illness (O'Connor 2003). We had created intensely powerful moments of image theatre and a young Maori woman, Tui, said we had created a feeling of "*oho mauri*."

She said, "*Oho mauri* is when the life force is awakened. When who we are, our *mauri*, the essence of ourselves becomes totally aware of itself." I said I wasn't exactly sure I understood, and she said:

> It's *oho mauri.* That is what happened. I'll give you a comparison so that you can liken the feeling to it. It's like sitting on the beach, in the still of the night, and all you can hear is just the sound of the waves hitting the shore. Now picture yourself in a moment like that, that's what you call *oho mauri*. Or sitting in the still of the night and all you can hear is the distinct call of the *reru*, or the night owl, it's just you and that night owl. It's that *oho mauri* that you can feel.

For Tui, the work had wakened the very essence of who we were as human beings. Myerhoff describes something similar in her discussions of the relationship between theatre and ritual where: "another state may come about, transcendence, where one is aware simultaneously of being in the flow as well as aware of his/her actions" (1990, 247). Csikszentmihalyi describes flow as:

> Where action and awareness merge, destroying a dualistic perspective, a performer becomes aware of his actions but not of the awareness itself. (cited in Myerhoff 1990, 247)

The power of drama then, may be simply to provide those moments where we may awaken, as Schechner describes, the "startling ability of human beings to create themselves, to change to become for better or for worse, what they ordinarily are not." (1993, 1)

The success of Everyday Theatre that evening was in not attempting to give a message or trying to save kids "at risk". It was about working to provide an uncontested space where people can use the language of drama to explore and share their stories about the issues of abuse and family violence. Everyday Theatre had silenced the surrounding noise that clutters and confuses us so we stop hearing those stories. In the stillness of the work—in the *oho mauri*—we finally got to hear each other.

In our current tour of Northland, we are contracted to provide our program free to a diverse range of community groups, as well as schools. On Tuesday next week, we spend the evening exploring the story of Bernie and April with the local youth drama group. The final level will be adapted so that it creates a video dance game where the decisions and issues are shifted into dance performance. On the Wednesday, we will be working with the Northland Deaf Association for the day. With two interpreters we will explore through the game the issues as they bring them to us. On Thursday after a morning back with a group of Year Seven and Eight students, we set up our stall in the car park of the local supermarket. The levels of the game will become a variation of forum theatre as passers-by work to resolve the issues of the family. In our work in the morning we will be visited by the National Manager of Education for the New Zealand

Police, who is interested in how Everyday Theatre might work alongside their program called Keeping Ourselves Safe which runs in 80 percent of New Zealand schools. In the weeks that follow we will work with the Men Beyond Violence Group, we will spend a day in the local Child, Youth and Family Youth Justice Centre, a few days with the local tribal group, the Northland Disability Centre and the school for teen mums. Earlier this year we visited and worked in the secure units of Child, Youth and Family residences throughout the country. As we travel we are invited to work with more and more groups. Because we travel with a process rather than a message, it's about how we adapt the process for each new context that gives us this flexibility of approach.

Until recently I was the National Facilitator for Drama with the New Zealand Ministry of Education. In that role I was responsible for the introduction of a compulsory drama curriculum into New Zealand schools. This national role carried considerable status and I enjoyed the opportunity to write texts for schools, produce posters and DVDs about drama, and lead a team of twelve advisers in the six universities throughout the country. However, I took an active role in the Everyday Theatre tour of the secure unit residences in May this year. By the end of the tour I had decided to resign from the Ministry and work full-time with Everyday Theatre. If I'm honest with myself, it wasn't just because I could see I could make a greater difference. It was more because I simply enjoy working with marginalized groups.

The reason why, I think, is that I feel more comfortable working with people who are pissed off with the world than working with those who are doing okay. Perhaps I feel more at ease with "at risk" young people because I have a sense of what it is to be given the label. And perhaps, most importantly for me, I do my best work there. On the edge, on the margins, is where I have to push my art and craft harder for often less return. I enjoy it because it's where I have to rely on who I am, rather than my status, to get things to happen in that classroom or hall. And perhaps if I am honest, like the women who came with the food baskets, I get as much, if not more, from the interchange. I learnt so much last week in my work with Everyday Theatre and I know I will learn more next week. I will learn about how drama can function to provide a space for people to meet and share their stories. I will be able to risk bringing my own story to the space, new stories will be created and my story will be changed. I can only guarantee one person is changed each time I work in Everyday Theatre: myself.

An ancient Maori proverb suggests:

"Nau te rourou, maku to rourou, ka ora ai te iwi."

("With your food basket and mine we will feed each other.")

Works Cited

Bolton, Gavin. 1999. *Towards a Theory of Drama in Education*. Harlow: Longman.

Bishop, Russell, and Ted Glynn. 1999. *Culture Counts: Changing Power Relationships in Education*. Palmerston North: Dunmore Press.

Giroux, Henri. 2004. *Public Time and Educated Hope: Educational Leadership and the War Against Youth.* Retrieved May 1 2004, http:www.ciconline.com/wo4-democracy.

Myerhoff, Barbara. 1990. "The Transformation of Consciousness in Ritual Performances: Some Thoughts and Questions." In *Intercultural Studies of Theatre and Ritual,* edited by Richard Schechner and William Appel. Cambridge: Cambridge University Press.

O'Connor, Peter. 2005. *The Lost Bag: Mental Health Matters for Years 7-8*. Auckland: Mental Health Foundation of New Zealand.

—. 2003. *Reflection and Refraction. The Dimpled Mirror of Process Drama: How Process Drama Assists People to Reflect on their Attitudes and Behaviours Associated with Mental Illness*. PhD dissertation. Brisbane, Australia: Griffith University.

Schechner, Richard. 1993. *The Future of Ritual: Writings on Culture and Performance*. London and New York: Routledge.

CONTRIBUTORS

Martina Boese is a honorary research fellow at the School of Political Science, Criminology and Sociology at Melbourne University, and a researcher at the Research and Policy Centre of the Melbourne-based charity Brotherhood of St Laurence. She completed her PhD in Sociology and has contributed to national and international research projects in the UK and Austria on the cultural economy, cultural diversity, migration and employment. She has published several articles in these fields.

Shirley Brice Heath is Professor at Large, Watson Institute for International Studies, at Brown University, and Margery Bailey Professor of English and Dramatic Literature, Emerita and Professor of Linguistics, Emerita, at Stanford University.

Mark Brown teaches criminology at the University of Melbourne, Australia. He has written on a number of aspects of corrections and penal history and theory. He is currently engaged in research on the process of women's desistance from offending and is writing a book on penal power and colonial rule.

Bruce Burton is an academic, teacher, playwright and director with an international reputation in the fields of drama education and applied theatre. He has been the recipient of five Australian Research Council Linkage grants in the past seven years, and is the author of eight books in the field of drama education. In 2007 he won the national Carrick Award for university teaching in the Humanities and the Arts. He is currently Chair in Applied Theatre in the Faculty of Education at Griffith University, Queensland, Australia.

Helen Cahill is the Deputy-Director of the Youth Research Centre at The University of Melbourne, Australia. She works in education and health research, specializing in the use of drama techniques as radical pedagogy and in border crossing research and learning partnerships between youth and adults. Her Masters thesis focused on using drama to enhance resilience in young people and her PhD study investigates the use of poststructuralist drama techniques to enhance communication between teachers, doctors and adolescents.

Kiersten Coulter is a criminologist and social researcher completing her doctoral research in the School of Political Science, Criminology and Sociology at the University of Melbourne, Australia. She has over fifteen years experience of working and researching in adult and juvenile custodial facilities with both male and female offenders. Her main areas of interest include theories of offending and desistance; prison education and programs; policy; the custodial space; drug use, mental health and offenders; and gender and diversity.

Kate Donelan is Head of Drama in the Melbourne Graduate School of Education at The University of Melbourne. She is well known within Australia and internationally in the field of drama education and has held leadership positions in peak arts organizations. Her recent published research focuses on drama, theatre and learning in a context of cultural pluralism and intercultural exchange, and the social impact of the creative arts. In 2007 she received the American Alliance for Theatre and Education Distinguished Dissertation award for her ethnographic study of intercultural arts education in a multicultural secondary school.

Anna Hickey-Moody is a Lecturer in Creative Arts Education in the Faculty of Education at Monash University, Australia. She is a writer, teacher and performance maker. Anna's university teaching has been in the areas of Gender Studies, Cultural Studies and Education. She is co-author of *Masculinity Beyond the Metropolis* (Palgrave Macmillan UK 2006) and co-editor of *Deleuzian Encounters: Studies in Contemporary Social Issues* (Palgrave Macmillan UK 2007).

Sharon Hogan is a consultant, researcher and facilitator specializing in the design of innovative learning solutions and professional development. Sharon liaises with clients to create programs for groups or individuals concentrating on developing leaders, supporting organizational, personal and cultural change, and building learning communities. Sharon has held leadership roles in public and private sectors of education, academia and the creative industries. She is currently completing a research masters in professional ethics education.

Mat Howard graduated from the University of Sydney, Australia with First Class Honours in Performance Studies in 2004. Mat has since worked as a theatre director, playwright, actor, educator and administrator in Australia, the United States, Thailand and Canada.

John Hughes is the Pro Dean, Faculty of Education and Social Work, University of Sydney, Australia. John has research and teaching interests in drama pedagogy, youth performance festivals, drama as a learning medium, and teacher professional development in arts education. Between 2001 and 2005 he was Chair of the Education Committee, Shakespeare Globe Centre Australia Youth Festival. He is co-editor (with Michael Anderson and Jacqueline Manuel) of *Drama in English Teaching: Imagination, Action and Engagement* (Oxford University Press 2008).

Dave Kelman is a theatre maker and drama educator working in inner Melbourne, Australia, where he is Artistic Director of an artists-in-schools program for Western Edge Youth Arts. For over twenty years he has been a teacher, actor, writer and director working with young people in inner city contexts in the United Kingdom and Australia. He is currently completing his PhD at the University of Melbourne based on his research practice.

Angela O'Brien is Deputy Dean of the Melbourne School of Graduate Research at The University of Melbourne and Chair of Creative Arts. Her research interests are in theatre history, theatre for young people and the social impact of the arts. She is also a qualified lawyer with an interest in restorative justice. In 2007, with Kate Donelan, she was awarded The University of Melbourne's inaugural Knowledge Transfer Excellence Award for *Risky Business* - Arts and Youth "At Risk".

Peter O'Connor is a co-director of Applied Theatre Consultants Ltd. in New Zealand. The company holds contracts with various government agencies to use applied theatre programs as part of public health campaigns. He is also an adjunct Associate Professor at the University of Sydney, Australia.

INDEX